Corporate Governance in Action

Over time we have seen large corporations, in many cases with multinational operations, begin to play an increasingly significant role in modern society. This in turn has put the governance of these corporations into focus.

Against the this background, *Corporate Governance in Action* helps provide a framework for examining corporate governance through a focus provided by external pressures on large corporations. It also brings together the approach of economics and finance with theories in organization studies, such as aspects of resource dependency theory. This framework takes into consideration not only the market relations of modern corporations but also their dependence on regulators and different kind of scrutinizers.

This thoughtful book is a complete research guide that provides a new understanding and applicable framework for advanced students, academics and researchers in the area of corporate governance and the related disciplines.

Lars Engwall is Professor Emeritus at Department of Business Studies, Uppsala University, Sweden.

Routledge Studies in Corporate Governance

For a full list of titles in this series, please visit www.routledge.com

4 **Corporate Governance and Resource Security in China**
The transformation of China's global resources companies
Xinting Jia and Roman Tomasic

5 **Internal and External Aspects of Corporate Governance**
Ahmed Naciri

6 **Green Business, Green Values, and Sustainability**
Edited by Christos N. Pitelis, Jack Keenan and Vicky Pryce

7 **Credit Rating Governance**
Global Credit Gatekeepers
Ahmed Naciri

8 **Mergers and Acquisitions and Executive Compensation**
Virginia Bodolica and Martin Spraggon

9 **Governance and Governmentality for Projects**
Enablers, Practices, and Consequences
Edited by Ralf Müller

10 **The Making of Shareholder Welfare Society**
A Study in Corporate Governance
Alexander Styhre

11 **Resource Security and Governance**
The Globalisation of China's Natural Resources Companies
Edited by Xinting Jia and Roman Tomasic

12 **Corporate Governance in Action**
Regulators, Market Actors and Scrutinizers
Edited by Lars Engwall

Corporate Governance in Action

Regulators, Market Actors and Scrutinizers

Edited by Lars Engwall

Routledge
Taylor & Francis Group
NEW YORK AND LONDON

First published 2018
by Routledge
605 Third Avenue, New York, NY 10017

and by Routledge
2 Park Square, Milton Park, Abingdon, Oxon OX14 4RN

First issued in paperback 2020

Routledge is an imprint of the Taylor & Francis Group, an informa business

Library of Congress Cataloging-in-Publication Data
A catalog record for this title has been requested

ISBN 13: 978-0-367-73544-9 (pbk)
ISBN 13: 978-1-138-28566-8 (hbk)

Typeset in Sabon
by Apex CoVantage, LLC

Contents

Figures

Tables

Tables

Abbreviations

ABF	Amnesty Business Forum
ABG	Amnesty Business Group
ACI	Airports Council International
AGM	Annual General Meeting
ATM	Air Traffic Management
BAA	British Airport Authority (Now Heathrow Airport Holdings)
CAEP	Committee on Aviation Environmental Protection (within ICAO)
CEMP	The Creation of European Management Practice
CEO	Chief Executive Officer
CFO	Chief Financial Officer
CSO	Civil Society Organization
CSR	Corporate Social Responsibility
DG	Directorates-General (within the European Union)
EBP	European Business Press
ECGI	European Corporate Governance Institute
EMOT	European Management and Organization in Transition
EPA	Environment Protection Agency
ESG	Environmental, Social and Governance
ESMA	European Securities an Markets Authority
ETI	European Transparency Initiative
EU	European Union
EUPERA	European Public Relations Education and Research Association
EU ETS	European Union Emissions Trading Scheme
FLA	Fair Labor Association
FTSE	Company owned by the *Financial Times* and the London Stock Exchange
GAO	Government Accountability Office (in the United States)
GC	Global Compact
GEMS	Global Enterprises Managing Stakeholders
GRI	Global Reporting Initiative
H&M	Hennes & Mauritz AB

IASB	International Accounting Standards Board
ICAO	International Civil Aviation Organization
ICC	International Chamber of Commerce
ICGN	International Corporate Governance Network
ICIJ	International Consortium of Investigative Journalists
IFRS	International Financial Reporting Standards
IGU	Internal Governance Units
ILO	International Labour Organization
IPCC	Intergovernmental Panel on Climate Change
IPRA	International Public Relations Association
IR	Investor Relations
ISO	International Organization for Standardization
ISS	Institutional Shareholder Services
MSCI	Formerly Morgan Stanley Capital International
MSF	Médecins sans frontiers
NAPF	National Association of Pension Funds
NASDAQ	National Association of Securities Dealers Automated Quotations
NGO	Non-Governmental Organization
OECD	Organisation for Economic Co-operation and Development
PRI	Principles for Responsible Investment
PRSA	Public Relations Society of America
SEC	Securities and Exchange Commission
SMSI	Sourcing & Manufacturing Sustainability Index
SRI	Socially Responsible Investment
TREO	Transnational Governance and the Transformation of States
UN	United Nations
UNFCCC	United Nation Framework Convention on Climate Change
UNICEF	United Nations Children's Fund
UNPRI	United Nations Principles for Responsible Investment
USAS	United Students Against Sweatshops
WRC	Worker Rights Consortium

Preface

This monograph is an illustration of the long-term character of scientific work. Basically, it is the result of the research program "Global Enterprises and Mediators in Society" (GEMS) funded by the Bank of Sweden Tercentenary Foundation. However, this project in turn is clearly based on the earlier research programs "European Management and Organization in Transition" (EMOT; 1991–1997) with support from the European Science Foundation, the Creation of European Management Practice (CEMP; 1997–2001) funded by the European Union and "Transnational Governance and the Transformation of States" (TREO; 1995–1999) funded by the Swedish Research Council. The final analysis and writing up of the project had support from yet another project funded by the Swedish Research Council on Roles of Corporations in Global Society. All these projects have aimed at a better understanding of the role of various management principles in modern society.

GEMS itself was a five-year research program, involving a dozen researchers, that has produced four Ph.D. dissertations and a large number of other publications. This volume is an effort to bring the research results together. We have worked with what we describe as a networked approach to research. Individual projects have pursued specific agendas and research questions, yet we have coordinated the projects through frequent meetings throughout the project. In these sessions, our common questions have been continually reiterated and developed, and following revisions, the individual projects have developed. For example, after our initial studies the role of the media became increasingly important for the project, and new subprojects were launched that revolved around the creation of business news.

We acknowledge the financial support for the research with gratitude and wish to express our deep appreciation to colleagues in the Department of Business Studies at Uppsala University as well as in our international network for continuous stimulating exchanges. We are also very grateful to Donald MacQueen for assisting us in the language editing of the text.

About the Contributors

Lead Authors

Lars Engwall is professor emeritus of management at Uppsala University, Sweden. His research has been directed toward institutional change as well as the production and diffusion of management knowledge. Since the 1960s, he has continuously published his research in monographs, journal articles and edited books. Among his more recent publications can be mentioned *Reconfiguring Knowledge Production* (ed. with Richard Whitley and Jochen Gläser, OUP, 2010), *Bibliometrics: Use and Abuse in the Review of Research Performance* (ed. with Wim Blockmans and Denis Weaire, Portland, 2014), *From Books to MOOCs?* (edited with Erik De Corte and Ulrich Teichler, Portland, 2016) and *Defining Management* (with Matthias Kipping and Behlül Üsdiken, Routledge, 2016). He is an elected member of a number of learned societies and has received honorary degrees from Åbo Akademi University and the Stockholm School of Economics.

Jaan Grünberg is senior lecturer at the Department of Business Studies at Uppsala University. In his Ph.D. from Uppsala University in 2002, he analyzed CEO exits in large Swedish publicly traded corporations. His subsequent research has been directed toward corporate governance. Jaan Grünberg has been the director of doctoral studies as well as department chair in the Department of Business Studies at Uppsala University.

Josef Pallas is professor at the Department of Business Studies, Uppsala University. He defended his thesis, *Talking Organizations: Corporate Media Work and Negotiation of Local Practice*, at Uppsala University in 2007. His subsequent research has mainly focused on the increased mediatization of Western societies and its implications for the governance of modern organizations. He is the co-editor of a number of books, among them *Organizations and the Media: Organizing in a Mediatized World* (Routledge, 2014) and co-author of many book chapters as well as journal articles dealing with mediatization, corporate communications and corporate governance.

Kerstin Sahlin is professor of public management at the Department of Business Studies at Uppsala University. Presently, she is secretary-general of humanities and social sciences at the Swedish Research Council. Between 2006 and 2011, she was deputy vice-chancellor of Uppsala University. Kerstin Sahlin has published widely in the fields of organizational institutionalism, organizational reform, public management, project management and corporate social responsibility, as well as on the global expansion of management ideas and the development of global standards and regulations. Her current research interests include the role and governance of universities, public sector reforms, the role of corporations in global society and the public-private divide in societies.

Linda Wedlin is professor at the Department of Business Studies, Uppsala University. She received her Ph.D. in business studies in 2004 from Uppsala University with the dissertation *Playing the Ranking Game: Field Formation and Boundary-work in European Management Education*. It was published internationally by Edgar Elgar in a revised version in 2006 as *Ranking Business Schools*. The same year Linda Wedlin was awarded the Nils Klim Prize for young Nordic researchers in the areas of arts and humanities, social sciences, law and theology. She has subsequently presented her research in several journal articles and book chapters on regulation and governance, most notably in the field of higher education.

Contributing Authors

Stefan Arora-Jonsson is Professor at the Department of Business Studies, Uppsala University. He defended his Ph.D. thesis in Business Administration, *Making and Breaking Norms: Competitive Imitation Patterns in the Swedish Mutual Fund Industry*, at the Stockholm School of Economics in 2003. His has since published in the *Administrative Science Quarterly*, *Organization Science*, *Sociological Theory*, the *Strategic Management Journal* and the *International Economic Review*, as well as contributed a chapter on diffusion and isomorphism in the *SAGE Handbook of Organizational Institutionalism*. In 2007–2010, he served as the Counsellor of Science and Technology at the Swedish Embassy in New Delhi.

Helena Buhr received a Ph.Lic. in Business Studies from Uppsala University in 2006 with her study *Multi-stakeholder Partnerships and the Dynamics of Fields*. In 2010, she attained a Ph.D. in sociology from the University of Michigan with the dissertation *Network Dynamics in Small Business Financing*. After her doctorate, Helena Buhr was a postdoctoral researcher at the Kellogg School of Management, Northwestern University, focusing particularly on the developments of institutions and network structures in new industries and their effects on firm performance. She is presently an external faculty member at the Northwestern Institute on Complex Systems.

Katarina Buhr defended her dissertation *Bringing Aviation into the EU Emissions Trading Scheme: Institutional Entrepreneurship at Windows of Opportunity* in business studies at Uppsala University in 2008. After a postdoc at the Center for Climate Science and Policy Studies, Linköping University, she is presently working for an environmental research institute firm. She is particularly dealing with international climate policy, carbon capture storage and sustainable urban development.

Magnus Frostenson is Associate Professor at Örebro University School of Business and an associated researcher with the Department of Business Studies at Uppsala University. He has a Ph.D. in business administration (2006) from the Stockholm School of Economics. The primary focus of his research is on business ethics and corporate social responsibility. He has published several monographs and articles in journals such as the *Journal of Business Ethics*, *Business Ethics: A European Review*, *Philosophy of Management* and the *Journal of Cleaner Production*.

Ingemund Hägg is Professor Emeritus at the Department of Business Studies, Uppsala University. His research has mainly been directed toward behavioral accounting and corporate governance. Among his publications are *Institutioner som aktieägare* (Institutions as Corporate Owners, co-authored, SNS, 1985), *Att äga stora företag* (The Ownership of Large Corporations, ed., SNS, 1987) and *Issues in Empirical Investment Research* (ed. with Esbjörn Segelod, Elsevier, 1992).

Laurence Romani earned her Ph.D. from the Stockholm School of Economics in 2008. She is Associate Professor at the Centre for Advanced Studies in Leadership at the same school. Her work focuses on issues of representation and interaction with the cultural Other in respectful and enriching ways. She considers contributions from critical management, feminist and postcolonial organization studies to further cross-cultural management and diversity management research and teaching. Laurence Romani has published in *Organizational Research Method*, the *Journal of Business Ethics* and the *International Journal of Cross-Cultural Management* as well as co-edited *Cross-cultural Management in Practice: Culture and Negotiated Meanings* (Edward Elgar, 2011).

Lars Strannegård is President of the Stockholm School of Economics in Sweden since 2014. He is Professor and holder of the Bo Rydin and SCA Chair in Leadership. His research interests focus on aspects of leadership, aesthetics, branding and organization. Lars Strannegård has carried out research on organizing and management practice in multinational organizations. His work has been published in journals such as *Organization*, the *Journal of Organization Change Management*, the *European Journal of Marketing*, *Leadership* and the *Annals of Tourism Research and Marketing Theory*. He has been a Visiting Scholar at Stanford University and Professor at Uppsala University.

Karolina Windell is Associate Professor in business studies at Score—Stockholm Centre for Organizational Research—at Stockholm School of Economics and Stockholm University. Her research deals with corporate social responsibility and sustainable business. A key question in her research is the ongoing mediatization of organizational life and, in particular, the role of media when it comes to circulating ideas and shaping the agenda for corporate responsibilities.

1 Resituating Corporate Governance

Lars Engwall, Jaan Grünberg, Josef Pallas, Kerstin Sahlin, Linda Wedlin, Stefan Arora-Jonsson, Helena Buhr, Katarina Buhr, Magnus Frostenson, Ingemund Hägg, Laurence Romani, Lars Strannegård and Karolina Windell

Introduction

Corporate governance has become a widely discussed and researched area in the recent decades (cf., e.g., Shleifer and Vishny 1997; Fligstein and Choo 2005; Wright et al. 2013; McGahan 2014). Often these discussions and research have been, and still are, concentrated on a few well-established mechanisms (e.g., incentive systems), on regulation (e.g., financial markets frameworks) and on particular actors (e.g., investors)—i.e., a strong focus on the financial aspects. In an effort to add to the earlier discourse, the present volume aims to provide an understanding of the governance of business corporations that includes institutions and processes beyond those that are generally denoted as corporate governance. In this way we are responding to the call from Tihanyi, Graffin and George (2014: 1539)

> to consider emergent, contextual trends that are reshaping . . . governance in organizations [by broadening] conceptions of governance [thereby raising] new research avenues on the effectiveness and efficiency of nongovernmental organizations, governmental bodies, proprietorships, and other forms in the creation of value through the deployment of organizational resources.

Our effort draws inspiration from the insights of the early management and organizational scholars who showed that understanding organizations entailed looking beyond the formal organization and pointed to how organizations functioned in action (Gouldner 1954; Dalton 1959; Thompson 1967). In this way, we offer an analysis of governance that includes considerable institutional complexity and ambiguity, as well as the actions and efforts to handle and contain such complexity and ambiguity.

In the following, we will first provide a brief overview of extant approaches. We will then discuss three significant changes that we consider to be important reasons for developing a broader framework for the analysis of corporate governance landscape. In a subsequent section, we will illustrate, by means of three empirical cases, how these changes have put new demands on the analysis of corporate governance. Against this backdrop, we then briefly summarize our proposed approach, which will be more extensively presented in Chapter 2. Finally, in this chapter, we will recapitulate the contents of the book.

Extant Approaches

Theoretical considerations concerning corporate governance were long the domain of legal theorists. Such models sprung from the formulations of corporate law in the nineteenth century. The twentieth century saw the arrival of economic theories of corporate governance. Although some of the early work was in the area of institutional economics (e.g., Veblen 1899 and 1904), in the latter part of the last century, the financial conception of corporate governance had become dominant. In such models and theories, the issue of corporate governance is often seen as a matter of the interplay between owners and managers (see, e.g., Alchian and Demsetz 1972; Fligstein 1990; Keasey, Thompson and Wright 1997; Barca and Becht 2001; Carlsson 2001). Some others have instead chosen to focus on the relations between corporations and their various stakeholders (see, e.g., Freeman 1984; Aoki, Gustafsson and Williamson 1990; Freeman et al. 2010). However, a problem with this approach is the definition of stakeholders. Freeman et al. 2010: 208) thus point out that the common definition of stakeholders is too inclusive:

> Indeed, on this definition, one could imagine virtually anyone, or any organization . . . Given such a wide view of what the term might mean, the notion of stakeholder risks becoming a meaningless designation. If all are stakeholders, then there is no point in using the term.

More recently alternative approaches have started to appear, as demonstrated by the contributions in the handbook by Wright et al. (2013) and a textbook (Goergen 2012) that includes a chapter on gatekeepers—i.e., financial analysts, credit rating agencies, corporate governance rating agencies, etc. However, the focus is still on the financial aspects of corporate governance.

A stream of writings by organizational scholars interested in the diffusion, variation and adoption of governance practices across areas and settings has also opened avenues for more institutionally inspired models of corporate governance (cf., e.g., Fiss 2008; Tihanyi, Graffin and George 2014). Such studies have covered issues such as governance processes of boards of directors (McNulty and Pettigrew 1998; Cowen and Marcel 2011), the political dynamics surrounding CEOs (Ocasio 1999; Zhang and Wiersema 2009; Gomulya and Boeker 2014) and the decoupling associated with the spread of governance mechanisms (Zajac and Westphal 1995). Studies focusing on the diffusion of corporate governance practices have shown how these are significantly embedded in normative and cultural values and framings. For instance, Davis and Greve (1997), in a study of practices to counter hostile takeovers by firms, found that poison pills spread rapidly through shared directorships, while golden parachutes were slower to spread through local and regional élite groups and networks. Furthermore, studies by Fiss and Zajac (2004) demonstrate the international spread of the shareholder value principles. Westphal and Zajac (1994), for their part, show that incentive plans for management are adopted by corporations in different settings, sometimes decoupled from actual governance practices (see also Belogolovsky and Bamberger 2014). However, although decoupling may occur, corporate governance processes are also adapted to fit local circumstances and contexts, leading to variation in corporate governance practices (Fiss and Zajac 2004). Other studies have also noted processes of translation and adaptation of corporate governance principles and practices in the rapid worldwide diffusion of corporate governance codes (Aguilera and Cuervo-Cazurra 2004; Enrione, Mazza and Zerboni 2006). In addition, corporate governance research has also come to look at the legitimacy of governance processes and the impact of governance on corporate reputations (Bates and Hennessy 2010; Delgado-García, De Quevedo-Puente and De La Fuente-Sabaté 2010; McDonnell and King 2013) and the way that media plays a role in corporate governance (Bednar 2012; Jansson 2013). Finally, changes in the corporate governance landscape are starting to enter research through studies of the role of activism from shareholders as well as various interest organizations (King 2008; Crespi and Renneboog 2010; Judge, Gaur and Muller-Kahle 2010).

Despite the fact that the aforementioned research, and other work in these traditions, largely focuses on relatively traditional actors involved in corporate governance—such as boards of directors, CEOs and managers and investors—and the relations between them, they nevertheless point to an increasing awareness of the need to include new mechanisms and processes for understanding corporate governance. Such studies include political, social and cultural processes linked to corporate governance practices. These studies show how corporate governance mechanisms and principles are neither stable nor uniform systems that can be understood without reference to their social and institutional contexts and settings, and without recognition of the multitude of interorganizational and interpersonal relationships that make up the structure of such governance systems.

Together these later studies point to the need for a broader approach to the governance of corporations, recognizing both a broader set of actors, interests and forces that shape corporate behavior and the processes that construct both meaning and practices of corporate governance. In so doing, it is very important to recognize that the corporate governance landscape has undergone considerable changes in the past few decades. In the following section, we will discuss three such changes that we consider particularly significant.

Three Significant Changes in the Corporate Governance Landscape

In developing extant approaches to analyze the governance of modern corporations, we need to acknowledge that the corporate governance landscape has changed. Our analysis has pointed to three such broad developments in modern society that have been particularly significant:

First, transnationalization, i.e., increasing relationships and interactions between various national actors across country borders as well as the development of transnational regulation (cf., e.g., Bruszt and Holzhacker 2009; Iriye 2014).

Second, regulatory changes, i.e., waves of deregulation—since the 1980s facilitating movements of capital and goods and increasing marketization, but also occurrences of re-regulation (cf., e.g., Morgan and Knights 1997; Balleisen and Moss 2010; MacAvoy and Schmalensee 2014).

Third, the rise of scrutinization, the increasing tendency of examining and inspecting modern organizations, corporations as well as public organizations, through formal arrangements (auditors), critical reporting (media) or various kinds of protests (voluntary organizations) (cf., e.g., Power 1997; Doh and Teegen 2003; Hjarvard 2013).

Transnationalization

Although transnational corporations were important in the world economy even before World War II, the period after 1945 has been a boom time for transnational corporations (Casson 1990; Tolentino 2000). They have increased both in number and in size. Following the deregulation of financial markets in the 1980s, with a subsequent increase in rapid capital flows around the world, the global corporations could grow not only organically but also, largely, through mergers and acquisitions. As a consequence, corporations, as well as the settings in which they operate, have grown and developed transnationally (cf., e.g., Hubbard 2013).

The observation that corporations as well as their environments are increasingly transnationalized is supported by the development of less nationally bounded corporate boards. In a data set of almost 150 of the world's largest companies for the period 1995–2005, Staples (2008) thus found that boards of directors in these companies grew more heterogeneous in terms of nationality during the period. The main driver for the increase in heterogeneity pointed out by Staples is transnational acquisitions, with already heterogeneous boards having a greater propensity for such deals, thus creating a mutually reinforcing process. Staples also points out that these globalized boards are much more common in corporations based within the European Union in comparison to the United States and Japan.

Similar evidence is provided by Carroll (2002), who focused on Canadian boards of directors in which the tight nationally oriented networks of directors became more international and the traditional relations to banks became more "episodically enacted" (p. 339). Carroll points to changes in governance and regulation, changing norms in the business community and the transnationalization of capital as driving forces.

The aforementioned development of transnationalization has been reinforced by the evolution of modern information and communication technology. It has facilitated global financial markets with a concentration in a few significant stock exchanges such as those on Wall Street in New York and the City of London, but also the transnational NASDAQ. The business world has also experienced an altered mix of ownership, where both private equity and institutional ownership are becoming increasingly important. In addition, there has been the rise of a number of new, sophisticated financial instruments, which, like the other changes, have been of great importance to both companies and governments. Their significance, complexity and, in particular, their risks became dramatically evident during the financial crisis in the wake of the bankruptcy of Lehman Brothers in 2008, which made markets shudder all over the world (Williams 2010).

However, modern information technology has been important not only for the development of financial markets. It has also contributed significantly to the emergence of a highly concentrated transnational media industry with some very powerful actors controlling different kinds of media channels (see Engwall, Kipping and Üsdiken 2016, particularly Chapter 15). These in turn have become significant for corporations both as scrutinizers and as partners.

Because of the aforementioned factors, the analysis of corporate governance must reach beyond national borders and acknowledge how modern corporations are subject to transnational demands. Corporate governance is no longer simply a national phenomenon.

Regulatory Changes

As corporations have grown larger and increasingly global, the limits of national regulation of such entities have become evident. National legislations are thus sometimes played out against each other in the competition for international investors. In addition, an increasing share of regulation takes place between and among nations. Such transnational regulations do not rely on the coercive power of the nation-state, but rather evolve in processes of negotiation (Djelic and Sahlin-Andersson 2006) and take the form of standards (Brunsson, Jacobsson and Associates 2000) and other legally non-binding soft rules (Mörth 2004). Therefore, there have been attempts to move beyond a state-centered perspective on regulation. As an alternative to focusing on the state alone (Baldwin and Cave 1999), efforts have been made to open up for the multitude of interest groups involved in regulation (Marks, Hooghe and Blank 1996). Such groups may include non-governmental organizations (NGOs) (Boli and Thomas 1999; Hedmo 2004), international organizations (Braithwaite and Drahos 2000), business interest groups (Pulver 2004), civil society groups, think tanks (Stone 1996; McGann 2016) and professional associations and standardizing bodies (Djelic and Sahlin-Andersson 2006; Hedmo, Sahlin-Andersson and Wedlin 2006).

The aforementioned does not mean that regulation is stateless, however. Rather than a state in retreat (Strange 1996) or "the end of the nation-state" in favor of globalization (Ohmae 1995), what we are seeing is that a great deal of regulation still has important origins from governments and nation states. Despite significant societal changes such as European integration, the nation-state remains a dominant and sometimes even strengthened actor (Moravcisk 1993; Milward 1999). However, while the state is, and most likely will continue to be, an important regulator (Hirst and Thompson 1996), it is likely to take on new roles in the increasingly transnational regulatory processes. Among activities in society that appears to attract increasing attention from the state are those of the welfare sector, such as health care and education.

Another important actor in regulatory processes appears to be corporations themselves. New means and modes of regulation, relying in part on voluntary principles and mechanisms for compliance, have entailed that corporations engage in self-regulation, voluntary agreements, self-evaluations and certifications, etc., actively participating in the regulatory process (Ayres and Braithwaite 1992; Hedmo, Sahlin-Andersson and Wedlin 2006). Research has also noted how corporations are actively taking part in rule-setting activities, through interest representation, lobbying, official stakeholder consultations and other activities (Coen 1998; Jutterström 2004; Buhr, K. 2008). This means that corporations are taking an active part in policy-making and regulatory activities and interacting with regulators to develop and refine regulatory mechanisms and processes.

The aforementioned implies a challenge to the perception of corporations as "recipients" of rules and regulations, or as rule-followers, and paves the way for a view of them as proactive in the shaping of regulatory mechanisms and principles. In other words, regulatory changes provide another strong argument to further develop extant theories of corporate governance.

The Rise of Scrutinization

The past few decades have also seen the rise of a number of mechanisms and techniques for evaluating and scrutinizing the performance of companies and other kinds of organizations. They have been reflected in the work that has followed Michael Power's introduction of the notion of the audit society (Power 1997), work on rankings (Wedlin 2006) and research on standardization (Brunsson, Rasche and Seidl 2012).

The range of scrutinizing also extends into moral and ethical social dimensions (Boli 2006). Thus, in the past few decades, corporate social responsibility has emerged as a global trend incorporating business corporations, states, international organizations and, in particular, NGOs (Sahlin-Andersson 2006; Carroll 2008). With this trend, sets of NGOS put pressure on corporations to act and to present themselves in certain ways. Hence, it is important for modern corporations to deal with those norms. As a result, the pressure on corporate actors to answer questions about the consequences and legitimate scope of their actions becomes part of, and is mixed with, other aspects of corporate governance. Various kinds of organizations push corporations to be accountable, not only for abiding with laws and providing consumers with decent products but also for external effects of corporate activity as well as the role of the corporations with regard to human well-being and social and environmental responsibility in general. The ability to handle such confrontations seems to become increasingly important for corporations, not least to obtain and maintain legitimacy (Dowling and Pfeffer 1975; Pfeffer 1978; Pfeffer and Salancik 1978; Suchman 1995).

A significant feature of the rise of scrutinization is the mediatization of society. Corporations, and other organizations for that matter, are being more and more closely scrutinized by the media and are thus quite sensitive about their reputation. As a result, the role of the media in corporate governance has changed dramatically in the last few decades through a strong expansion of business coverage in the media (cf., e.g., Grafström 2006; Pallas, Strannegård and Jonsson 2014). A particularly significant change in the present century has been the explosion of various social media channels and platforms, as they are not only adding to the number of scrutinizers but also changing the way scrutiny is undertaken (cf., e.g., Meikle 2016).

The media is sometimes described as being everywhere, shaping and reflecting our lives, tastes and aspirations. In contrast, the media remains surprisingly absent in theories and studies of corporate governance, which have tended to leave the media outside the core business of governance, control and management. However, in present times the various media have become significant scrutinizers of corporations. All too often, what is missing from the conceptualizations of the role of the media is the fact that the objects of media attention, the corporations, are far from passive. Communication departments, media strategists, communication consultants and public relations specialists are omnipresent in society. They shape agendas, channel attention and craft arguments. They need to be taken into account if contemporary corporate governance is to be understood, and in order to achieve this, we need a concept of the business corporation that allows for such an analysis (Grünberg and Pallas 2013).

The rise of scrutinization as well as the aforementioned transnationalization and regulatory changes constitute further strong reasons, in addition to what we said by means of introduction, to further develop extant approaches to corporate governance. In order to further emphasize this, before introducing our approach, we will provide some examples illustrating their significance.

Three Cases of Corporate Governance in Action

Since we in the present volume are emphasizing corporate governance in action, it is appropriate to present cases that illustrate the reasoning of the previous section but also add evidence to the argument for a broader approach to corporate governance. First, we present the TeliaSonera case, that is, the corporate governance problems of the Swedish-Finnish telecommunications company in relation to its expansion into Eurasia. Our second case is that of Volkswagen and the disclosure that the company had cheated in some of its emission tests, while the third case is constituted by the International Consortium of Investigative Journalists (ICIJ) and its revelations of tax evasions. At the end of the section, we will provide some conclusions that will pave the way for the following brief summary of our approach, which will be presented more extensively in Chapter 2.

TeliaSonera

In the wave of regulatory changes of the telecommunications industry, the earlier state monopolies in Finland (Post-och televerket) and Sweden (Televerket) were partly privatized in 1997 and 2000, turning into Sonera and Telia, respectively. In 2002, the Swedish company acquired Sonera, thereby creating the TeliaSonera Corporation, still with a degree of considerable state ownership from the two nations (History of Telia Company 2016). In this way, a transnational company emerged. It was transnational not only through its owners and its operations in Finland and Sweden, however. The company was also quite active on other international markets. At the end of 2005, it thus had 80 million customers (23 million in the Nordic countries and 57 million in the international market) (Annual Report of Telia Sonera 2005)—a figure that had increased to 157 million in 2010 (Annual Report of TeliaSonera 2010).

A particular expansion had occurred in Euroasia in countries like Afghanistan, Tadzhikistan, Turkey and Uzbekistan. These markets in general, and Uzbekistan in particular, turned out to be associated with a number of problems, however (Hedelius 2015: esp. 161–205, see also Milne 2013). In April 2012, a Swedish television team broke the news that the company had collaborated with the secret service of Uzbekistan, and in a second program in September 2012, they told viewers that considerable amounts of money had been paid out to the eldest daughter of the Uzbekistan dictator Islam Karimov. This led to extensive coverage in other media, but also actions from the Swedish Police (investigating bribery) as well as the Swedish Ministry of Finance in its capacity as part owner of the company. The company responded by taking advice from a communication consultancy and by commissioning an investigation by a law firm. The latter, in a report in late January 2013, concluded that it had not been able to detect any illegal activities but could not exclude that this had been the case. As a result, the CEO resigned and the Swedish Ministry of Finance, again as part owner, reshuffled the board, allowing only two members of the old board to stay on. The new board came to rely on formal policies on ethics as well as membership in the UN Global Compact to assure that TeliaSonera had changed its behavior. In 2015, the company even decided to leave Eurasia, which is expected to take some time (Annual Report of TeliaSonera 2015). However, the earlier actions still haunt the company: In September 2016, the *Financial Times* reported that Dutch and US authorities intended to fine the company about USD 1.4 billion for its alleged briberies in Uzbekistan (Milne 2016).

The TeliaSonera case clearly illustrates the three changes in the corporate landscape discussed in the previous section. The TeliaSonera Company was obviously part of a transnational development and experienced regulatory changes. It also became subject to increasing scrutinization, in this case by the media, and responded by seeking external expertise. Although it has yet not been determined whether the company was involved in illegal actions, it is evident from the development that it had broken norms and thereby had to act in the field of governance. Obviously, the case shows how corporate governance goes beyond the principal-agent relationship and financial matters. In this particular case, it is also evident that roles are blurred: the government, which is supposed to be the regulator, was also a part owner.

Volkswagen

The history of the German Volkswagen goes back to the late 1930s. Since then it has become a very significant employer in Germany and one of the world's largest vehicle manufacturers (Bowler 2015). In the latter capacity, it has sold vehicles all over the world, including the United States, where stricter emission standards for motor engines took effect in 2009. The year before, Volkswagen had introduced its new Clean Diesel, which the company claimed would meet the standards. The cars were also passing laboratory tests with flying colors. In this way, the company in the following years won several environmental rewards and even received tax breaks (Ayapana 2015).

However, in 2013, a research center pointed out, "Sensors and electronic components in modern light-duty vehicles are capable of 'detecting' the start of an emissions test in the laboratory" (Weiss et al. 2013: 31). In other words, vehicles passing the laboratory tests may very well produce much higher emissions on the road. Later reports from researchers at the University of West Virgina (Franco et al. 2014 and Thompson et al. 2014) showed this to be the case.

These findings and other evidence prompted the Environmental Protection Agency (EPA) to issue a Notice of Violation to Volkswagen on

September 18, 2015, followed by a second EPA Notice of Violation on November 2, 2015 (for this and the following, see US Environmental Protection Agency 2016). Seventeen days later, on November 19, 2015, these notices forced Volkswagen to acknowledge, "The defeat device has existed in all of its U.S. 3.0 liter diesel models since 2009." This was followed by a complaint by the Department of Justice on behalf of EPA against Volkwagen for alleged violations of the Clean Air Act. Consequently, on June 28, 2016, Volkswagen entered into a multi-billion-dollar settlement, which was approved on October 25, 2016, by the US District Court for the Northern District of California. In addition, the company had to recall many millions of cars for adjustment.

Thus, in a period of about twelve months Volkswagen had been accused of cheating on its emission tests, had admitted that the company had done so, had to recall millions of cars and had to pay out large sums of money. Obviously, this had considerable consequences for corporate governance. The Volkwagen CEO, Martin Winterkorn, tried to stay on, but had to resign on September 23, 2015, declaring, "I am doing this in the interests of the company even though I am not aware of any wrongdoing on my part" (Winterkorn 2015). Later on, other top executives in Volkswagen also had to go. In the process, the negative media coverage all over the globe was vast (cf. *New York Times*, September 23, 2015). Needless to say, Volkswagen stock prices experienced a dramatic decline.

It should be obvious that the Volkswagen case also points to the transnationality of corporate governance. However, it also emphasizes the significant role of regulation, in this case a regulation that the company tried to evade. Another very strong feature of the case is the role of scrutinizers, in this case researchers and inspection agencies. Once again, the complexity of modern corporate governance is evident.

The International Consortium of Investigative Journalists

In 1997, the American journalist, Charles Lewis, started an organization called the ICIJ. It grew out of the Washington based Center for Public Integrity, founded in 1989, describing itself as "one of the country's oldest and largest nonpartisan, non-profit investigative news organizations" with the mission to "serve democracy by revealing abuses of power, corruption and betrayal of public trust by powerful public and private institutions, using the tools of investigative journalism" (Center for Public Integrity 2016). The creation of ICIJ meant an internationalization of these activities and a focus "on issues that do not stop at national frontiers: cross-border crime, corruption, and the accountability of power." This organization is built on a collaboration of roughly two hundred journalists in 65 countries (ICIJ 2016a). Among its many projects, we will here focus on leaks regarding tax evasion.

On November 5, 2014, ICIJ attracted considerable news attention for what has been labeled the Luxembourg Leaks. Based on an examination of almost 28,000 pages of documents, ICIJ in this project revealed that

340 multinationals—among them companies such as Pepsi, IKEA, AIG, Coach, Deutsche Bank, Abbott Laboratories—had evaded taxes through secret deals with the Luxembourg government. They also demonstrated how the global accounting firm PricewaterhouseCoopers had been a significant consultant to the multinationals to obtain more than 500 tax rulings. As a result, some companies had paid less than 1 percent in taxes by exploiting tax mismatches and using hybrid loans. At the same time, many of them had limited presence in Luxembourg, which is demonstrated by the fact that more than 1,600 companies can be found at one address: 5, rue Guillaume Kroll (ICIJ 2016b; see also Houlder 2014).

About a month after the first report, on December 9, 2014, ICIJ came out with a second report that added another 30 companies to the list of tax evaders, among them the Walt Disney Company and the US multinational conglomerate Koch Industries. The reports also revealed that PricewaterhouseCoopers had not been the only advisor to the tax-evading companies. The three other accounting firms in the Big Four group—Ernst & Young, Deloitte and KPMG—had also been assisting these companies (ICIJ 2016b).

The Luxembourg Leaks led to considerable media attention but also actions from the European Parliament and the European Commission. For the latter, it was particularly sensitive that the then newly elected European Commission President Jean-Claude Juncker had been the Luxembourg Prime Minister at the time of the deals (Houlder 2014).

So far, the legality of the revealed tax arrangements has not been questioned. On the other hand, legal actions have been taken against the employees of the accounting firms that had acted as whistle-blowers. Two of them were given suspended sentences and small fines in June 2016, while a third was acquitted (Bowers 2016). However, even if the companies have not been brought to court, the Luxembourg Leaks have had quite negative consequences for the companies in question, both the tax-evading companies and the Big Four advising them, sparking considerable criticism regarding unethical behavior.

Problems similar to those of the multinationals in the Luxembourg Leaks affected the Swiss bank HSBC in February 2015 as ICIJ, in what has been called the Swiss Leaks, made public information about 100,000 of the bank's clients. It was revealed that the bank had offered services to "clients who had been unfavorably named by the United Nations, in court documents and in the media as connected to arms trafficking, blood diamonds and bribery" (ICIJ 2016c). Needless to say, this was not favorable for the image of the Swiss bank. It had not only taken money that had been earned illegally, but it had also helped these clients evade taxes.

The ICIJ case further emphasizes the three changes mentioned earlier, but particularly how a scrutinizing organization can play a very significant role in corporate governance. Again, it should be evident that corporations are not only subject to market forces but also the object of scrutiny by the media and interact with regulators.

Some Further Evidence

The three cases presented have demonstrated the significance of transnationalization, regulatory changes and the rise of scrutinization. However, they have also pointed out how corporations relate to advisors and other external actors in order to manage their reputation. This can be further illustrated by adding the case of the German corporation Siemens. After facing media reports in 2006 that it had systematically used consultancy fees for briberies of almost EUR 500 million, it turned to external bodies for help. Siemens approached Michael Hershman, co-founder of Transparency International, and engaged him as an advisor. In addition, a law firm was commissioned to perform an investigation, and substantial funds were allocated to a long-term program with the aim of supporting non-profit organizations that are fighting corruption (Dietz and Gillespie 2012).

The earlier actions are not limited to corporations that have been scandalized, however. Adding just two examples, we can first mention the Anglo-Dutch multinational consumer goods company Unilever's work with UNICEF to improve sanitation worldwide and to stop the spread of disease-causing germs (UNICEF 2016). In a similar effort to demonstrate social responsibility, the Swedish retail-clothing multinational H&M communicates that the production processes of the clothes in their stores do not involve child labor (H&M 2016):

> We take a clear stand against all use of child labour and it is a minimum requirement for all factories producing for H&M. Today it is rare that we discover any workers below the statutory minimum age in our supplier factories. We continuously monitor compliance with this essential requirement in all factories. If we discover any person below the statutory minimum age we have a clear policy in place that guides us to act in the best interests of the child.

A multitude of other examples could be added, thereby further underlining that international organizations, NGOs, business associations, institutional investors, different kinds of advisors and the media all play an increasingly important role in shaping business activities both nationally and internationally. Our conclusion is, therefore, that the governing of modern corporations constitutes a globalized and organized landscape with actors, interests and expectations that are new or have become more salient in putting pressures on corporations. In order to make sense of the governing of corporations in the modern world, we therefore need to develop a systematic understanding of the interplay among all these actors, interests and expectations.

Our Approach

Against the aforementioned background, the central argument of this book, which we will develop further in Chapter 2, is that business corporations are embedded in a field of governance that basically includes three types of actors, namely (1) regulators, (2) market actors and (3) scrutinizers (media, NGOs, auditors, etc.). The structure and organizing of this field has significant consequences for how corporate governance plays out in practice. This means that we shift the focus from the narrow view of corporate governance, which according to Shleifer and Vishny (1997: 737) is simply "the way in which suppliers of finance to corporations assure themselves of getting return on their investment." We also go beyond the approach of business corporations as bundles of resources (Wernerfelt 1984) or nexuses of contracts (Aoki, Gustafsson and Williamson 1990). Instead, we stress the role of embeddedness and reciprocity in the field of governance. Hence, embeddedness means that our suggested approach focuses on the various demands on corporations in the field of governance. In addition, reciprocity means that our approach takes into consideration the two-way interaction between the governors and corporations. In other words, it is not simply that corporations are impacted by regulators, market actors and scrutinizers; companies, in turn, are at pains to shape and control the multiple interests that confront them.

Our approach means that new actors, beyond principals and agents in the traditional corporate governance literature, are in focus for the analysis. Their activities bring new values, norms and ideals to the standards and practices of corporate activities. Therefore, it is becoming more and more important and necessary for corporations to relate to them. Particularly, corporations are paying more and more attention to social and environmental concerns, in addition to more traditional ideals such as shareholder value and their financial evaluation. This is also changing the relationships and processes of governance in contemporary corporations. Similar processes are also in evidence in government agencies, professional organizations, academic institutions and other organizations. Through the analysis of governance surrounding business corporations as well as corporate responses to various kinds of governors, the present volume will therefore bring attention to governance processes that are of broad significance throughout society.

The approach we present in this volume should be seen as complementary, rather than contradictory, to the established traditions. Our effort to study corporate governance does not exclude conflicts of motivation as a fundamental governance problem; such conflicts have always existed and will exist in the future. However, we argue that it is important to take into consideration the fact that investors are not monoliths with one clear view of adequate corporate actions. Instead, investors constitute a conglomerate of different groups with varying interests and time horizons. Therefore, even the simple relationship between investors and corporate leadership is a matter for continuous negotiation and interaction. Such continuous interaction also occurs between corporations and other actors in society. Among the latter, too, there are multitudes of actors that have different interests in relation to corporations.

As we tried to sketch out earlier, contemporary corporations are largely governed in new constellations of organizations, interests and forces.

Models that depict corporate governance as a fairly stable set of relations and processes that are uniform across contexts and settings are therefore less adequate for understanding contemporary governance. From what many observers have noted about the changes in the organizing of global financial systems and markets, we can no longer assume that corporate governance processes are concerned only with single, isolated and stable relations and dependencies, or that they are only concerned with the workings of the capital market, whether national or transnational.

The title of the book, *Governance in Action*, alludes to James Thompson's (1967) seminal work *Organizations in Action*, where he emphasized that organizations are exposed to contradictory goals, environmental pressures, technological shifts and coordination problems. We find his insights into how organizations relate to and interact with others to be the key to understanding not only how organizations operate but also to how corporate governance is enacted in contemporary society.

Our purpose with this volume is to further elaborate the understanding of modern corporate governance by asking the following question:

What are the significant characteristics of modern corporate governance?

Dealing with this question, we have made use of the extant literature but also to a large extent empirical research, using a wide range of data-collection methods. Most prominent among these are interviews, which have been employed to understand both highly contemporary and historical processes of governance. The empirical material rests on hundreds of interviews, altogether twelve weeks of participant observation (of financial analysts, business journalists and communications executives). In addition, the analysis of documents has been a significant feature of the research. The results from these earlier studies have been presented separately in a number of dissertations by members in the research team (see Buhr, H. 2006; Buhr, K. 2008; Frostenson 2006; Grafström 2006; Göthberg 2007; Pallas 2007; Petrelius Karlberg 2007; Wedlin 2004; Windell 2006) as well as in other publications (e.g., Buhr and Grafström 2007; Grafström, Göthberg and Windell 2008; Grafström et al. 2006; Grafström and Pallas 2007; Grünberg and Pallas 2009, 2013; Hedmo, Sahlin-Andersson and Wedlin 2006; Jonsson, Greve and Fujiwara-Greve 2009; Kjaer, Erkama and Grafström 2007).

This empirical research and the extant literature have made it possible to develop the framework that we will present in more detail in the following chapter. Before turning to this presentation, in the final section of this first chapter we will summarize the contents of the chapters to come.

Outline of the Book

In the next chapter, as mentioned, we will develop the theoretical arguments for resituating corporate governance as a process embedded in an organizational field containing regulators, market actors and scrutinizers. We will spell out a set of ideal types that characterize each governing relation. However, we will also emphasize that, in practice, governing relations do not work in isolation from each other but rather in interaction and interplay.

After Chapter 2, follows four chapters (Chapters 3–6) where we deal with corporate governance in relation to the three aforementioned types of governors (regulators, market actors and scrutinizers). Again, it is important to keep in mind that we recognize that they are interrelated and embedded not only in each other but also in the institutions of global society. Nonetheless, it is essential to see their distinctive features first. Our approach can thus to a certain extent be seen as similar to that of the British author Lawrence Durrell, who in his famous Alexandria Quartet, including the novels *Justine* (1957), *Mountolive* (1958a), *Balthazar* (1958b) and *Clea* (1960), portrayed the same social interactions from different perspectives. Thus our approach focuses on a set of interrelated governing relations. We expect to find that the governing relations often overlap, interplay, intertwine and even conflate with each other. The chapters of this volume all depict corporate governance as embedded, but they do so from different standpoints.

Chapter 3 analyzes the relationships between corporations and *regulators*. Recent research has pointed to dramatic changes in these relations. While many corporate regulations are nationally based, as mentioned earlier, we see an expansion of transnational regulations. Such regulations are often soft in nature, building on both voluntariness and the active participation of the regulated. There is also a prevalence of overlapping regulations, often with elements of reciprocity and self-regulation. Corporations are thus not only subject to regulations but also increasingly take part in developing and sustaining regulation and regulatory mechanisms. The chapter analyzes the main features of contemporary, particularly transnational, regulation and its implications for the governance of businesses and corporations. Two empirical cases are studied in detail. First, the UN Global Compact, which illustrates how the interpretation of the agreement's principles evolved in reciprocal dialogues and how the roles between those regulating and those being regulated became blurred in the process. The second case is that of aviation in the European Union Emissions Trading Scheme, which points to the same kind of process being present in an instance of formal regulation.

In Chapter 4, we deal with *market actors* by focusing on the classic governance relation between investors and corporations. It is true that we have pointed out earlier that traditional corporate governance models are inadequate, in that they focus almost entirely on such relations. However, a study of corporate governance should not, and cannot, exclude these relations as unimportant for the governance of corporations. Nevertheless, these relations need to be understood as being embedded in a whole set of other governing relations, and to wider processes of societal change and development. In the chapter, we give a detailed account of the interaction between the top management of large Swedish corporations and their investors. In so doing, we identify three groups of owners: cross-border investors, national block-holders and national retail owners, and point to the significant roles of informal discussions, road shows and annual general meetings for the interaction with these investors. Furthermore, we show how corporate governance ideas are articulated through corporate governance codes, global organizations and networks as well as intermediaries in the form of rating institutes and proxy advisory services.

In Chapter 5, we turn to *scrutinizers*, with a primary focus on NGOs. Their emergence has entailed that corporations have to deal with demands for what has become labeled as corporate social responsibility (CSR). This has appeared as a global trend encompassing business corporations, states, international organizations and various organizations of civil society. Our analysis specifies the roles assumed in these evolving governing relations, and the resulting necessity for businesses and corporations to participate in such governing relations in order to organize and to meet challenges that follow from them. Through case studies, it is shown how the interaction modes can span from criticism through activism, over collaboration toward common goals, to dependence relations. It is demonstrated how normative ideas about the role of business in global society shape governing relations.

In Chapter 6, we further develop our analysis of scrutinizers through an analysis of the role of the media. We start out with a discussion of the role of media as embedded in institutional processes and then provide an historical overview of the growth of both business media and the coverage of businesses in traditional media. Next, using empirical studies, we present four roles of business media in relation to corporations: (1) scrutinizing, (2) informing, (3) agenda-setting and (4) legitimizing. In relation to these roles, we have identified three types of corporate responses: (1) news providing, (2) organizing of media interactions and (3) co-creating of field-level practice that guides the long-term corporate media interactions. The processual dynamics are found to be reminiscent of those in typical governance relations: mutual dependence and negotiation of solutions. The interaction between the media and corporations is characterized by "embedded agency."

In Chapter 7, against the background of the four preceding chapters, we turn to the relations between regulators, market actors and scrutinizers, on the one hand, and corporations, on the other, in the field of governance. We start out with direct relations between corporations and governors and then turn to indirect relations by means of commercial and non-commercial intermediaries, such as consultants, corporate interest organizations, etc. In addition to these, we show in the chapter that corporations handle their relations to governors by means of boundary-spanning units such as offices for public relations, investor relations and media relations. In this context, we identify three main corporate strategies: persuasion in relation to regulators, promotion in relation to market actors and protection in relation to scrutinizers. Finally, we introduce the concept of the editing corporation.

In Chapter 8, we summarize and discuss our results. We especially point to the significance of embeddedness and reciprocity in the field of governance, whereby corporations interact with regulators, market actors and scrutinizers. Finally, we present implications of our research beyond the corporation, for organization theory, for further studies, for management education and for management.

References

Aguilera, R. and Cuervo-Cazurra, R., 2004, "Codes of Good Governance Worldwide: What Is the Trigger?" *Organization Studies*, 25(3): 415–443.

Alchian, A. A. and Demsetz, H., 1972, "Production, Information Costs and Economic Organization," *American Economic Review*, 62(5): 777–795.

Annual Report of TeliaSonera 2005, Stockholm: TeliaSonera.

Annual Report of TeliaSonera 2010, Stockholm: TeliaSonera.

Annual Report of TeliaSonera 2015,Stockholm: TeliaSonera.

Aoki, M., Gustafsson, B. and Williamson, O. E., 1990, *The Firm as a Nexus of Treaties*, London: Sage.

Ayapana, E., 2015, "Taxpayers Paid $51M in Green Car Subsidies Linked to VW Diesels," *Motortrend*, 23 September <www.motortrend.com/news/taxpayers-paid-51m-in-green-car-subsidies-linked-to-vw-diesels/> accessed on December 7, 2016.

Ayres, I. and Braithwaite, J., 1992, *Responsive Regulation*, Oxford: Oxford University Press.

Baldwin, R. and Cave, M., 1999, *Understanding Regulation: Theory, Strategy and Practice*, Oxford: Oxford University Press.

Balleisen, E. J. and Moss, D. A. (eds.), 2010, *Government and Markets: Toward a New Theory of Regulation*, New York: Cambridge University Press.

Barca, F. and Becht, M., 2001, *The Control of Corporate Europe*, Oxford: Oxford University Press.

Bates, K. and Hennessy, D., 2010, "Tilting at Windmills or Contested Norms?: Dissident Proxy Initiatives in Canada," *Corporate Governance: An International Review*, 18(4): 360–375.

Bednar, M. K., 2012, "Watchdog or Lapdog?: A Behavioral View of the Media as a Corporate Governance Mechanism," *Academy of Management Journal*, 55(1): 131–150.

Belogolovsky, E. and Bamberger, P., 2014, "Signaling in Secret: Pay for Performance and the Incentive and Sorting Effects of Pay Secrecy," *Academy of Management Journal*, 57(6): 1706–1733.

Boli, J., 2006, "The Rationalization of Virtue and Virtuosity in World Society," in: Djelic, M.-L. and Sahlin-Andersson, K. (eds.), *Transnational Governance: Institutional Dynamics of Regulation*, Cambridge: Cambridge University Press, pp. 95–118.

Boli, J. and Thomas, G., 1999, *Constructing World Culture*, Stanford, CA: Stanford University Press.

Bowers, S., 2016, "LuxLeaks Whistleblower Avoids Jail after Guilty Verdict," *The Guardian*, June 29, 2016 <www.theguardian.com/world/2016/jun/29/luxleaks-pwc-antoine-deltour-avoids-jail-but-is-convicted-of-theft> accessed on December 11, 2016.

Bowler, T., 2015, "Volkswagen: From the Third Reich to Emissions Scandal," *BBC News*, October 2, 2015 <www.bbc.com/news/business-34358783> accessed on August 9, 2017.
Braithwaite, J. and Drahos, P., 2000, *Global Business Regulation*, Cambridge: Cambridge University Press.
Brunsson, N., Jacobsson, B. and Associates, 2000, *A World of Standards*, Oxford: Oxford University Press.
Brunsson, N., Rasche, A. and Seidl, D., 2012, "The Dynamics of Standardization: Three Perspectives on Standards in Organization Studies," *Organization Studies*, 33(5–6): 613–632.
Bruszt, L. and Holzhacker, R. (eds.), 2009, *The Transnationalization of Economies, States, and Civil Societies: New Challenges for Governance in Europe*, New York, NY: Springer.
Buhr, H., 2006, *Multi-stakeholder Partnerships and the Dynamics of Fields: GAVI's Attempts to Create a Healthy Vaccine Market*, Licentiate Thesis 44 from the Department of Business Studies, Uppsala: Uppsala University.
Buhr, H. and Grafström, M., 2007, "The Making of Meaning in the Media: Corporate Social Responsibility in the Financial Times, 1988–2003," in: den Hond, F., de Bakker, F. G. A. and Neergaard, P. (eds.), *Managing Corporate Social Responsibility in Action: Talking, Doing and Measuring*, Aldershot: Ashgate, pp. 15–31.
Buhr, K., 2008, *Bringing Aviation into the EU Emissions Trading Scheme: Institutional Entrepreneurship at Windows of Opportunity*, Doctoral Dissertation No. 140 from the Department of Business Studies, Uppsala: Uppsala University.
Carlsson, R. H., 2001, *Ownership and Value Creation: Strategic Corporate Governance in the New Economy*, Chichester: Wiley.
Carroll, A. B., 2008, "A History of Corporate Social Responsibility: Concepts and Practices," in: Crane, D., McWilliams, A., Matten, D., Moon, J. and Siegel, D. S. (eds.), *The Oxford Handbook of Corporate Social Responsibility*, Oxford: Oxford University Press, pp. 19–46.
Carroll, W. K., 2002, "Does Disorganized Capitalism Disorganize Corporate Networks?" *Canadian Journal of Sociology*, 27(3): 339–371.
Casson, M. (ed.), 1990, *Multinational Corporations*, Aldershot: Elgar.
Center for Public Integrity, 2016, "About the Center for Public Integrity" <www.publicintegrity.org/> accessed on December 7, 2016.
Coen, D., 1998, "The European Business Interest and the Nation State: Large-firm Lobbying in the European Union and Member States," *Journal of Public Policy*, 18(1): 75–100.
Cowen, A. P. and Marcel, J. J., 2011, "Damaged Goods: Board Decisions to Dismiss Reputationally Compromised Directors," *Academy of Management Journal*, 54(6): 509–527.
Crespi, R. and Renneboog, L., 2010, "Is (Institutional) Shareholder Activism New?: Evidence From UK Shareholder Coalitions in the Pre-Cadbury Era," *Corporate Governance: An International Review*, 18(4): 274–295.
Dalton, M., 1959, *Men Who Manage: Fusions of Feeling and Theory in Administration*, New York: John Wiley.
Davis, G. F. and Greve, H. R., 1997, "Corporate Elite Networks and Governance Changes in the 1980s," *American Journal of Sociology*, 103(1): 1–37.

Delgado-García, J. B., De Quevedo-Puente, E. and De La Fuente-Sabaté, J. M., 2010, "The Impact of Ownership Structure on Corporate Reputation: Evidence From Spain," *Corporate Governance: An International Review*, 18(6): 540–556.
Dietz, G. and Gillespie, N., 2012, "Rebuilding Trust: How Siemens Atoned for Its Sins," *theguardian.com*, March 26, 2012 <www.theguardian.com/sustainable-business/recovering-business-trust-siemens> accessed on August 9, 2017.
Djelic, M.-L. and Sahlin-Andersson, K. (eds.), 2006, *Transnational Governance: Institutional Dynamics of Regulation*, Cambridge: Cambridge University Press.
Doh, J. P. and Teegen, H. (eds.), 2003, *Globalization and NGOs: Transforming Business, Government, and Society*, Westport, CT: Praeger.
Dowling, J. B. and Pfeffer, J., 1975, "Organizational Legitimacy: Social Values and Organizational Behavior," *Pacific Sociological Review*, 18(1): 122–136.
Durrell, L., 1957, *Justine*, London: Faber & Faber.
Durrell, L., 1958a, *Mountolive*, London: Faber & Faber.
Durrell, L., 1958b, *Balthazar*, London: Faber & Faber.
Durrell, L., 1960, *Clea*, London: Faber & Faber.
Engwall, L., Kipping, M. and Üsdiken, B., 2016, *Defining Management: Business Schools, Consultants, Media*, New York: Routledge.
Enrione, A., Mazza, C. and Zerboni, F., 2006, "Institutionalizing Codes of Governance," *American Behavioral Scientist*, 49(7): 961–973.
Fiss, P., 2008, "Institutions and Corporate Governance," in: Greenwood, R., Oliver, C., Sahlin, K. and Suddaby, R. (eds.), *The Sage Handbook of Organizational Institutionalism*, London: Sage, pp. 389–410.
Fiss, P. and Zajac, E. J., 2004, "The Diffusion of Ideas Over Contested Terrain: The (Non)Adoption of a Shareholder Value Orientation Among German Firms," *Administrative Science Quarterly*, 49(4): 501–534.
Fligstein, N., 1990, *The Transformation of Corporate Control*, Cambridge, MA: Harvard University Press.
Fligstein, N. and Choo, J., 2005, "Law and Corporate Governance," *Annual Review of Law and Social Science*, 1(1): 61–84.
Franco, V., Sánchez, F. P., German, J. and Mock, P., 2014, *Real-World Exhaust Emissions From Modern Diesel Cars: A Meta-Analysis of PEMS Emission Data From EU (EURO6) and US (Tier 2 BIN 5/ULEV II) Diesel Passenger Cars. Part 1: Aggregated Results*, Berlin: International Council on Clean Transportation <www.theicct.org/sites/default/files/publications/ICCT_PEMS-study_diesel-cars_20141010.pdf> accessed August 10, 2017.
Freeman, R. E., 1984, *Strategic Management: A Stakeholder Approach*, Boston: Pitman.
Freeman, R. E., Harrison, J. S., Wicks, A. C., Parmar, B. L. and de Colle, S., 2010, *Stakeholder Theory: The State of the Art*, Cambridge: Cambridge University Press.
Frostenson, M., 2006, *Legitimationskontrollen: en studie av etiska värderingars roll i gränsöverskridande förvärv och fusioner* (The Control for Legitimacy: A Study of the Role of Ethical Values in Cross-Border Acquisitions and Mergers), Dissertation from the Stockholm School of Economics, Stockholm: EFI.
Goergen, M., 2012, *International Corporate Governance*, Harlow: Pearson Education.
Gomulya, D. and Boeker, W., 2014, "How Firms Respond to Financial Restatement: CEO Successors and External Reactions," *Academy of Management Journal*, 57(6): 1759–1785.

Göthberg, P., 2007, *Varför projekt överlever: En studie av Skandias Idéer för livet* (Why Projects Survive: A Study of Skandia's Ideas for Life), Licentiate Dissertation, Department of Business Studies, Uppsala: Uppsala University.

Gouldner, A. W., 1954, *Patterns of Industrial Bureaucracy*, Glencoe, IL: Free Press.

Grafström, M., 2006, *The Development of Swedish Business Journalism: Historical Roots of an Organisational Field*, Doctoral Dissertation No. 121 from the Department of Business Studies, Uppsala: Uppsala University.

Grafström, M., Göthberg, P. and Windell, K., 2008, *CSR: Företagsansvar i förändring* (CSR: Corporate Responsibility in Flux), Malmö: Liber.

Grafström, M., Grünberg, J., Pallas, J. and Windell, K., 2006, *Ekonominyhetens väg: Från kvartalsrapporter till ekonominyheter* (The Route of the Business News: From Quarterly Reports to Business News), Stockholm: SNS Förlag.

Grafström, M. and Pallas, J., 2007, "The Negotiation of Business News," in: Kjaer, P. and Slaatta, T. (eds.), *Mediating Business: The Expansion of Business Journalism*, Copenhagen: Copenhagen Business School Press, pp. 217–233.

Grünberg, J. and Pallas, J., 2009, "Barbarians at the Gates?: Organizations Protecting and Promoting their (non)Technical Cores Through Institutional Boundary Spanning," in: Wedlin, L., Sahlin, K. and Grafström, M. (eds.), *Exploring the Worlds of Mercury and Minerva: Essays for Lars Engwall*, Acta Universitatis Upsaliensis. Studia Oeconomiae Negotiorum 51, Uppsala: Uppsala University, 243–256.

Grünberg, J. and Pallas, J., 2013, "Beyond the News Desk: The Embeddedness of Business News," *Media, Culture & Society*, 35(2): 216–233.

Hedelius, P., 2015, *Telia: alliansregeringen och korruptionen* (Telia: The Alliance Government and the Corruption), Stockholm: Massolit.

Hedmo, T., 2004, *Rule-making in Transnational Space*, Doctoral Thesis No. 109 from the Department of Business Studies, Uppsala: Uppsala University.

Hedmo, T., Sahlin-Andersson, K. and Wedlin, L., 2006, "The Emergence of a European Regulatory Field of Management Education," in: Djelic, M.-L. and Sahlin-Andersson, K. (eds.), *Transnational Governance*, Cambridge: Cambridge University Press, pp. 308–328.

Hirst, P. and Thompson, G., 1996, *Globalization in Question: The International Economies and the Possibilities of Governance*, Cambridge: Cambridge University Press.

History of Telia Company <www.teliacompanyhistory.com/> accessed on December 7, 2016.

Hjarvard, S., 2013, *The Mediatization of Culture and Society*, London: Routledge.

H&M, 2016, "A Clear Stand Against Child Labour" <http://sustainability.hm.com/en/sustainability/commitments/choose-and-reward-responsible-partners/code-of-conduct/clear-stand-against-child-labour.html> accessed on December 6, 2016.

Houlder, V., 2014, "Leak Reveals Scale of Corporate Tax Deals With Luxembourg," *FT.com*, November 6, 2014 <www.ft.com/content/93e75c1a-6545-11e4-91b1-00144feabdc0> accessed on December 8, 2016.

Hubbard, N., 2013, *Conquering Global Markets: Secrets From the World's Most Successful Multinationals*, London: Palgrave Macmillan.

ICIJ, 2016a, "About ICIJ" <www.icij.org/about> accessed on December 8, 2016.

ICIJ, 2016b, "Luxembourg Leaks: Global Companies' Secrets Exposed" <www.icij.org/project/luxembourg-leaks> accessed on December 8, 2016.

ICIJ, 2016c, "Swiss Leaks: Murky Cash Sheltered By Bank Secrecy" <www.icij.org/project/swiss-leaks> accessed on December 11, 2016.

Iriye, A. (ed.), 2014, *Global Interdependence: The World After 1945*, Cambridge, MA: The Belknap Press of Harvard University Press.

Jansson, A., 2013, "'Real Owners' and 'Common Investors': Institutional Logics and the Media as a Governance Mechanism," *Corporate Governance: An International Review*, 21(1): 7–25.

Jonsson, S., Greve, H. R. and Fujiwara-Greve, T., 2009, "Lost Without Deserving: The Spread of Legitimacy Loss in Response to Reported Corporate Deviance," *Administrative Science Quarterly*, 54(2): 195–228.

Judge, W. Q., Gaur, A. and Muller-Kahle, M. I., 2010, "Antecedents of Shareholder Activism in Target Firms: Evidence From a Multi-Country Study," *Corporate Governance: An International Review*, 18(4): 258–273.

Jutterström, M., 2004, *Att påverka beslut—företag i EUs regelsättande* (Influencing Decisions: Companies in the Rule-Making of the European Union), Doctoral Dissertation from the Stockholm School of Economics, Stockholm: EFI.

Keasey, K., Thompson, S. and Wright, M., 1997, "Introduction. The Corporate Governance Problem: Competing Diagnoses and Solutions," in: Keasey, K., Thompson, S. and Wright, M. (eds.), *Corporate Governance: Economic, Management, and Financial Issues*, Oxford: Oxford University Press, pp. 1–17.

King, B. G., 2008, "A Political Mediation Model of Corporate Response to Social Movement Activism," *Administrative Science Quarterly*, 53(3): 395–421.

Kjaer, P., Erkama, N. and Grafström, M., 2007, "Transforming Business News Content: A Comparative Analysis," in: Kjaer, P. and Slatta, T. (eds.), *Mediating Business: The Expansion of Business Journalism*, Copenhagen: Copenhagen Business School Press, 131–158.

MacAvoy, P. W. and Schmalensee, R. (eds.), 2014, *The Causes and Effects of Deregulation*, Cheltenham: Edward Elgar.

Marks, G., Hooghe, L. and Blank, K., 1996, "European Integration From the 1980s: State-centric v. Multilevel Governance," *Journal of Common Market Studies*, 34(3): 341–378.

McDonnell, M.-H. and King, B. G., 2013, "Keeping Up Appearances: Reputational Threat and Impression Management After Social Movement Boycotts," *Administrative Science Quarterly*, 58(3): 387–419.

McGahan, A. M., 2014, "AOM 2015 Theme: Opening Governance. Theme for the 75th Annual Meeting of the Academy of Management, Vancouver, BC, Canada" <http://aom.org/uploadedFiles/Meetings/annualmeeting/2015/AOM2015Theme-OpeningGovernance.pdf> accessed on December 12, 2016.

McGann, J., 2016, *The Fifth Estate: Think Tanks, Public Policy, and Governance*, Washington, DC: Brookings Institution Press.

McNulty, T. and Pettigrew, A., 1998, "Strategists on the Board," *Organization Studies*, 20(1): 47–74.

Meikle, G., 2016, *Social Media: Communication, Sharing and Visibility*, New York: Routledge.

Milne, R., 2013, "TeliaSonera Eyes Shake-up as Chief Quits," *FT.com*, February 1, 2013 <www.ft.com/content/a21c6812-6c53-11e2-b73a-00144feab49a?mhq5j=e1> accessed August 11, 2017.

Milne, R., 2016, "Telia to Cop $1.4bn Fine Over Corruption in Uzbekistan," *Financial Times*, September 15, 2016 <www.ft.com/content/1b02bb34-9350-3751-a6e1-153b3b06b424?mhq5j=e1> accessed on August 9, 2017.

Milward, A. S., 1999, *The European Rescue of the Nation-State*, London: Taylor & Francis.

Moravcisk, A., 1993, "Preferences and Power in the European Community: A Liberal Intergovernmental Approach," *Journal of Common Market Studies*, 31(4): 473–524.

Morgan, G. and Knights, D. (eds.), 1997, *Regulation and Deregulation in European Financial Services*, Basingstoke: Macmillan.

Mörth, U. (ed.), 2004, *Soft Law in Governance and Regulation*, Cheltenham: Edgar Elgar.

New York Times, "What Was Volkswagen Thinking?" September 23, 2015 <www.nytimes.com/2015/09/23/opinion/what-was-volkswagen-thinking.html?_r=0> accessed on December 7, 2016.

Ocasio, W., 1999, "Institutionalized Action and Corporate Governance: The Reliance on Rules of CEO Succession," *Administrative Science Quarterly*, 44(2): 348–416.

Ohmae, K., 1995, *End of the Nation State: The Rise of Regional Economies*, London: HarperCollins.

Pallas, J., 2007, *Talking Organizations: Corporate Media Work and Negotiations of Local Practice*, Doctoral Dissertation No. 133 from the Department of Business Studies, Uppsala: Uppsala University.

Pallas, J., Strannegård, L. and Jonsson, S. (eds.), 2014, *Organizations and the Media: Organizing in a Mediatized World*, London: Routledge.

Petrelius Karlberg, P., 2007, *Den medialiserade direktören* (The Medialized Manager), Doctoral Dissertation from the Stockholm School of Economics, Stockholm: EFI.

Pfeffer, J., 1978, *Organizational Design*, Arlington Heights, IL: AHM Publishing Corporation.

Pfeffer, J. and Salancik, G. R., 1978, *The External Control of Organizations*, New York: Harper and Row.

Power, M., 1997, *The Audit Society: Rituals of Verification*, Oxford: Oxford University Press.

Pulver, S., 2004, *Power in the Public Sphere: The Battle Between Oil Companies and Environmental Groups in UN Climate Change Negotiations 1991–2003*, Dissertation Submitted in Partly Satisfaction of a Doctor of Philosophy in Sociology in the Graduate Division of University of California, Berkeley, Fall 2004.

Sahlin-Andersson, K., 2006, "Corporate Social Responsibility: A Trend and a Movement, But of What and for What?" *Corporate Governance*, 6(5): 595–608.

Shleifer, A. and Vishny, R. W., 1997, "A Survey of Corporate Governance," *Journal of Finance*, 52(2): 737–783.

Staples, C. L., 2008, "Cross-border Acquisitions and Board Globalization in the World's Largest TNC, 1995–2005," *Sociological Quarterly*, 49(1): 31–51.

Stone, D., 1996, *Capturing the Political Imagination: Think Tanks and the Policy Process*, London: Frank Cass.

Strange, S., 1996, *The Retreat of the State: The Diffusion of Power in the World Economy*, Cambridge: Cambridge University Press.

Suchman, M. C., 1995, "Managing Legitimacy: Strategic and Institutional Approaches," *Academy of Management Review*, 20(3): 571–610.

Thompson, G. J., Carder, D. K., Besch, M. C., Thiruvengadam, A. and Kappanna, H. K., 2014, *In-Use Emissions Testing of Light-Duty Diesel Vehicles in the United*

States, Center for Alternative Fuels, Engines & Emissions, Morgantown: University of West Virginia.
Thompson, J. D., 1967, *Organizations in Action*, New York: McGraw-Hill.
Tihanyi, L., Graffin, S. and George, G., 2014, "Rethinking Governance in Management Research," *Academy of Management Journal*, 57(6): 1535–1543.
Tolentino, P. E. E., 2000, *Multinational Corporations: Emergence and Evolution*, London: Routledge.
UNICEF, 2016, "UNICEF's Corporate Partnerships" <www.unicef.org/corporate_partners/index_82186.html> accessed on December 6, 2016.
US Environmental Protection Agency, 2016, "Volkswagen Light Duty Diesel Vehicle Violations for Model Years 2009–2016" <www.epa.gov/vw> accessed on December 7, 2016.
Veblen, T., 1899, *The Theory of the Leisure Class: An Economic Study of Institutions*, New York: B. W. Huebsch.
Veblen, T., 1904, *The Theory of Business Enterprise*, New York: C. Scribner's Sons.
Wedlin, L., 2004, *Playing the Ranking Game: Field Formation and Boundary-work in European Management Education*, Doctoral Dissertation 108 from the Department of Business Studies, Uppsala: Uppsala University.
Wedlin, L., 2006, *Ranking Business Schools: Forming Fields, Identities and Boundaries in International Management Education*, Cheltenham: Edgar Elgar.
Weiss, M., Bonnet, P., Hummel, R. and Steiniger, N., 2013, *A Complementary Emissions Test for Light-Duty Vehicles: Assessing the Technical Feasibility of Candidate Procedures*, European Commission JRC Scientific and Policy Reports, Report EUR 25572 EN, Brussels: European Commission.
Wernerfelt, B., 1984, "A Resource-based View of the Firm," *Strategic Management Journal*, 5(2): 171–180.
Westphal, J. D. and Zajac, E. J., 1994, "Substance and Symbolism in CEO's Long-term Incentive Plans," *Administrative Science Quarterly*, 39(3): 367–390.
Williams, M. T., 2010, *Uncontrolled Risk: The Lessons of Lehman Brothers and How Systemic Risk Can Still Bring Down the World Financial System*, New York: McGraw-Hill.
Windell, K., 2006, *Corporate Social Responsibility under Construction: Ideas, Translations, and Institutional Change*, Doctoral Dissertation No. 123 from the Department of Business Studies, Uppsala: Uppsala University.
Winterkorn, M., 2015, "Statement by Prof. Dr. Winterkorn" <www.volkswagenag.com/en/news/2015/9/Statement.html> accessed on December 7, 2016.
Wright, M., Siegel, D. S., Keasey, K. and Filatotchev, I. (eds.), 2013, *The Oxford Handbook of Corporate Governance*, Oxford: Oxford University Press.
Zajac, E. J. and Westphal, J. D., 1995, "Who Shall Govern?: CEO/Board Power, Demographic Similarity, and New Director Selection," *Administrative Science Quarterly*, 40(1): 60–83.
Zhang, Y. and Wiersema, M. F., 2009, "Stock Market Reaction to CEO Certification: The Signalling Role of CEO Background," *Strategic Management Journal*, 30(7): 693–710.

2 A Field Approach to Corporate Governance

Lars Engwall, Jaan Grünberg, Josef Pallas, Kerstin Sahlin, Linda Wedlin, Stefan Arora-Jonsson, Helena Buhr, Katarina Buhr, Magnus Frostenson, Ingemund Hägg, Laurence Romani, Lars Strannegård and Karolina Windell

Introduction

As was pointed out in Chapter 1, a basic point of departure for this book is the felt need to develop a new approach to corporate governance. This is particularly the case in relation to the principal-agency approach. As demonstrated by the three cases in the previous chapter, there is a crying need to take a wider perspective and take into consideration that other actors than the principals and their agents are important for the governance of corporations. This means that corporate governance is associated with considerable complexity. In order to address this complexity, research has provided a valuable approach by introducing the field concept—i.e., pointing out that all organizations, corporations included of course, are parts of *organizational fields*. However, they are not only parts of fields; their situation is also characterized by *embeddedness*—that is, they have all sorts of relationships with other actors in their particular field, as, again, was demonstrated by our three cases in Chapter 1. In addition, it is important to note that the relationships are not only unilateral, as modeled in the principal-agency model, where the principal is signaling the agent. The relationships are characterized by *reciprocity*, meaning that the various actors influence each other bilaterally or even multilaterally. This means that it is important for our analysis of corporate governance to discuss in more detail three central concepts for our analysis: (1) organizational fields, (2) embeddedness and (3) reciprocity. We will do this in the following three sections, where we also present our approach step-by-step.

A Field of Governance

The Field Concept

Field theories and models in the social sciences provide a way of exploring and explaining the complex interplay among actors, meanings and activities, thus specifying the character and form of the organizational and institutional embeddedness of action. Field models aim to explain the relations and interdependence among a large set of actors and to understand overarching social regularities that can be observed in actions and processes over time (Martin 2003) and are therefore particularly suitable for addressing the complicated governance relations we exemplified in Chapter 1.

The field concept situates actions and relations in an analytical space between actors, be they individuals or organizations and society (Wooten and Hoffman 2008) with the aim to capture "the totality of relevant actors" that influence and shape individual actions and activities (DiMaggio and Powell 1983: 148). In later developments of the field concept, particularly within the strand of organizational institutionalism (Greenwood et al. 2008a), the term organizational field has come to focus on those actors that make up a "recognized area of institutional life" (DiMaggio and Powell 1983: 148). In these fields, the behavior of organizations is guided by various other organizations. In this way, more or less taken-for-granted repetitive social behavior is underpinned by normative systems and cognitive understandings. These in turn give meaning and stability to social exchange that enables the self-reproduction of the social order (Scott 1995, Greenwood et al. 2008b: 4). These other organizations, while providing guidance for action, at the same time both constrain and enable individual actions and relations within the field (Djelic and Sahlin-Andersson 2006a: 23). Modern corporate governance is obviously characterized by these features.

The field concept needs additional clarification, however. If we briefly go back to the early developments of the concept in the social sciences, we find at least two important dimensions that are essential to our argument. They are (1) the structural and (2) the cognitive dimensions of fields.

As far as *the structural dimension* is concerned, early field theorists, such as Kurt Lewin and Roland Warren, developed the concept of field in order to analyze the mutual interdependence of the "totality of coexisting facts" that affect the behavior of actors at any given time (Lewin 1951: 240). Warren, building on Lewin, developed the concept of interorganizational fields to observe that "interaction between two organizations is affected, in part at least, by the nature of the organizational pattern or network in which they find themselves" (Warren 1967: 397). While these theories clearly put the emphasis on relationships and interconnectedness, these are deemed to consist largely of intra-field interactions and dependencies, suggesting that the field is almost synonymous with networks (Djelic and Sahlin-Andersson 2006b). These definitions of fields thus stress the relational and "spatial" view of fields—as interacting and interconnected actors and organizations. As we will show next, these interactions are important for modern corporate governance.

In terms of *the cognitive dimension*, Scott and Meyer (1983) revisited and recombined Warren's work (1967, 1972) to talk about the duality of space and meaning associated with the organization and development of societal sectors. This conceptualization of fields is closer to and partly inspired by

Bourdieu's (1977) use of the field concept. He introduced the notion of meaning and common belief systems into the analysis, specifically noting how fields are defined and held together by a common recognition of the importance of certain activities. A coherent pattern of action and meaning thus develops without any single actor intentionally striving for coherence or conformity. In Bourdieu's notion of a field, it is constituted by the ongoing struggle among its members to define the value and positions within the field. Such struggles, often explained as the struggle between dominant and dominated actors, are both for position and influence and for a common and dominant understanding and meaning of the field itself. When this notion of field was brought into the neo-institutional theories—through DiMaggio (1983) and DiMaggio and Powell (1983)—it became associated with the Weberian concept of rationalization, iron cage and spheres of value. DiMaggio and Powell thus pointed out that organizations may be influenced by each other, and develop in similar ways, without ever being in direct contact or interaction with one another. Thus, as important as interaction and direct relations are, organizations also change through cultural and normative forces and through changes in identities and positions. As we will show later in this chapter, we have been strongly influenced by the reasoning of DiMaggio and Powell (1983) in developing our approach to corporate governance.

Field theories thus teach us to pay attention to both structural and cognitive dimensions of the embeddedness of corporations. Yet empirical research following the field tradition has tended to give prominence to either one or the other of these aspects (Djelic and Sahlin-Andersson 2006a; Mohr 2003). In one strand of the institutional literature directly following on the work of DiMaggio and Powell (1983), the understanding of fields as networks and interaction patterns among a set of increasingly homogeneous organizations dominates (Greenwood and Meyer 2008). In the other strand, researchers have tried in particular to understand how cultural frames, ideas, or patterns of meaning shape and constitute new structures as well as new modes of action and interaction across the world (e.g., Meyer and Scott 1983; Thomas et al. 1987; Meyer et al. 1997). This separation is also evident in the literature on corporate governance. Many institutionally inspired studies have focused on the role of personal relations and networks, such as in studies of board interlocks (Davis 1991; Haunschild 1993; Haunschild and Beckman 1998; Gulati and Westphal 1999; Bizjak, Lemmon and Whitby 2009). On the other hand, a major current of research has at the same time focused on the cultural and cognitive embeddedness of governance relationships, often with specific reference to field models. Mostly, the political and legal dimensions of market creation and functioning have been studied (Edelman 1990, 1992; Stone Sweet 1999; Fligstein 2001). This research has particularly emphasized the symbiotic development of political and market structures, and rule systems (Fligstein and Stone Sweet 2002).

Following Djelic and Sahlin-Andersson (2006a), we note that a field framework can, and indeed should, combine and integrate studies of individual behavior, interaction and processes with studies of institutional and cultural forces, which are the forces that shape and structure both patterns of behavior and patterns of interaction (see also Martin 2003; Mohr 2003). Our conception of the field of governance incorporates both of these aspects and views these fields as the set of organized actors and processes constraining and enabling the way in which business corporations are governed. Individual actions should thus be understood as dependent on the characteristics of the field and on the positions that individual actors hold in relation to other actors in the field. Thus field theories posit that we need to study the relational positions, meanings, and activities that make up a certain field. In this work, there will be a particular focus on the latter in accordance with our notion of corporate governance in action.

Our Approach

In Chapter 1, we mentioned the limitations of the principal-agency approach, with its focus on just one governing body: the owners. We also pointed to the problems of the stakeholder approach due to the difficulty of defining stakeholders. Our approach in defining the field of governance is in a way between the principal-agency approach and the stakeholder approach, as our point of departure is the political science literature and its focus on two modes of governance: politics and markets (cf., e.g., Lindblom 1977). This means a distinction between collective decisions made by elected politicians on behalf of the electorate (politics) and individual decisions based on economic considerations in the market (markets). Significant actors in those two systems of governance are *regulators* and *market actors*. However, as was discussed in Chapter 1, there are also other actors present in the governance of modern organizations: the media, NGOs, auditing organizations, etc. Together they play an important role in corporate governance as *scrutinizers*.

Regulators

The issue of regulation has become particularly visible in recent decades due to strong tendencies to diffuse market principles (Djelic 2006) and open up markets (Yergin and Stanislaw 1998). However, this development has not implied the abandonment of regulation (deregulation) but rather changes in the rules of the game (re-regulation). Nevertheless, regulators are still significant actors, as they always have been. And with the recurrent financial crises, the need for regulations has been articulated.

We noted earlier that re-regulation has meant that softer forms of regulations—with considerable elements of self-regulation, voluntariness, and social control. Even at this early juncture, we get an idea of how the ideal types of governance overlap and mix in practice. As legal frameworks have undergone continuous change as a result of internationalization, the balance of power between the different levels of government has shifted. In discussions related to the European Union, it has been common to speak of Europe as a multilevel governance system, where national, regional, and European levels are interrelated (Marks, Hooghe and Blank 1996; Jacobsson 2006; Mörth 2006). Regulation by national governments, too, has become more differentiated. The levels are definitely not disconnected. European competition policies, for instance, have been copied by national governments, and the expansion of rule-making into different layers significantly changes the environments for businesses (Djelic and Kleiner 2006). However, as pointed out earlier, the relationship between corporations and governments is reciprocal. It is not only governments that influence corporations; corporations also influence governments (see further in the next section).

Although the many regulatory actors may seem to be diverse, a striking convergence is appearing across sectors and across territories. Sectors as diverse as the defense industry, labor markets, higher education, health care, public management and the social responsibility of corporations are increasingly governed in a similar way: transnationally.

Market Actors

In terms of markets actors, investors play a particularly significant role since they represent the owners with their specific rights and interests as well as power over significant financial resources. Prime examples are private investors, pension funds and mutual funds. Therefore, there has been a strong focus on the role of investors in the past few decades. As was pointed out in Chapter 1, in traditional agency theories, they have been looked upon as principals trying to deal with agents (managers) in their own best interest. As the former have delegated operations to the latter, the models point out, that they run the risk of the managers not acting entirely in the interests of the principals. Therefore, in principal-agency models, the issue of corporate governance is seen, also as mentioned, as an issue of owners monitoring managers. This idea was developed by Alchian and Demsetz (1972), Jensen and Meckling (1976) and Fama (1980), followed by a number of important studies in the 1990s (Fligstein 1990; Roe 1994; Blair 1995; Monks and Minow 1995; Keasey, Thompson and Wright 1997).

Empirical studies in the area, stimulated by an interest in practice, came to take a broader view, focusing on investor relations. More than 20 years ago, Useem (1996) thus coined the term "relational investing," and Tainio et al. (2003) noted the impact of actors such as analysts in formulating corporate policy. In addition, over several decades important institutions, particularly in the United States, have developed practices of shareholder activism (Smith 1996). In addition, regulatory developments have spurred changes in interactional patterns. Kaplan and Holmstrom (2004), for example, draw attention to the dropping by the Securities and Exchange Commission (SEC) of the rule forcing owners to file proxies if communicating with more than ten other shareholders.

Although investors are very important for modern corporations, they are not the only significant type of market actors. Others, which also have considerable influence on corporate behavior, are providers of human, physical and financial resources—that is, the workforce, suppliers of inputs and various financial institutions, particularly banks. They provide opportunities for as well as constraints on the corporation by their conditions for input to the operations. Finally, as pointed out earlier, the behavior of competitors constitutes a significant force of governance.

Scrutinizers

The stress of regulators in itself implies an extension of the focus for corporate governance. Another significant addition is the introduction of scrutinizers as governing bodies. Among these, we have identified two groups of actors as particularly significant: (1) non-governmental organizations (NGOs) and (2) the media.

In terms of the NGOs, such as Amnesty International, Greenpeace and CorpWatch, their activities are closely associated with the concept of corporate social responsibility (CSR). It is to a large extent related to a critique of corporate behavior in the Third World in the wake of a growing discourse of globalization. It then got a foothold in the corporate world and developed into a powerful management concept (Windell 2006). Social responsibility is often even presented as a business opportunity rather than an obstacle to corporate profitability. Corporations largely communicate their social responsibility in their annual reports, communiqués and websites. In addition, the use of codes of conduct is spreading in the business community.

One of the explanations behind the diffuseness of the CSR concept is the multitude of actors directing their interest to the concept, which was open to interpretation and void of any consensus meaning. Governments, grassroot organizations and investors have exerted demands on corporations to behave responsibly and expand their actions to go far beyond producing return on the capital of investors. Windell (2006) showed that the concept has gained in usage largely due to a broader group of actors jumping on the bandwagon with their own contributions. In addition, management consultants and the media have been visible in their treatment of CSR issues, expanding both the audience and the group of active participants (Windell 2006). Furthermore, corporations themselves have been active in placing CSR high on corporate agendas. Rather than being merely passive receivers of pressures, corporations have interacted with others in the field and co-produced the meaning-creation and popularization of CSR. Again, we should thus note the interactive character of governance in practice.

In addition to NGOs, the media have come to play an important role in scrutinizing corporations. As a matter of fact, we can relate this governance relation to the ideal types of political science: the media (earlier the press) has since long been mentioned in the literature as the fourth branch of government in addition to the executive, the legislative and the judicial branches (Siebert, Peterson and Schramm 1956). The media thus constitute another group of actors that is scrutinizing all the other processes of governance. They monitor and report on the actions of the main actors (regulators, market actors, but also other scrutinizers). For actors in all governing relations, it is important to be aware of the attention of the media and to be prepared to act in relation to media.

Needless to say, the media landscape has changed dramatically over time. Print newspapers faced their first competition from radio, and later television. However, these were governed in the same way as the print media, with strong editorial functions. Today, in contrast, social media have exploded with limited control of "what is fit to print" to allude to the slogan of the *New York Times*. Facebook, Twitter, WikiLeaks, etc., have considerable impact on the field of governance, sometimes giving rise to serious investigations by reporters, sometimes providing what the Trump administration has labeled "alternative facts." (For analyses of social media, see, e.g., the contributions in Hendricks and Noor Al-Deen 2012, particularly Chapters 8–10 on strategic communication.)

In conclusion, our approach is thus based on the idea that corporations are part of a field of governance, where they are subject to the impact of three major groups of actors—namely, regulators, market actors and scrutinizers. As pointed out, this governance occurs through their embeddedness in the field, a topic we will turn to next.

Embeddedness

The Concept of Embeddedness

The second significant concept for our analysis is *embeddedness*. It means a recognition that corporations are situated in collectives, amidst a set of relations that influence how corporations act. Again, we can refer back to our examples in Chapter 1 as illustrations. They demonstrated how the corporations in question were embedded in numerous relations to regulators, market actors and, particularly, scrutinizing organizations, such as media companies, universities and law enforcement agencies.

The term embeddedness, which traces back to the writings of Polanyi (1944), was made popular in more recent scholarly writings by Granovetter (1985) and was later given different interpretations (Krippner and Alvarez 2007). Granovetter, for his part, focused on the "networks of interpersonal relations" that influence economic transactions, and used it to counter the dominant neoclassical economics view of market transactions as independent of the social and relational ties of the actors involved (Granovetter 1985: 504). Together with Polanyi's efforts to challenge the understanding of the "economy" as analytically autonomous and thus a "sphere" that is separate from society in general (Polanyi 1944; Krippner and Alvarez 2007), these writings have formed the basis for a relational and sociological approach to economics and the study of economic transactions (cf. Davis 2005).

The aforementioned means a recognition that governance is embedded in systems of norms and relations that reside largely outside individual corporations and relations, and are both culturally and socio-politically constructed (Fiss 2008: 390). Such embeddedness implies that governance processes are guided not by fixed systems of rules and principles, but by the ongoing interaction and interrelation among the actors involved. The meaning as well as the practice of corporate governance is created in such interactions. Furthermore, this implies that corporate governance needs to be understood as embedded in permeable and changeable systems of meaning, subject to institutional logics (Fiss 2008).

The recognition of the embeddedness of corporate governance practices in wider societal and relational systems also opens the analysis to include multiple actors and interests affecting the governance of contemporary corporations. Particularly focusing on the ongoing and continuous construction of corporate governance mechanisms and practices, it has been suggested that

> rather than focusing merely on executives and directors, such work could take seriously how governance is constructed at the intersection of various influence spheres, including those of inside and outside constituents and the attempts of corporate actors to actively manage such groups.
>
> (Fiss 2008: 403)

The complexity that these developments present, to both corporations and to the researchers trying to understand them, has resulted in a considerable interest in the connections between corporations and their environment. Although many classical contributions have recognized these connections, including those by Thompson (1967), Pfeffer and Salancik (1978) and the early institutionalists, there are still a number of unanswered questions.

In an effort to answer some of these questions Fligstein and McAdam (2012) have developed a comprehensive theory of the strategic action field, which is reminiscent of our conception of governance field but broader. In their perspective, organizations can be seen as "Russian dolls" where a large number of strategic action fields are nested into each other. However, a core part of their theory is the idea of fields forming internal governance units (IGU). These units "seek to promote the long-term stability and routine reproduction of the field" (Fligstein and McAdam 2012: 78). They achieve this through activities such as lobbying, external liaison, administration, information, regulation, enforcement and certification. A distinct contribution from this perspective is that Fligstein and McAdam point to mechanisms for organizing fields beyond the well-explored role of so-called institutional entrepreneurs. A similar kind of organizational form is found in the concept of field governing bodies (Van Wijk et al. 2013). In relation to our analysis, the aforementioned internal units—which we will label boundary-spanning units next, inspired by Thompson (1967)—are very important to uncover if we are to understand the embeddedness of corporations.

These IGU can be contrasted with the idea of elites and centralized power. Zald and Lounsbury (2010) have called for the study of command posts, a term which they use to denote both "traditional centers of societal power . . . and other formal bodies of governance" (Zald and Lounsbury 2010: 964). They emphasize the embeddedness of such centers of power in organizational fields and thereby their being shaped and constituted by field-level influences, which provides a more "fluid" or "nuanced and multidimensional approach to power" (Zald and Lounsbury 2010: 974). The staffing of experts and the communities of that shape expert discourse are critical for these command posts.

Finally, we should note that the embeddedness of organizations does not always mean that they have direct relations. In many cases the relationships between corporations and other significant actors in the field involve various kinds of intermediaries, such as consultants and interest organizations (see, e.g., the contributions in Kipping and Clark 2012). The observation earlier that organizational fields are in part structured by intermediaries has important consequences for our study.

Our Approach

The embeddedness in the field of governance means that corporations are subject to various forces from regulators, market actors and scrutinizers. These can be analyzed by means of the institutional ideas that constitute a main part of the theoretical foundations for the present volume (e.g., Meyer and Rowan 1977; Zucker 1977; DiMaggio and Powell 1983; and Meyer and Scott 1983). We then find that regulators signal by means of rules, market actors through benchmarks and scrutinizers through norms (Table 2.1).

Looking more closely at the three governors, we find that regulators (Table 2.1, cell A1) are signaling by rules, which are associated with what DiMaggio and Powell (1983) label as coercive forces (cell B1) and what Scott (1995)

Table 2.1 Characteristics of Three Types of Governance

Governor	*Regulators (1)*	*Market Actors (2)*	*Scrutinizers (3)*
Signals of Governance (A)	Rules	Benchmarks	Norms
Isomorphic Force (B)	Coercive	Mimetic	Normative
Organizational Pillar (C)	Regulative	Cognitive	Normative
Governance Process (D)	Obedience	Adaptation	Norm Following
Non-Compliance Measure (E)	Punishments	Market Verdict	Naming and Shaming

later labeled the regulative pillar (cell C1). The governance process is obedience (cell D1), and the measures for non-compliance (cell E1) are punishments. These could be in the form of imprisonment or fines, and in the worst case even execution in some countries. Actors pursuing this mode of governance are primarily political bodies at local, national and international levels.

While the relationship between politics and the institutional framework is obvious, the relationship between markets and the same framework is less clear. As a matter of fact, DiMaggio and Powell (1983) argue that competitive isomorphism "is most relevant for those fields in which free and open competition exists" (p. 150), and they therefore concentrate on the institutional isomorphism, leaving the competitive isomorphism aside. However, even if there is no "free and open competition," we can observe mimetic behavior. As early as the 1930s, Chamberlin (1933) and Robinson (1933), independently of each other, presented models of oligopolistic pricing behavior based on the observation that firms in oligopolies can observe each other and therefore follow each other in pricing. Such mimetic behavior is not limited to pricing, however. Studies of newspaper competition (Engwall 1981, 1985), bank internationalization (Engwall and Wallenstål 1988), lending in the deregulated banking markets (Engwall 1994; 1997), recruitment of university presidents (Engwall 2007) and diffusion of management ideas (Engwall and Kipping 2006) provide evidence of mimetic forces in markets. This means that we find it appropriate to associate market actors with benchmarks (Table 2.1, cell B1), which constitute mimetic forces (cell B2) and the cognitive organizational pillar (cell C2). These actors are part of a governance process of adaptation (cell D2). The non-compliance measure is simply the market verdict (cell E2), in the worst case, bankruptcy.

While regulators and market actors provide rules and benchmarks, respectively, scrutinizers signal by norms (Table 2.1, cell A3). This means that they provide a normative isomorphic force (Table 2.1, cell B3) and constitute the normative organizational pillar (cell C3). In terms of the governance process they are central for norm following (cell D3), while the non-compliance measure in relation to scrutinizers is constituted by naming and shaming (cell E3), that is, damage to reputation.

The embeddedness thus means that corporations are subject to various signals of governance from regulators, market actors and scrutinizers that work in isolation. However, the field of governance is also characterized by reciprocity among regulators, market actors, and scrutinizers as well as between corporations and the aforementioned governors. We will therefore now turn to that phenomenon.

Reciprocity

The Concept of Reciprocity

The fact that corporations are part of a field of governance where they are embedded in a multitude relations means that they are subject to a number of different signals. However, as mentioned earlier, these signals are not always unilateral but can be bilateral or even multilateral. In this way, modern corporate governance is characterized by *reciprocity*, which is a third significant concept for our analysis.

In recent years, the concept of reciprocity has been increasingly applied by economists, particularly those working with game theory and experiments. It has thus become quite fashionable. Nevertheless, there seems to be good reason to agree with the statement of Alvin Gouldner from more than 50 years ago: "There are . . . few concepts in sociology which remain more obscure and ambiguous" (Gouldner 1960: 161). Similarly Lawrence C. Becker (1990: 3–4) pointed out that reciprocity has been the subject of study in many fields such as ethnography, psychology, social anthropology and political theory, thereby leading to disagreement on the definitions of reciprocity. For his own part, he defined it as a moral virtue—that is,

> That we should return good for good, in proportion to what we receive; that we should resist evil, but not do evil in return; that we should make reparation for the harm we do; and that we should be disposed to do things as a matter of moral obligation.
>
> (Becker 1990: 4)

Game theorists and experimental economists have taken another stand by focusing on "a behavioral response to perceived kindness and unkindness, where kindness comprises both distributional fairness as well as fairness intentions" (Falk and Fischbacher 2006: 294). The issue in this tradition is thus whether actors are exclusively self-interested or whether they are responding to kind behavior from counterparts with reciprocal kind actions or to unkind behavior in a tit-for-tat mode. Studies into this kind of reciprocity have particularly been undertaken by the Austrian behavioral economist Ernst Fehr (see, e.g., Fehr, Gächter and Kirchsteiger 1997; Fehr and Gächter 2000; Fehr, Fischbacher and Gächter 2002; Fehr and Schmidt 2006) who with the passage of time has garnered many followers (see, e.g., Bolton, Greiner and Ockenfels 2013). A particular issue in this tradition is the strength of reciprocity (see, e.g., Fehr and Fischbacher 2003).

The wide use of the concept of reciprocity is also demonstrated by West, Griffin and Gardner (2007), who, from an evolutionary perspective, dealt with altruism, cooperation, mutualism, strong reciprocity and group selection. Like Gouldner and Becker, they point out that there are variations in the definitions of the concepts they are analyzing: "Different people [are] using the same term to mean different things, or different terms to mean the same thing" (West, Griffin and Gardner 2007: 415).

An important reason for the confusion around the concept reciprocity appears to be its complexity. In the words of Serge-Christophe Kolm (2008: 2): "reciprocity has several different psychological motives and various social structures, and most of these motives consist in a dynamic combination of a number of more elementary sentiments." He also presents a number of different types of reciprocity characterized by balance, liking, continuation, relations, imitation and extension (Kolm 2008: Chapters 6–8).

Our Approach

The previous section has obviously demonstrated that reciprocity is a concept that has had many interpretations. Without going further into the different definitions, we have found it appropriate for our analysis to use reciprocity to denote "the mutual interaction between the actors in the field of governance." This means an acknowledgment that actors are mutually constructed through interactions and interrelationships where they both structure and are structured by other actors involved (Djelic and Sahlin-Andersson 2006b: 12). In such reciprocal processes, actors as well as actorhood itself are constituted and shaped by cultural and institutional processes. Organizations receive cultural codes and benchmarks for action from the institutional context in which they are active, but at the same time, the activities reinforce or change the institutional context. Governing relations are thus relations of action, meaning production, identity construction, elaboration and change.

Regarding reciprocity, it is first appropriate to point out that regulators, market actors and scrutinizers are not only involved in interaction with corporations but also with each other (Figure 2.1). Regulators thus

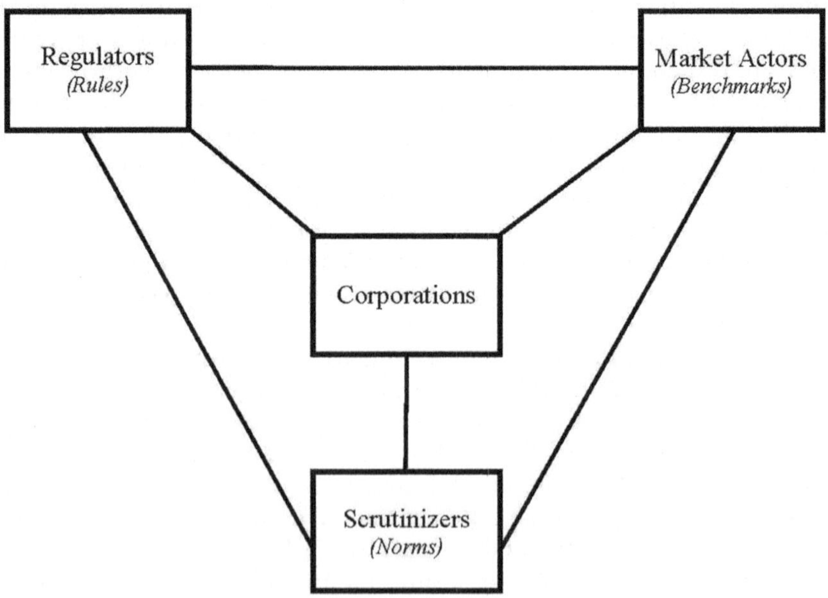

Figure 2.1 Reciprocal Relationships in the Field of Governance

provide rules for market actors and scrutinizers, market actors offer benchmarks for regulators and scrutinizers and scrutinizers communicate norms to regulators and market actors (cf., e.g., Fligstein and Stone Sweet 2002). Of course, this in turn has implications for corporations in the form of indirect governance from the three types of governors. Regulators govern not only directly through their rules but also indirectly through market actors and scrutinizers. Similarly, market actors govern indirectly through regulators and scrutinizers, whereas scrutinizers govern indirectly through regulators and market actors. As we will show in more detail in Chapter 7, this reciprocity also holds true for corporations through their counteractions vis-à-vis the governors.

Conclusions

Our basic argument in this chapter has been that corporations and their governors are embedded in a field of governance where they influence each other through constant interaction processes. We have also pointed out the need to integrate the structural and cognitive dimensions of fields. Against this backdrop, we have developed our basic framework for analyzing contemporary corporate governance, pointing out the three ideal types of governors: regulators, market actors and scrutinizers, and their signaling through rules, benchmarks, and norms, respectively.

As mentioned in Chapter 1, in the following four chapters we will now focus specifically on the respective groups of governors. In so doing, we will pay particular attention to scrutinizers by devoting separate chapters to two them, one to NGOs and another to the media. After that, in Chapter 7, we will discuss governance relations before we present the overall conclusions in Chapter 8.

References

Alchian, A. A. and Demsetz, H., 1972, "Production, Information Costs and Economic Organization," *American Economic Review*, 62(5): 777–795.

Becker, L. C., 1990, *Reciprocity*, Chicago: University of Chicago Press.

Bizjak, J., Lemmon, M. and Whitby, R., 2009, "Option Backdating and Board Interlocks," *Review of Financial Studies*, 22(11): 4821–4847.

Blair, M. M., 1995, *Ownership and Control: Rethinking Corporate Governance for the Twenty-First Century*, Washington: Brookings.

Bolton, G., Greiner, B. and Ockenfels, A., 2013, "Engineering Trust: Reciprocity in the Production of Reputation Information," *Management Science*, 59(2): 265–285.

Bourdieu, P., 1977, *Outline of a Theory of Practice*, Cambridge: Cambridge University Press.

Chamberlin, E., 1933, *The Theory of Monopolistic Competition*, Cambridge, MA: Harvard Economic Studies.

Davis, G. F., 1991, "Agents Without Principles?: The Spread of the Poison Pill Through the Intercorporate Network," *Administrative Science Quarterly*, 36(4): 583–613.

Davis, G. F., 2005, "New Directions in Corporate Governance Research," *Annual Review of Sociology*, 31: 143–162.

DiMaggio, P. J., 1983, "State Expansion and Organizational Fields," in: Hall, R. H. and Quinn, R. E. (eds.), *Organizational Theory and Public Policy*, Beverly Hills, CA: Sage, pp. 142–172.

DiMaggio, P. J. and Powell, W. W., 1983, "The Iron Cage Revisited: Institutional Isomorphism and Collective Rationality in Organizational Fields," *American Sociological Review*, 48(2): 147–160.

Djelic, M.-L., 2006, "Marketization: From Intellectual Agenda to Global Policy-Making," in: Djelic, M.-L. and Sahlin-Andersson, K. (eds.), *Transnational Governance: Institutional Dynamics of Regulation*, Cambridge: Cambridge University Press, pp. 53–73.

Djelic, M.-L. and Kleiner, T., 2006, "The International Competition Network: Moving Towards Transnational Governance," in: Djelic, M.-L. and Sahlin-Andersson, K. (eds.), *Transnational Governance: Institutional Dynamics of Regulation*, Cambridge: Cambridge University Press, pp. 287–307.

Djelic, M.-L. and Sahlin-Andersson, K. (eds.), 2006a, *Transnational Governance: Institutional Dynamics of Regulation*, Cambridge: Cambridge University Press.

Djelic, M.-L. and Sahlin-Andersson, K., 2006b, "Introduction: A World of Governance: The Rise of Transnational Regulation," in: Djelic, M.-L. and Sahlin-Andersson, K. (eds.), *Transnational Governance: Institutional Dynamics of Regulation*, Cambridge: Cambridge University Press, pp. 1–28.

Edelman, L. B., 1990, "Legal Environments and Organizational Governance: The Expansion of Due Process in the American Workplace," *American Journal of Sociology*, 95(6): 1401–1440.

Edelman, L. B., 1992, "Legal Ambiguity and Symbolic Structures: Organizational Mediation of Civil Rights Law," *American Journal of Sociology*, 97(6): 1531–1576.

Engwall, L., 1981, "Newspaper Competition: A Case for Theories of Oligopoly," *Scandinavian Economic History Review*, 29(2): 145–154.

Engwall, L., 1985, *Från vag vision till komplex organisation* (From Vague Vision to Complex Organization), Acta Universitatis Upsaliensis. Studia Oeconomiae Negotiorum 22, Uppsala: Almqvist & Wiksell.

Engwall, L., 1994, "Bridge, Poker and Banking," in: Fair, D. E. and Raymond, R. J. (eds.), *The Competitiveness of Financial Institutions and Centres in Europe*, Amsterdam: Kluwer, pp. 227–239.

Engwall, L., 1997, "The Swedish Banking Crisis: The Invisible Hand Shaking the Visible Hand," in: Morgan, G. and Knights, D. (eds.), *Regulation and Deregulation in European Financial Services*, London: Macmillan, pp. 178–200.

Engwall, L., 2007, "The Universities, the State and the Market: Changing Patterns of University Governance," *Higher Education and Policy*, 19(3): 87–104.

Engwall, L. and Kipping, M., 2006, "Management Education, Media and Consulting vs. Management Practice," *Innovation—The European Journal of Social Science Research*, 19(1): 93–104.

Engwall, L. and Wallenstål, M., 1988, "Tit for Tat in Small Steps: The Internationalization of Swedish Banks," *Scandinavian Journal of Management*, 4(3/4): 147–155.

Falk, A. and Fischbacher, U., 2006, "A Theory of Reciprocity," *Games and Economic Behavior*, 54(2): 293–315.

Fama, E., 1980, "Agency Problems and the Theory of the Firm," *Journal of Political Economy*, 88(2): 288–307.

Fehr, E. and Fischbacher, U., 2003, "The Nature of Human Altruism," *Nature*, 425(6960): 785–791.

Fehr, E., Fischbacher, U. and Gächter, S., 2002, "Strong Reciprocity, Human Cooperation, and the Enforcement of Social Norms," *Human Nature*, 13(1): 1–25.

Fehr, E. and Gächter, S., 2000, "Fairness and Retaliation: The Economics of Reciprocity," *Journal of Economic Perspectives*, 14(3): 159–181.

Fehr, E., Gächter, S. and Kirchsteiger, G., 1997, "Reciprocity as a Contract Enforcement Device: Experimental Evidence," *Econometrica*, 65(4): 833–860.

Fehr, E. and Schmidt, K. M., 2006, "The Economics of Fairness, Reciprocity and Altruism—Experimental Evidence and New Theories," in: Kolm, S.-C. and Ythier, J. M. (eds.), *Handbook of the Economics of Giving, Altruism and Reciprocity*, 1, Amsterdam: Elsevier, pp. 615–691.

Fiss, P., 2008, "Institutions and Corporate Governance," in: Greenwood, R., Oliver, C., Sahlin, K. and Suddaby, R. (eds.), *The Sage Handbook of Organizational Institutionalism*, London: Sage, pp. 389–410.

Fligstein, N., 1990, *The Transformation of Corporate Control*, Cambridge, MA: Harvard University Press.

Fligstein, N., 2001, *The Architecture of Markets*, Princeton, NJ: Princeton University Press.

Fligstein, N. and McAdam, D., 2012, *A Theory of Fields*, Oxford: Oxford University Press.

Fligstein, N. and Stone Sweet, A., 2002, "Constructing Polities and Markets: An Institutionalist Account of European Integration," *American Journal of Sociology*, 107(5): 1206–1243.

Gouldner, A. W., 1960, "The Norm of Reciprocity: A Preliminary Statement," *American Sociological Review*, 25(2): 161–178.

Granovetter, M., 1985, "Economic Action and Social Structure: The Problem of Embeddedness," *American Journal of Sociology*, 91(3): 481–510.

Greenwood, R. and Meyer, R. E., 2008, "Influencing Ideas: A Celebration of DiMaggio and Powell (1983)," *Journal of Management Inquiry*, 17(4): 258–264.

Greenwood, R., Oliver, C., Sahlin, K. and Suddaby, R. (eds.), 2008a, *The Sage Handbook of Organizational Institutionalism*, London: Sage.

Greenwood, R., Oliver, C., Sahlin, K. and Suddaby, R., 2008b, "Introduction," in: Greenwood, R., Oliver, C., Sahlin, K. and Suddaby, R. (eds.), *The Sage Handbook of Organizational Institutionalism*, London: Sage, pp. 1–46.

Gulati, R. and Westphal, J. D., 1999, "Cooperative or Controlling?: The Effects of CEO—Board Relations and the Content of Interlocks on the Formation of Joint Ventures," *Administrative Science Quarterly*, 44(3): 473–506.

Haunschild, P. R., 1993, "Interorganizational Imitation: The Impact of Interlocks on Corporate Acquisition Activity," *Administrative Science Quarterly*, 38(4): 564–592.

Haunschild, P. R. and Beckman, C. M., 1998, "When Do Interlocks Matter?: Alternate Sources of Information and Interlock Influence," *Administrative Science Quarterly*, 43(4): 815–844.

Hendricks, J. A. and Noor Al-Deen, H. S. (eds.), 2012, *Social Media: Usage and Impact*, Lanham, MD: Lexington.

Jacobsson, B., 2006, "Regulated Regulators: Global Trends of State Transformation," in: Djelic, M.-L. and Sahlin-Andersson, K. (eds.), *Transnational Governance: Institutional Dynamics of Regulation*, Cambridge: Cambridge University Press, pp. 205–224.

Jensen, M. C. and Meckling, W. H., 1976, "Theory of the Firm: Managerial Behavior, Agency Costs and Ownership Structure," *Journal of Financial Economics*, 3(4): 305–360.

Kaplan, S. N. and Holmstrom, B., 2004, *The State of U.S. Corporate Governance 2004*, Related Publication 04–02, AEI Brookings Joint Center for Regulatory Studies and The University of Chicago <www.researchgate.net/profile/Bengt_Holmstroem/publication/46454276_The_State_of_Corporate_Governance_2004/links/552668a10cf21e126f9daa4a/The-State-of-Corporate-Governance-2004.pdf> accessed on August 10, 2017.

Keasey, K., Thompson, S. and Wright, M., 1997, "Introduction: The Corporate Governance Problem: Competing Diagnoses and Solutions," in: Keasey, K., Thompson, S. and Wright, M. (eds.), *Corporate Governance: Economic, Management, and Financial Issues*, Oxford: Oxford University Press, pp. 1–17.

Kipping, M. and Clark, T. (eds.), 2012, *The Oxford Handbook of Management Consulting*, Oxford: Oxford University Press.

Kolm, S.-C., 2008, *Reciprocity: An Economics of Social Relations*, New York: Cambridge University Press.

Krippner, G. R. and Alvarez, A. S., 2007, "Embeddedness and the Intellectual Projects of Economic Sociology," *Annual Review of Sociology*, 33: 219–240.

Lewin, K., 1951, *Field Theory in Social Science: Selected Theoretical Papers*, New York: Harper and Row.

Lindblom, C. E., 1977, *Politics and Markets: The World's Political-Economic Systems*, New York: Basic Books.

Marks, G., Hooghe, L. and Blank, K., 1996, "European Integration From the 1980s: State-Centric vs Multilevel Governance," *Journal of Common Market Studies*, 34(3): 341–378.

Martin, J. L., 2003, "What Is Field Theory?" *American Journal of Sociology*, 109(1): 1–49.

Meyer, J. W., Boli, J., Thomas, G. and Ramirez, F., 1997, "World Society and the Nation-State," *American Journal of Sociology*, 103(1): 144–181.

Meyer, J. W. and Rowan, B., 1977, "Institutionalized Organizations: Formal Structure as Myth and Ceremony," *American Journal of Sociology*, 83(2): 340–363.

Meyer, J. W. and Scott, W. R., 1983, *Organizational Environments: Ritual and Rationality*, Beverly Hills, CA: Sage.

Mohr, J., 2003, *Implicit Terrains: Meaning, Measurement, and Spatial Metaphors in Organizational Theory*, Unpublished Paper, Department of Sociology, Santa Barbara: University of California.

Monks, R. A. and Minow, N., 1995, *Corporate Governance*, Cambridge, MA: Blackwell.

Mörth, U., 2006, "Soft Regulation and Global Democracy," in: Djelic, M.-L. and Sahlin-Andersson, K. (eds.), *Transnational Governance: Institutional Dynamics of Regulation*, Cambridge: Cambridge University Press, pp. 119–135.

Pfeffer, J. and Salancik, G. R., 1978, *The External Control of Organizations*, New York: Harper and Row.

Polanyi, K., 1944, *The Great Transformation: The Political and Economic Origins of Our Time*, Boston: Beacon.

Robinson, J., 1933, *The Economics of Imperfect Competition*, London: Macmillan.

Roe, M. J., 1994, *Strong Managers, Weak Owners: The Political Roots of American Corporate Finance*, Princeton, NJ: Princeton University Press.

Scott, W. R., 1995, *Institutions and Organizations*, London: Sage.

Scott, W. R. and Meyer, J. W., 1983, "The Organization of Societal Sectors," in: Meyer, J. W. and Scott, J. W. (eds.), *Organizational Environments: Ritual and Rationality*, Beverly Hills, CA: Sage, pp. 129–154.

Siebert, F. S., Peterson, T. and Schramm, W., 1956, *Four Theories of the Press*, Urbana, IL: University of Illinois Press.

Smith, M. P., 1996, "Shareholder Activism by Institutional Investors: Evidence From CalPERS," *Journal of Finance*, 51(1): 227–252.

Stone Sweet, A., 1999, "Judicialization and the Construction of Governance," *Comparative Political Studies*, 32(2): 147–184.

Tainio, R., Huolman, M., Pulkkinen, M., Ali-Yrkkö, J. and Ylä-Anttila, P., 2003, "Global Investors Meet Local Managers: Shareholder Value in the Finnish Context," in: Djelic, M.-L. and Quack, S. (eds.), *Globalization and Institutions: Redefining the Rules of the Economic Game*, Cheltenham: Edward Elgar, pp. 37–56.

Thomas, G., Meyer, J. W., Ramirez, F. and Boli, J., 1987, *Institutional Structure*, Newbury Park, CA: Sage.

Thompson, J. D., 1967, *Organizations in Action*, New York: McGraw-Hill.

Useem, M., 1996, *Investor Capitalism: How Money Managers Are Changing the Face of Corporate America*, New York: Basic Books.

Van Wijk, J., Stam, W., Elfring, T., Zietsma, C. and den Hond, F., 2013, "Activists and Incumbents Structuring Change: The Interplay of Agency, Culture, and Networks in Field Evolution," *Academy of Management Journal*, 56(2): 358–386.

Warren, R. L., 1967, "The Interorganizational Field as the Focus for Investigation," *Administrative Science Quarterly*, 12(3): 396–419.

Warren, R. L., 1972, *The Community in America*, Chicago: Rand McNally.

West, S. A., Griffin, A. S. and Gardner, A., 2007, "Social Semantics: Altruism, Cooperation, Mutualism, Strong Reciprocity and Group Selection," *Journal of Evolutionary Biology*, 20(2): 415–432.

Windell, K., 2006, *Corporate Social Responsibility Under Construction: Ideas, Translations and Institutional Change*, Doctoral Dissertation 123 from the Department of Business Administration, Uppsala: Uppsala University.

Wooten, M. and Hoffman, A. J., 2008, "Organizational Fields: Past, Present and Future," in: Greenwood, R., Oliver, C., Sahlin, K. and Suddaby, R. (eds.), *The Sage Handbook of Organizational Institutionalism*, London: Sage, pp. 130–147.

Yergin, D. and Stanislaw, J., 1998, *The Commanding Heights: The Battle Between Government and the Marketplace that Is Remaking the Modern World*, New York: Simon & Schuster.

Zald, M. N. and Lounsbury, M., 2010, "The Wizards of Oz: Towards an Institutional Approach to Elites, Expertise and Command Posts," *Organization Studies*, 31(7): 963–996.

Zucker, L. G., 1977, "The Role of Institutionalization in Cultural Persistence," *American Sociological Review*, 42(5): 726–743.

3 Regulators

Linda Wedlin, Katarina Buhr and Kerstin Sahlin

Introduction

The global economic crisis of the past decade put significant focus on the issue of regulation, and particularly transnational regulations. Whether seen as part of the cause of the breakdown or a remedy for the problems of global financial markets, regulations of transnational financial institutions and transactions were significantly developed in the wake of the global financial crisis. Even before that, however, many observers had noted the strong, and seemingly increasing, role and presence of regulation in contemporary society, so much so that our time has been dubbed the "golden era of regulation" (Levi-Faur and Jordana 2005). Not only have regulations increased in number, but, as suggested by the concept of "regulatory capitalism" (Braithwaite 2008), they are taking on a fundamental governing role in modern societies and economies, and not only in relation to financial markets.

This is supported by much empirical observation that suggests an increasingly complex regulatory landscape facing businesses and corporations (see, for example, Kohler-Koch and Eising 1999; Bache and Flinders 2004; Djelic and Sahlin-Andersson 2006a). Regulatory activities have expanded into new areas of previously virgin territory. They have changed form, as they are no longer necessarily linked to legal sanctions but may be based on collectively shaped normative values. Regardless of form, they have a significant impact on corporate activities. In addition, regulatory activities unfold across national borders and arenas for intergovernmental negotiations, and involve activities and interactions among interest groups, governments and many other actors involved in regulation and policy making.

Observations of these kinds indicate the significance of regulation and regulatory activity for the governance of contemporary corporations, and at the same time, they suggest a need to revisit our understanding of the modern regulatory landscape and it entailments. *First*, we need to apply a broader definition of regulation beyond a "legal-state" perspective on rule-making. Previous research tells us that social mechanisms of control are equally powerful for the governance of corporations as traditional command-and-control approaches (Baldwin and Cave 1999; Jacobsson and Sahlin-Andersson 2006). *Second*, we need to direct attention to the relationship between the multitude of actors involved in regulation and distinguish an analytically rewarding context in which regulation unfolds that is not delimited to governments or a specified geographical area, in order to study the relevant organizational interaction through which regulation emerges. *Third*, corporations are not only subject to the governance of this multitude of actors. As we pointed out in Chapters 1 and 2, the governing and regulation of corporations is clearly characterized by reciprocity. Therefore, it is equally important to explore the role of corporations themselves in shaping regulations and the regulatory patterns that follow.

To address the aforementioned issues, we will begin by focusing on important aspects of contemporary regulation, namely how it covers new issues and areas and widens its form to include both hard and soft law. We will then proceed to a more in-depth review of the literature on changing actors involved in multilevel forms of regulation. To analyze the interrelatedness and embeddedness of regulatory actors and processes, we thereafter present two empirical case studies of contemporary transnational regulatory processes that we have explored in our research: the EU Emissions Trading Scheme and the UN Global Compact.

In accordance with the model developed in Chapter 2, we will analyze the political system of governance. It is a system of regulators and regulations, interacting with businesses and corporations and with each other. This analysis highlights the interrelationship among these multiple actors involved in regulation geared to ensuring a regulatory impact on a specific area or problem. The analysis furthermore directs our understanding to how relations are embedded in and shaped by those institutionalized forces that permeate the system. Although we analytically distinguish regulatory actors and relations, these are inevitably interrelated and intertwined with other actors and relations in the wider field of governance that we have discussed in Chapter 1 and 2. We close the chapter with some conclusions on the relations between regulators and the influence of the wider field of governance.

A Changed Regulatory Landscape

Insights From Soft Regulation

Rules and regulations are constantly entering new areas of concern, and organizations are expected to handle previously unregulated issues in for example ethical, social and environmental aspects of corporate activities (e.g., Cutler, Haufler and Porters 1999; Kirton and Trebilcock 2004; Gulbrandsen 2010) and administrative procedures (Brunsson, Jacobsson and Associates 2000; Beck and Walgenbach 2002), interpreted into vast systems such as accounting procedures, employment rules, competition laws, product quality and safety standards and trade agreements. At the same time, many of these areas are not regulated through traditional instruments with legal sanctions but are rather built on normative and cognitive elements that prescribe appropriate corporate behavior. Such new forms of regulation include the setting of standards and guidelines (Brunsson, Jacobsson and Associates 2000), the creation of audits and evaluations (Power 1997) and the formulation of codes of conduct and recommendations (Jenkins 2001; Kolk and van Tulder 2002). As such, corporations today are asked to adhere to ethical standards and corporate governance codes, report on the social and environmental impact of their businesses and activities, and standardize their reporting and financial accounting systems, to name just a few examples. These forms of regulations are "soft" in the sense that they are not legally binding and there are no formal sanctions associated with non-compliance (Mörth 2004). This makes regulation appear more "voluntary" and informal, and provides more room for interpretation and adjustment by those being regulated (Djelic and Sahlin-Andersson 2006b).

We draw on two main insights from this work on soft regulations to build our argument in this chapter. *First*, we revise the understanding of the state and state agencies as the most influential regulators of corporate activities and procedures dominating in the state-centered and intergovernmentalist perspectives to put increasing focus on a wider set of regulatory actors. *Second*, we recognize the active role of businesses and corporations in processes of regulation and regulatory activities.

The Role of the State and Business in Regulation

With the perspective of the state-centered and intergovernmentalist traditions, decision making and regulation are carried out mainly through bargaining among state representatives (Hoffmann 1982). Societal changes like European integration have not changed this, and it has been argued that the nation-state remains a dominant and even strengthened actor in these processes, as national preferences and powers of the nation-state are important for shaping EU level governance (Moravcisk 1993; Milward 1999). In this view, parliaments, local authorities, central government departments or agencies, directors general or courts and tribunals all become important regulators (Baldwin and Cave 1999).

Another perspective, which we align ourselves with, is to open up for the multitude of actors involved in regulation, including interest groups, non-governmental organizations (NGOs), international organizations and others, and be attentive to how they may not only have an impact on regulation but in fact can be seen as important co-creators of it (Marks, Hooghe and Blank 1996). Previous research has pointed to the global expansion of NGOs (Boli and Thomas 1999), the increasing role of international organizations in regulatory processes (Braithwaite and Drahos 2000), the expansion and influence of business interest groups in global policy making (Pulver 2004), and the role of think tanks (Stone 1996) and other "policy professionals" inside and outside the government system (Svallfors 2017). Also, professional associations, standardizing bodies and scrutinizing organizations can play a role in regulatory processes (Brunsson, Rasche and Seidl 2012; Djelic and Sahlin-Andersson 2006a; Hedmo, Sahlin-Andersson and Wedlin 2006).

A number of concepts have been proposed to describe the observed phenomena in which states no longer have a monopoly on rule-making activities. We find for instance concepts such as "policy networks" (Marsh 1998), which are strictly defined by their function to formulate and implement policy; "epistemic communities" (Haas 1992), which merely refers to communities of experts influencing policy; and "advocacy networks," a term that evokes highly structured actions bound together by shared and common values, discourses and exchanges in a way that emphasizes agreement and ignores struggles (Keck and Sikkink 1998). The more widely used term of "governance" includes not only formal policy making but also a number of organizing, discursive, and monitoring activities found in the broader organizational interplay as well (Rosenau and Czempiel 1992). Even more so, the term "interactive governance" (Torfing et al. 2012) emphasizes the interaction between actors involved in governance processes. In this view, states interact with other societal actors to construct governance, such as networks, market actors and other governments. Thus, retaining the importance of governmental and state actors in governance, this perspective suggests that their positions in governance cannot be assumed a priori but should be analyzed and the processes of governance understood, in relation to other actors in the field. States should thus be analyzed as one type of actor among others (Katzenstein, Keohane and Krasner 1998). While the state is, and most likely will continue to be, an important regulator (Hirst and Thompson 1996), it is taking on new roles in the regulatory process through increasing interaction with other actors and regulatory entities. This interaction forms an important part of contemporary regulatory processes.

Our second recognition of the active role of businesses and corporations in processes of regulation and regulatory activities is an important implication of bringing in a perspective of regulators beyond states. New means and modes of regulation, relying in part on voluntary principles and mechanisms for compliance, have entailed that corporations engage in self-regulation, voluntary agreements, self-evaluations and certifications, etc., thus actively participating in the regulatory process (Ayres and Braithwaite 1992; Hedmo, Sahlin-Andersson and Wedlin 2006). Research has also noted how corporations are actively taking part in rule-setting activities, through interest representation, lobbying, official stakeholder consultations and other activities (Coen 1998; Jutterström 2004; Buhr 2008). This means that corporations are taking an active part in policy-making and regulatory activities, and interact with regulators to develop and refine regulatory mechanisms and processes. Such observations lead us to challenge the perception of corporations as "recipients" of rules and regulations, or as rule-followers, and analyze the new roles and responsibilities, but also opportunities, for corporations in this regulatory landscape and the relationships that help to create, shape and sustain regulatory mechanisms and principles.

Building partly on these two important recognitions, there is yet another challenge for understanding regulation. This is the fact that regulation does not exclusively unfold within the boundaries of the nation-state. Globalization scholars have emphasized "the intensification of economic, political, social and cultural relations across borders" (Holm and Sørensen 1995:1), and, although such processes are not new to the world, there is a broad agreement that such relations have increased in number and importance (Holton 1998) and that globalization and European integration have had implications for patterns of governance and regulation (Schneiberg and Bartley 2008). Regulation is, in fact, often formulated and organized according to sectors such as telecommunications rather than a specific national concern (Levi-Faur and Jordana 2005).

Among scholars interested in EU policy (Kohler-Koch and Eising 1999; Marks 1993), multilevel approaches have gained a strong foothold proposing that authority is not centralized in either national governments or supranational actors but dispersed and interconnected across levels (Marks, Hooghe and Blank 1996). Such a perspective allows recognition of how actors may move more freely between arenas of governance, and the fact that states are not the only interface between supranational and subnational actors; interests may mobilize directly into a supranational arena with or without state intervention. From this, we learn to involve multiple arenas and governance levels into an analytical framework that can explain regulatory processes and how various actors interact to form new governance modes. This will be further explored empirically in the following section.

Transnational Regulatory Processes

Building on the field approach as set out in Chapter 1, in the following sections we will turn to an analysis of transnational regulatory processes. In so doing, we will focus on the interaction among a multitude of actors involved in regulation, how these relations evolve and how they shape the regulations that ensue. Three recognitions of field processes are particularly stressed. *First*, we focus on the reciprocity of field processes, thus how relations as well as actors and their interests are formed and develop in these interactions, and how corporations are both influenced by and also influence processes of regulation. *Second*, we show how both activity and meaning are formed in these regulatory processes. The regulations that develop are both highly embedded in, and thus influenced by, existing norms, understandings and assumptions about the specific activities and functions of corporations, but common meanings are also formed, and reformed, among organizations as the regulatory processes evolve. *Third*, we point to the way fields come to be organized and structured over time, where regulation both provides a structuring mechanism in itself and contributes to further processes of organizing and ordering relations among actors and interests in the field of governance.

We base our analysis on two empirical case studies of contemporary transnational regulatory processes, the first dealing with European regulation and the second involving global regulation. The first case is the process of bringing international aviation into the EU Emissions Trading Scheme (EU ETS). Our analysis is based on a study conducted by Katarina Buhr (2008), who examined the policy development process in-depth up until the initial EU proposal in 2005. Through interviews (26 in total) and a range of documents, from official policy papers to various communications, reports, position papers and press releases, the study aimed to cover a wide range of interests and actors, including the European Commission as well as various interest groups, organizations and corporations that took an active part in the process.

The second case builds on several studies of the United Nations Global Compact initiative. We build on the research of Karolina Windell (2006) and Kerstin Sahlin-Andersson (2006), who mainly used documents and public information available to document the process of setting up the initiative. This case can be seen as an institutionalization of views expressed within a growing civil society activism, which we will discuss further in Chapter 5. But the Global Compact initiative can also be seen as a more encompassing soft regulatory framework significantly influencing the conduct and relations of businesses, governments and other actors (Sahlin-Andersson 2004, 2006). This is particularly evident, as we, for the purpose of this chapter, have done a follow-up study (in 2008–2009) of the Global Compact initiative and its governing framework.

European Regulation: Aviation in the EU Emissions Trading Scheme

In January 2009, an EU Directive was presented in which all airlines departing from or arriving at EU airports are prescribed to participate in the EU Emissions Trading Scheme as of 2012, buying and selling pollution permits on a market for emission rights as a means to control CO_2 emissions (Official Journal of the European Union, January 13, 2009). This piece of legislation represents the first non-domestic regulation to target the greenhouse gas emissions of aviation. Although it had been made an environmental scapegoat in the public debate for a number of years, the aviation sector was generally treated as an exception in an emerging climate change regulatory package due to extraordinary challenges to agree on a number of scientific, political, technological and economic aspects and issues. In the following, we analyze the development of this regulatory initiative as it took shape in an interactive process between regulators, corporations and their many stakeholders.

Multiple Policy Alternatives

With the creation of the United Nations Framework Convention on Climate Change (UNFCCC) in 1992, the UN established itself as the foremost arena for global climate change talks. As additional structures for political progress was set up under UNFCCC auspices throughout the 1990s, the Intergovernmental Panel on Climate Change (IPCC) prepared a Special Report to comprehend aviation's contribution to climate change. When the Kyoto Protocol was formulated in 1997, international aviation was explicitly excluded. Instead, the UN body International Civil Aviation Organization (ICAO) was given the mandate to come up with a regulatory response to address the climate change impact of international aviation. This reallocation of responsibility, from the UNFCCC to the ICAO, marked an important watershed in regulatory developments. The task to address aviation's contribution to global warming was mainly discussed in ICAO's Committee on Aviation Environmental Protection (CAEP), formed by both members and observers representing states, businesses, international organizations and environmental NGOs. However, progress was slow within ICAO, and the Council of the European Union called for the European Commission to proceed with unilateral action if no significant breakthrough had been reached within ICAO to address the greenhouse gas emissions from international aviation by 2002 (European Commission 2001).

Inspiration for a climate policy for the aviation sector was sought in the emerging environmental and climate change regime, though it also involved measures specific to air traffic. A range of policy instruments, not necessarily mutually exclusive, were suggested and examined over the years and taken into account throughout the policy formulation process. Making existing operations more environmentally efficient was an essential regulatory cornerstone and held significant potential for reducing greenhouse gas emissions. Another important efficiency variable was that of improving air traffic management (ATM) systems, which are used to coordinate aircraft movements. These were important steps, but the question was whether such efficiency improvements would be sufficient or whether an economic instrument would be required to control the greenhouse gas effects of this expansive industry. Economic instruments, or market-based instruments, had been increasingly used in environmental policy making for a number of years (Jordan et al. 2003). Taxes and charges are longstanding means by which regulators attempt to "internalize externalities" and were used extensively in EU environmental policy (Golub 1998). Emissions trading is a market-based option that has attracted considerable interest in recent years, both in research and in practice (Baldwin 2008; MacKenzie 2009). The entry of emissions trading into the general climate change debate prompted consideration of whether this instrument should be imposed on the aviation sector.

Multiple Interests and Common Moves Toward Emissions Trading

The European Union (EU) took an early interest in regulating emissions of aviation, with significant discussion and research in the legislative engine of the European Commission as early as the mid-1990s. The issue overlapped the interests of several directorates-general (DG) in the European Commission, most notably DG Transport and Energy and DG Environment. An important input for the regulatory discussion was a report commissioned by the Commission to the consulting firm CE Delft, who performed in-depth studies of the three economic instruments taxes, charges and emissions trading. Nevertheless, aviation's climate change impact did not rise to the very top of the agenda until the United Kingdom announced that it would become a key issue during their EU presidency in the second half of 2005. The statement triggered an abundance of activities and discussions on the topic, and significant lobbying activities toward the European Commission were initiated. Platforms for debate were created by the Commission but also by other actors, exemplified by a conference on the topic hosted by three environmental NGOs—the European Federation for Transport and Environment, Milieudefensie (Friends of the Earth Netherlands) and the Aviation Environment Federation—in January 2005. An important event was also the public stakeholder consultation arranged by DG Environment between March and May 2005. A total of 5,564 responses from individuals and 198 responses from organizations were received, and their opinions were further discussed with stakeholders at the annual Green Week in June 2005, where an entire day was devoted to a discussion of aviation's climate change impact (European Commission 2005a).

Among interested actors in this process, we find some of the major airlines operating in Europe, but also other corporations with stakes in aviation matters, such as airports and manufacturers of aircraft and aero engines. These corporations group themselves according to various parameters such as function, geographical residence or business model, giving rise to overlapping industry coalitions. From the various reports and position papers produced in the consultation process, it is clear that corporations and their various interest organizations clearly favored emissions trading as the preferred policy alternative for this sector. In July 2005, six trade associations representing the European aviation industry launched a joint position paper that demonstrated their support for emissions trading as the most promising economic instrument. Even more enthusiasm for emissions trading was expressed in a position paper from January 2005 from the airports of Europe through the European branch of the major trade association Airports Council International (ACI-Europe).

As emissions trading received increasing support, the European Commission presented a communication in September of 2005, in which, for the first time, they suggested including aviation in the EU Emissions Trading Scheme. Besides the perceived broad industry support for emissions trading in Europe,

ICAO had by this point in time indicated an optimistic view of emissions trading, thus further supporting this position. This can be described as a common move by a number of organizations interested in having a say about a forthcoming regulation of aviation's climate change impact. Although dissents existed, collective support was shaped in favor of emissions trading in particular. With the launch of the communication, the European Commission also announced the setting up of an Aviation Working Group, consisting of invited stakeholders including companies within and beyond the aviation sector, the NGO community and member state representatives, which met to discuss the details of an emissions trading proposal that would inform the subsequent policy process (European Commission 2005b).

Across Levels—National Triggers for Transnational Policy Initiatives

Discussions of emissions trading also took place at the national level at this time, which significantly influenced developments within the EU. It found especially fertile ground in the United Kingdom. Even before the UK government announced its intentions to bring aviation into the EU Emissions Trading Scheme during its EU presidency, a collective of actors in and around the UK government had arrived at emissions trading as their preferred policy instrument to tackle the climate change impact of aviation, as early as 2003. In fact, ideas about this particular policy had been floated through British representatives in ICAO, in speeches and the media, and at various events throughout this time. At a multi-stakeholder conference arranged and hosted by the British airport operator BAA in October 2003, the then European Commissioner for the Environment, Margot Wallström, responded to the idea of emissions trading as something that meets "serious consideration" (Wallström 2003). A number of companies from the UK aviation sector recognized their strategic stake in climate change, connected to an ongoing and vibrant domestic debate that had escalated during the first years of the century as the UK government prepared a long-term strategy for airport expansion. In order to ensure legitimate growth while taking climate change seriously, the aviation industry expressed their support for emissions trading, working through industry-wide coalitions such as Freedom to Fly and Sustainable Aviation and their national as well as European trade associations. The airport expansion plans had been informed by major national public consultations that attracted huge interest, prompting some 500,000 responses in total, peaking with the launch of the White Paper on the Future of Air Transport in December 2003. In this document, emissions trading is said to be the best way forward, and, as mentioned earlier, the UK government was firm about working hand in hand with their stakeholders toward this objective during their six-month EU presidency in 2005. A fairly common ground, at least in terms of supporting emissions trading in principle, had thereby been achieved within the boundaries of a nation-state but in dialogue with a larger transnational collective. As the issue shifted its emphasis to the EU arena, influential actors were found not in the immediate vicinity of the policy process but within the same social sphere interested in the issue as the policy makers that eventually came to put the legislation in print.

Field Interaction in Regulatory Processes

The aforementioned shows how aviation was incorporated into an emissions trading proposal in the EU. Over the course of the first years of the new century, norms and values relating to the regulatory discussion took shape, calling for aviation to take responsibility for its climate change impact and for regulators to use an economic instrument to tackle the issue. The emissions trading proposal was not formulated by the European Commission in isolation; on the contrary; it was shaped in interaction between regulators and their stakeholders across levels. Given the transnational character of policy making in this area, several actors were engaged in discussions in ICAO, in the EU and at the national level, both within and around various governments. The content of the regulation emerged through these discussions and as relationships among actors developed. As noted earlier, the nation-state may still be an important context in which driving forces for legislation may be set in motion, although regulation, in this case, developed in the transnational context.

An important element of the regulatory activities was to identify an appropriate arena that offered a fruitful institutional context in which emissions trading could gain a foothold. Arena selection became imperative in the process studied. The EU formed an important arena for discussion and debate, and subsequently regulation and policy making, of aviation's climate change impact. This case clearly illustrates that there may be multiple arenas to advance policy and that selecting an arena for advancing emissions trading was an important element in forming regulation for aviation. The problem was widely seen as a global one, and it was desired that any policy arrived at be applied with the widest geographical scope possible. However, the many difficulties in agreeing at the global level did not appear to pose favorable regulatory conditions, and failure of the UN agency ICAO to take charge of regulating aviation's climate change impact raised opportunities for other actors to take the lead in other arenas. This way, the EU was targeted for regulatory initiatives, partly because climate change had achieved a high level of recognition within the EU, and because it has demonstrated strong leadership in its role as a negotiator in international climate talks (Oberthür and Roche Kelly 2008). Thus, the transnational process gained a foothold in an organizational arena in the EU in which policy could be advanced.

Global Regulation: The Global Compact Initiative

In our second empirical case, we focus our attention on the emergence of one of the most high-profile programs aimed to regulate and control the social and environmental responsibility of businesses in recent years: the United Nations Global Compact initiative. It is not only one of the more comprehensive and authoritative initiatives aimed to spread and legitimize ethical issues among corporations, but it has also invoked a great many national and/or local initiatives and programs and other activities (see further Chapter 5), making it an important element for the governance of corporations. It is distinct, however, in its specific aim to be a voluntary framework, resting on the willingness of the business world to take active responsibility for its social and environmental impact.

The Global Compact initiative was launched in 1999 by the then UN secretary-general Kofi Annan when he spoke at the World Economic Forum in a symbolic action to encourage the business leaders of the world to engage in responsible business operations by adhering to nine universal principles related to labor, human rights, and the environment. The principles were based on the content of several international declarations including the Universal Declaration of Human Rights, the International Labour Organization's Fundamental Principles on Rights at Work and the Rio Principles on Environment and Development. A tenth principle was added in 2004: targeting anti-corruption and building on the UN Convention against Corruption (for the ten principles, see Table 3.1).

The initiative is explicitly stated not to be a new regulation for businesses to follow, but rather a voluntary activity resting on principles of public

Table 3.1 The UN Global Compact's Ten Principles

Human Rights

1: Businesses should support and respect the protection of internationally proclaimed human rights; and
2: make sure that they are not complicit in human rights abuses.

Labour

3: Businesses should uphold the freedom of association and the effective recognition of the right to collective bargaining;
4: the elimination of all forms of forced and compulsory labour;
5: the effective abolition of child labour; and
6: the elimination of discrimination in respect of employment and occupation.

Environment

7: Businesses are asked to support a precautionary approach to environmental challenges;
8: undertake initiatives to promote greater environmental responsibility; and
9: encourage the development and diffusion of environmentally friendly technologies.

Anti-Corruption

10: Businesses should work against corruption in all its forms, including extortion and bribery.

Source: United Nations (2017a).

accountability and transparency and relying on companies' willingness to serve a general public good (United Nations 2008b):

> The Global Compact is not a regulatory instrument—it does not "police," enforce or measure the behavior or actions of companies. Rather, the Global Compact relies on public accountability, transparency and the enlightened self-interest of companies, labour and civil society to initiate and share substantive action in pursuing the principles upon which the Global Compact is based.

The Global Compact seeks to include organizations of all kinds, from governments and agencies, to civil society organizations (CSO) and private companies. Most of the participants signing on to the initiative represent the business sector, many of them large and well-known corporations. In July 2003, some 1,000 companies had signed on to the principles of Global Compact (Sahlin-Andersson 2004: 132), a figure that doubled in two years' time (Windell 2006: 72), and again more than doubled, to 5,200, by August 2009 (United Nations 2009a). Including non-business stakeholders in the count, there were over 6,700 participants. In 2017, those figures have increased to 9,000 companies and 4,000 non-businesses (United Nations 2017b).

A Global Arena for Regulating CSR

The Global Compact initiative was developed by the UN at a time when the CSR field was rapidly expanding and taking shape. The Global Compact was preceded or paralleled by a number of national as well as international attempts and practices to develop and establish CSR as a concept and a practice for corporate behavior. Among the national initiatives was a Danish CSR campaign launched by the then Minister for Social Affairs in 1994, and the subsequent creation of the Copenhagen Centre for Corporate Responsibility in 1998. This was an independent think tank started by the Danish government, geared to deal with the increasing interest in CSR issues and provide a platform for CSR partnerships and programs. Also in the United Kingdom, there was a lot of activity around CSR, with a minister for CSR issues being appointed in 2000 (Eberhard-Harribey 2006: 360). Among the most prominent international activities are the OECD Guidelines for Multinational Enterprises, established in 2000, and the International Labour Organization and its conventions for workplace practice (Eberhard-Harribey 2006; Sahlin-Andersson 2006). There were also previous attempts within the United Nations to regulate and monitor the social responsibility of corporations, for instance, through the UN Centre on Transnational Corporations. The UN project is thus part of a developing regulatory framework for CSR issues (see, e.g., Bendell and Visser 2003).

The Global Compact initiative was developed to address issues of corporate citizenship and to involve the business community in spreading "universal values and responsible business operations" (United Nations 2008b). To do this, the Global Compact drew on the overall principles and established and accepted values and norms of a large set of UN conventions and guidelines to create a regulatory framework for CSR. The initiation of the Global Compact was seen as a way for the UN to promote and ensure the implementation of its principles and declarations, and serve to help to fulfill the UN "Millennium Development Goals" established in 2000. Thus, it was part of an extensive program within the UN aiming at mobilizing and integrating stakeholders into its organization and in particular at stimulating responsible business practices to achieve its own objectives. In an article in the *Wall Street Journal*, the then secretary-general, Kofi Annan, stressed (Annan 1999),

> We need help from the private sector. Transnational companies have been the first to benefit from globalization. They must take their share of responsibility for coping with its effects. That's why, earlier this year, I proposed a Global Compact between business and the UN, under which we will help corporations to act in accordance with internationally accepted principles of human rights, labor standards, and environmental protection.

Rather than resting on the nation states and their legal authority to enforce the principles and guidelines of the framework, the Global Compact thus turned directly to the global corporations and asked for voluntary compliance to its principles. They rely on the business community both to promote and to enforce and uphold the values, standards and norms of the initiative. In doing so, the Global Compact has avoided much of the criticism that other regulatory attempts of CSR faced at this time (Utting 2002). State backing and legitimating was indeed important, both to get the program started and to uphold its status. It was originally financed by voluntary governmental contributions and was intended to be an ambitious experiment, whose content would emerge in dialogue with the participants. It has the continuous backing of national governments and states through the UN General Assembly, strengthened and sustained in the declaration "Towards Global Partnerships" (United Nations 2008a: 4):

> [The General Assembly] encourages the activities of the United Nations Global Compact as an innovative public-private partnership to advance United Nations values and responsible business practices within the United Nations system and among the global business community.

The Global Compact further inspired several national and local initiatives to spread the practice of CSR, and directly influenced many local initiatives and projects to deal with CSR issues. Among these, we find the Swedish governmental initiative "Globalt ansvar" (The Swedish Partnership for

Global Responsibility). Along the lines of the Global Compact, the Swedish initiative was a voluntary agreement that appealed to the business community to help improve working conditions, protect the environment, and develop human rights around the world (Ministry of Foreign Affairs 2002). Similar national initiatives are found also in other countries, not least in Europe (Windell 2006: 68). The EU has also been active in constructing and promoting CSR issues, mainly in the context of improving business practices and labor market functions within Europe (Windell 2006: 76). Through multiple stakeholder conversations and a broad inclusion of businesses and corporations, NGOs, trade unions, employers' organizations and international organizations (such as the ILO and the OECD), the EU aimed to create a "pole for excellence" on CSR issues (European Commission 2006a). Rather than a declaration to be signed, like the Global Compact, the European Commission created the "European Alliance for CSR" as a political process to "increase the uptake of CSR amongst European enterprises" (European Commission 2006a: 3). In this process, they both built on and supported the use and spread of the Global Compact as they actively encouraged and promoted this, and similar international frameworks, to European corporations.

Corporate Participation in Soft Regulation

Basing the Global Compact on existing UN principles and conventions has provided a distinct normative foundation, and, through its close interrelationship with the respective UN agencies and their work, wide acceptance of its principles has been secured. The Global Compact gains its credibility from the global reach and moral authority of the UN but also from the inclusion of additional actors and the created "community" around the principles issued. In this sense, the relationship between the regulators and those regulated in this regulatory framework is largely reciprocal, as the UN is dependent on the participants to create and sustain legitimacy for its regulatory framework.

Businesses are encouraged to participate in order to appear legitimate and to strengthen their own knowledge and work on CSR issues. The Global Compact webpage and brochures explicitly state a number of "benefits" believed to accrue to businesses participating in the initiatives. Among these, we find access to the UN knowledge structures and decision-making powers, and networking and learning opportunities through the meeting of other corporations as well as the United Nations, state governments, non-governmental organizations (NGOs), etc. More interesting, perhaps, are also the "indirect" benefits described, where things such as increased legitimacy, enhanced reputation, branding opportunities and similar things are stressed, along with accountability and transparency arguments (United Nations 2008b).

In subscribing to the initiative, organizations commit to change their business operations in such ways that the Global Compact principles form "an integral part of business, day-to-day operations, and organizational culture" (United Nations 2009c), and to describe, in writing annual reports on progress, how they support and work with the principles. They further agree to publicly advocate the principles in their policies and mission statements, as well as to announce their participation in such documents as their annual reports and in press releases. Participants are thus responsible both for advancing and "working" the UN principles within their own organizations and for promoting it to others.

Furthermore, great emphasis is placed on what are called "learning networks" and "policy dialogues," where business leaders, UN agencies, labor associations, governmental representatives, NGOs, academics and other groups are brought together to discuss and share experiences on specific issues. "Partnerships for development" is another important feature, encouraging companies to form partnerships with public organizations and with their stakeholders to work on common issues and projects that promote broader UN goals and support advancement in developing countries. Through these many networking activities and partnership programs, what is envisioned is the formation of a community in which each participant strives to appear appropriate in relation to the other members and to the society at large, which drives them to act according to the principles and established rules. Inclusion in this community is a crucial mechanism to make people adhere to the norms, but it is equally essential to reach a level of legitimacy for the effort as a whole to make it an important signal that members can use to show social responsibility to a wider audience. Inclusion is thus both the end and the means of the Global Compact.

From "Experiment" to Regulatory Framework

From the beginning, the Global Compact was seen as an "ambitious experiment," as a way to involve corporations and encourage them to take responsibility for global social and environmental issues. As the initiative has developed through dialogues among participants, the Global Compact has come to take on a clearer structure and form over the years. As one attempt to move the Global Compact "from its initial phase of experimentation to one of greater focus, transparency and sustained impact" (United Nations 2005: 1), a new governance framework for the initiative was adopted in 2005, giving an increasingly important role to corporations and other stakeholders in directing and governing the initiative. The new governance framework is described to be "light, non-bureaucratic and designed to foster greater involvement in, and ownership of, the initiative by participants and other stakeholders themselves" (United Nations 2010: 29). Alongside the Global Compact board—consisting of representatives from the four stakeholder groups: business, civil society, labor and the United Nations—the initiative gives significant influence to the Leaders' Summit and the Local Networks to influence its direction and content. The Leaders' Summit gathers the top executives of all participating organizations to set the strategic direction for the initiative. The Local Networks, in contrast, represent the local and regional initiatives within the Global Compact framework, and work to assist companies in implementing the Global Compact principles and to foster action in particular areas or regions. Through this governance framework, these bodies establish the rules for participation in the Global Compact and also oversee its main principles and procedures. In this way, the network guides the overall structure, development, and implementation of the initiative at the same time as its members are subject to the rules they establish.

The regulatory principles and the mechanisms for control and compliance have developed through reciprocal dialogues in these networks and relationships. This approach has led to a gradual development of the initiative, with an expansion of its scope with the inclusion of the tenth principle on anti-corruption, but also by establishing clearer rules and further guidelines for participation and non-compliance with the established principles. This has included a specification of the requirements of participants as well as several "integrity" measures. Examples can be found in the new governance framework (United Nations 2009b).

The main mechanism in the Global Compact is the Communication of Progress reports, which were instigated in 2003. These reports should contain a statement by the CEO or other senior representative of the company that expresses the continued support of the Global Compact and its principles—to "signify that the Global Compact is considered a commitment deserving of the highest level of attention" (United Nations 2005: 3)—and a description of the practical actions taken by the company to adhere to and implement the ten principles into its business operations. The report should also contain a measurement of outcomes or expected outcomes, recommending, although not requiring, the use of the metrics and indicators developed within the Global Reporting Initiative (see further Chapter 5). Furthermore, the reports should be shared with the corporate stakeholders as well as posted on the Global Compact website. Each company signing up to the Global Compact has to deliver a Communication of Progress report within two years of signing, and this report has to be updated annually (United Nations 2009d).

Since the United Nations has no enforcing capacity in any legally binding sense, it relies on the active participation of corporations in advancing the principles that it lays down. In addition, it relies on the active scrutiny of corporate activities, not only among corporations but also by the media, and civil society organizations—such as CorpWatch—that have as their task to scrutinize corporations. This means that a fundamental principle on which the Global Compact initiative builds is that of "naming and shaming." Corporations are encouraged to follow the issued principle so that they will not be subject to negative publicity. Or more generally framed, the

Global Compact rests on corporation's concern for reputational risk (see Power 2007 and Chapter 7).

Furthermore, the United Nations takes no responsibility for auditing or assessing corporations in terms of their activities in relation to the Global Compact, but simply makes sure that companies report on the progress and their adherence to the principles. However, after some debate and some problems in upholding the legitimacy and authority of the initiative, a number of "integrity measures" were developed and adopted in 2004. These included guidelines for the use of the UN and Global Compact name, emblem and logo to prevent misuse of the association with the Global Compact initiative; principles to handle allegations of abuse of the Global Compact overall aims and principles; and principles for handling failure to report progress. This last principle is perhaps the most pronounced means that the network has taken toward greater control of its regulatory function. It means that companies failing to produce or update their Progress Report will be marked as "non-communicating" or, after a year of not fulfilling this duty, will eventually be termed inactive and removed from the Global Compact database. This "delisting" policy was implemented in 2008, with a total of 630 companies being delisted in the first six months (United Nations 2008c).

With the development and implementation of these new governance mechanisms, the participating organizations have been given greater influence in the construction of the regulatory framework and a more prominent role in monitoring and upholding the regulatory function of the initiative. What are formed in this network are complex constellations of mobilizing, policy making, reporting and monitoring bodies, where the whole network, rather than individual organizations or regulations, forms a regulatory impact. Within this network, roles and relationships are unclear and individual actors may appear as rule setters, rule enforcers and rule-followers, as well as rule monitors. In these frameworks, no one has clear authority over any of the others.

Normative Diffusion

Earlier we explained how the Global Compact initiative in itself developed into a regulatory framework, as relations among those many actors involved are increasingly structured and stabilized. The most important regulatory impact of the Global Compact framework, however, comes perhaps from the normative diffusion of those principles in the field. The principles of the Global Compact have diffused far beyond its organized network. The principles have come to be widely used to argue for and demand corporate responsibilities. With the increased attention to and awareness of corporate social responsibility (CSR) among corporations and their counterparts, as examined in Chapter 5, demands have been raised among many groups to make sure that corporations are acting in socially responsible ways.

For example, the Swedish pension funds have adopted investment policies stating that they should not invest in corporations that break the Global Compact principles. In order to monitor these corporations, the investment funds purchase services from consultancies that specialize in such screening. These consultancies in turn base their screening on various sources, among them published reports by NGOs such as CorpWatch that, according to their mission, scrutinize the activities of corporations in relation to human rights, workers' rights, environmental concerns, etc. In addition, these organizations use the Global Compact principles as part of their template against which corporations are screened. The outcome of the screening are lists of corporations that violate the Global Compact principles. The main policy, however, is that rather than just putting corporations on a "blacklist," a dialogue is encouraged where the corporations that are found to be violating some of the Global Compact principles should be made aware of this and be asked to present a plan for how to improve their social responsibility (see, e.g., GES-Invest 2017).

With the described development, the norms that have been formulated and promoted with the Global Compact principles have diffused so that they now permeate the field of governance. These norms have become a template for monitoring and assessing the social responsibility of corporations. The United Nations, in this case, has clearly spurred a normative orientation in the field, which has come to pervade the field of governance. We can characterize the role of the United Nations as a norm entrepreneur as defined by Finnemore and Sikkink (1998). In terms of their terminology of norm "life cycle," the Global Compact has driven the cascading and integration of corporate social norms in the field of governance.

Actors, Roles and Relationships in Regulatory Fields

As we argued in the introduction to this chapter, regulations and regulatory relations are prominent elements of contemporary governance of corporations. Our two cases have demonstrated how a pair of transnational regulatory processes developed over time, particularly stressing the many and intertwined relationships and interdependencies that are involved in regulation, and how both activity and meaning are shaped in these processes.

To analyze these dynamics of contemporary regulation, we will return to the field concept as set out in Chapter 2. There, we particularly stressed its usefulness for explaining the embeddedness of corporations in a wider institutional environment, and how common meaning systems develop among organizations that are subject to field pressures and institutional forces. We will elaborate on these field processes here, with a particular focus on how they play out in relation to regulations and regulatory relations. In doing so, we will use the term "regulatory field." This is a depiction of the actors and relationships as well as the forces at play to exert a regulatory impact on a particular set of organizations, and in relation to specific issues and aspects of corporations. We further argue that the concept of regulatory field is particularly useful when analyzing regulations that develop in a transnational context (cf. Djelic and Sahlin-Andersson 2006a). In such contexts, we find many interacting actors, unclear and porous boundaries, and overlapping regulations. Thus the kind of regulations that tend to evolve in such contexts are often soft in nature; they develop in combinations so that individual regulations are embedded in each other, and they are backed by organizing, monitoring and expertise (cf. Jacobsson and Sahlin-Andersson 2006). With the concept of regulatory field, we would also like to draw attention to how regulations govern—namely, they tend to overlap and intertwine so that the governing of corporations is molded in the interrelation of various regulations. Those many intertwined regulations and the means of backing them combine into what we next term a "regulatory knot." This in turn has implications for how responsibility is distributed and on the impact of compliance with or deviance from individual regulatory schemes.

Regulation and the Development of Organizational Fields

The concept of regulatory fields serves to highlight the fact that regulations are dependent on field-specific relations and actors and are consequential for further field structuration and the shaping of common meaning systems within fields. Previous studies have pointed to this importance of several regulatory actors in the forming and development of organizational fields (DiMaggio and Powell 1983; DiMaggio 1987; Leblebici et al. 1991; Greenwood, Suddaby and Hinings 2002). As a key element in the institutional environment, regulatory agencies can exercise both coercive and normative pressures on organizations in a particular field, by providing rules and laws in a traditional sense but also, and perhaps more significantly, by providing support, resources and legitimacy to field actors and activities. DiMaggio (1983), for instance, showed that the state, by issuing rules for certain grants, exerted significant coercive pressure on organizations in the field of art. The most enduring impact of such state support, however, was the influence it had on the structuring of relations within the field (DiMaggio 1983: 148). Those organizations that gained state support came to be perceived by other organizations as more successful (DiMaggio 1983) and, hence, tended to be imitated more frequently (cf. DiMaggio and Powell 1983: 152; Sahlin-Andersson and Sevón 2003). Thus, also through mimetic processes among organizations, the field came to be configured around particular activities and actors that were indirectly legitimated by the state.

Regulations also exert normative pressures on organizations within fields. In these processes, professional organizations and associations play a particularly important role as regulatory actors (Greenwood, Suddaby and Hinings 2002). Professions and professional organizations also legitimate actors and practices, and they monitor compliance with normatively and coercively sanctioned expectations within fields (Greenwood, Suddaby and

Hinings 2002: 62). As such, they are important for shaping, reproducing and reforming collective beliefs and shared understandings among members of fields (DiMaggio and Powell 1983; Ruef and Scott 1998; Greenwood, Suddaby and Hinings 2002). For instance, professional organizations within the field of professional business services firms played important roles in legitimating change in the authority and structure of the large international accounting firms (Greenwood, Suddaby and Hinings 2002).

Furthering our understanding of the role of regulations for field development, Hedmo, Sahlin-Andersson and Wedlin (2006) argue that the interaction among regulators as well as the interrelations between regulators and those being regulated is particularly important. They show how professional organizations and the media—through accreditation programs and rankings—have significantly influenced the development of the field of management education, helping to construct an international, and a European, character and profile of management education. Without originally having been intended to serve a regulatory function, these mechanisms came to support and reinforce each other, and were developed in cooperation with business schools, in such ways that they together formed a "regulatory field" (Hedmo, Sahlin-Andersson and Wedlin 2006: 6):

> As the new monitoring and assessment efforts emerge, build on each other, and become intensely intertwined, they come to form a regulatory field that frames and influences individual actors—be they education providers, participants in educational programs, or rule setters or monitors of programs. Our studies show that the intertwined educational providers, regulators, and monitoring bodies develop in relation to each other, so that the whole field ends up constituting a "regulatory knot."

The concept of regulatory fields thus provides additional means to understand the complex interplay of actors and relationships in the forming of regulations, and their impact on field development and change. Redirecting our attention back to our two cases of contemporary regulations, in the following we will focus on some important findings of such processes.

Evolving Regulatory Fields

In both of our cases, it is clear that a large set of actors and the relationship among them form regulations—largely of a soft kind—and common meaning systems develop regarding appropriate practice and principles of regulation and corporate conduct. In the case of aviation, a common recognition of the problems of aviation's environmental impact took shape as a number of actors, including states, businesses, international organizations and environmental NGOs, engaged in discussions and policy formulation processes at the transnational level. Agreement on appropriate means for regulating greenhouse gas emissions of aviation developed in these processes, particularly as the idea of emissions trading gained increasing attention and support from various actors, both among aviation industry associations and individual corporations such as airlines, while climbing the agenda in the wider climate change debate. For these actors, emissions trading became the preferred policy alternative around which a large number of actors and their interests could coalesce.

The case of Global Compact further illustrates the interconnectedness of various actors and interests in forming regulatory principles and outcomes, and how shared recognitions of CSR developed through these relationships. The Global Compact initiative, while originating in the United Nations, was an explicit attempt to incorporate a large set of actors in framing issues of CSR, and to engage corporations in building a normative framework for the conduct of business through the proliferation of a set of established principles and guidelines in the global community. While not originally a regulatory initiative, it has come to constitute the cornerstone of a developing soft regulatory framework for CSR issues, as a large number of organizations have joined, and new regulatory initiatives have followed in its wake.

Our two cases particularly highlight the interdependence among regulators, as well as among regulators and those being regulated, and how both actors—their roles and interests—and activities are shaped in the interactions that arise among them. These relations and interactions develop as the regulatory process evolves. In both our cases, regulations are developing on the initiative of the transnational organizations, the EU and the United Nations, respectively. These can be conceptualized as arenas that provide an institutional setting and context for the developing regulations (March and Olsen 1984; Stone Sweet, Sandholtz and Fligstein 2001), providing legitimacy and resources as well as organizational settings for the developing regulations, which in turn help to shape the regulatory procedures and principles. Such arenas host debates and discussions and help structure relationships among organizations and actors involved in regulations (Woll and Artigas 2007), and they can provide both normative and cognitive guidance for developing regulations (Marcussen 2004).

However, it is clear from our cases that the authority and role of these arenas as regulators are not established beforehand, but develop in the process of constructing policies and principles for regulation. In the case of emissions trading in particular, we saw that the issue of regulating the environmental impact of aviation drifted across different levels and policy arenas before it landed in the EU, where the principles of emissions trading had already been established in other policy areas (Braun 2009) and where a number of actors could join to push this issue forward on the regulatory agenda. An important actor in putting this into the EU framework was the UK government, who put the issue on the agenda during their EU presidency. Here, national debates on airport expansion and an existing emissions trading program in the United Kingdom are among the factors that served as important triggers for the regulatory developments in the EU. In this case, the overlapping transnational and national institutional contexts and settings and the interrelations among actors and activities at different policy levels helped shape a regulatory outcome for this issue.

Embedded Regulatory Actors and Processes

The case of emissions trading highlights the embeddedness of regulatory actors and processes, in wider, and sometimes multiple, institutional contexts. In this case, the UK government is an important actor in pushing for and forming regulation in the transnational arena, where their role and interests is taking shape in relation to both national regulatory relations as well as transnational ones. Thus, we see that national and transnational institutional contexts for regulation are clearly interrelated and interdependent (cf. Djelic and Quack 2003). Through participation in transnational or supranational organizations and networks, states are embedded in broader institutional contexts and networks of regulation, where they make up participating units but also become subject themselves to rules, regulations and guidelines that form their respective roles, activities, and interests (Jacobsson 2006: 213–214). The embeddedness of states in transnational networks and organizations means an increasing interaction with these organizations and with other states, and the construction of states as participants in transnational regulatory activities (Djelic and Sahlin-Andersson 2006b).

The embeddedness of regulatory actors and processes, particularly national governments, in wider institutional contexts is further highlighted in the case of the Global Compact. It is evident in this case that the authority and role of governments in regulation can vary—and here, more clearly perhaps than ever—the mandate of the states to regulate corporations is challenged. Instead of relying on the authority of the state, the United Nations deliberately chose to appeal to corporations directly and to get them involved in the process of constructing, developing and upholding the regulatory principles and processes of the Global Compact. Here, states took the role of supporting or legitimizing the regulations developed by other actors rather than establishing their own regulatory frameworks. While states have supported the initiative, both financially and otherwise, it is the corporations and other organizations, backed by the legitimacy and support provided by the United Nations, who function as the main regulatory actors.

The corporations are in this case more active in regulatory activities than common conceptions of them as "rule-followers" admit. Rather than being passive recipients of or followers of rules and regulations, corporations are often actively involved in developing, refining and upholding systems of rules, regulations and self-regulation (cf. Hedmo, Sahlin-Andersson and Wedlin 2006). As was particularly evident in the case of the Global Compact, corporations have taken an active role in the development and structuring of the initiative, and the partnership between the Global Compact and the corporations is becoming more pronounced, organized and structured over time. This soft regulatory system thus rests on reciprocal relationships between those regulating and those being regulated, and it is dependent on the participation as well as the legitimacy and authority of both the regulating and the regulated organizations. Thus, it provides a cross-sectional soft form of regulation that is pursued in transformed interlinkages among states, business and international governmental organizations and NGOs, and the relationships and respective roles of these diverse types of organizations are formed as the regulatory principles and activities take shape.

It is not only states and other actors that are embedded in multiple institutional contexts, however. Our cases also show how the principles and mechanisms of regulation are embedded into the wider field of governance. In many instances, regulations give rise to new regulations, as well as link up to and (or) build significantly on other regulatory principles and procedures. The Global Compact initiative, for instance, both built on national initiatives and on existing conventions and guidelines developed within the United Nations, which helped to inform and establish the principles and governance framework for the initiative. More importantly, perhaps, the Global Compact initiative has also been explicitly linked to various standards and reporting guidelines, such as the Global Reporting Initiative and the ISO 14000 standards, both enhancing the legitimacy and the governing functions of the initiative. Furthermore, the Global Compact has led to many and various local and regional initiatives to regulate the issue of CSR, such as those initiated by the European Commission (Windell 2006: 73–79). Such embeddedness of regulatory processes is also visible in the aviation case, as was discussed earlier, where previous experiences with emissions trading at the national level as well as the existing EU trading program provided fertile ground for regulation in the aviation sector at the transnational level.

Organizing and Structuring of Regulatory Relations and Fields

As a field analysis suggests, we have seen that regulatory fields and the relationships among actors in such fields develop and are shaped over time. As regulatory processes evolve, the interests, roles and relationships of the regulating as well as regulated actors develop and are both shaped by and shape the regulatory outcomes. Fields become increasingly structured over time, as common meaning systems as well as principles of interaction and involvement develop (DiMaggio and Powell 1983). Such structuration processes develop at the field level through interactions, debates and struggles among organizations in the field, including professional associations (DiMaggio 1991; Greenwood, Suddaby and Hinings 2002), interest associations (Washington 2004), and regulatory actors.

Recognizing the multitude of actors and interests involved in regulatory activity, we can also note an increase in the organizing and structuring of the relationship between regulators and corporations, as well as between the multitude of interests and stakeholders involved in regulatory processes and developments. The Global Compact example clearly illustrated how such relationships are being formed within a soft regulatory framework, largely building on the voluntary participation of corporations and other organizations, and how these relationships took on a more formalized and distinct form as the initiative and its governance framework evolved and expanded. With the development of more detailed and developed procedures and guidelines for compliance, and thus for inclusion and exclusion, the relationship between corporations and the Global Compact was both elaborated and formalized, and the regulatory impact of the initiative was strengthened.

The case of emissions trading for aviation further highlights how relationships between formal regulatory bodies and various interest groups, industry associations, and individual companies are structured through both formal and informal interest representation. The involvement of these actors, all having a stake in the aviation industry and its development, clearly molded the regulatory process and its outcome. In part, these actors and interests took part in institutionalized procedures for formal and informal interest representation within the EU (Stone Sweet, Sandholtz and Fligstein 2001), including official stakeholder consultations established within the policy preparation system of the European Commission (Mazey and Richardson 1993a; Green Cowles 2003; Greenwood 2003). As part of these systems, corporations and interest organizations contributed both knowledge and information to the regulatory process, and put forward their own opinions and views of the regulatory principles discussed, clearly influencing the development of emissions trading as the favored regulatory option for the aviation sector.

The increasing involvement of corporations in regulatory processes of this kind—be they hard or soft principles and systems of regulation—have led, overall, to an increase in organizing and structuring of relations between corporations and various regulatory actors. This organizing takes many forms. Participation in and involvement with industry or trade associations is a common way for corporations to seek to influence public decision-making procedures (Wallace and Young 1997; Jutterström 2004). These can be organized within or across sectors and industries, and at both the national and the transnational levels. Large corporations may also have their own "governmental relations" or "public relations" offices, which seek to influence policy processes directly. Many of the large multinational corporations, for instance, even have their own offices or representatives in Brussels to be able to observe and take part in important policy-making and regulatory processes (Mazey and Richardson 1993b: 7). One of the most striking developments, in the EU context at least, is the rapid increase in the number of professional lobbyists, consultant companies, and law firms working with professional lobbying for corporations and other organizations that are not themselves represented in Brussels (Mazey and Richardson 2006:

249). Such intermediaries form important ways for corporations to influence and take part in regulatory and policy-making processes (see further Chapter 7).

The increasingly important role of corporations and their intermediate organizations in rule-making activity particularly at the European level has led to further changes in the relationship between the EU and its many stakeholders. In a specific effort to organize, and perhaps also "regulate," the influence of corporations in policy-making processes, the EU has launched a register for interest organizations lobbying the European Commission and the Council. The register was developed and launched as part of the European Transparency Initiative (ETI) in 2005 in an effort to increase, and perhaps also restore, legitimacy for European institutions (European Commission 2006b). Unlike the register that for many years has been compulsory for accreditation to lobby the European Parliament, the register developed under ETI is voluntary. It asks interest organizations and corporations to disclose information about what their mission is, who they represent, and how they are funded, and also to sign and abide by a Code of Conduct regulating the relationship between lobbyists and the public officials (European Commission 2007). Through this initiative, the EU has recognized the importance of lobbying activities and seeks to make it a legitimate part of the rule-making and policy-making process.

Conclusions

The expansion of regulation into new areas, and alterations of its forms, calls for the development of analytical tools through which contemporary regulation and its impact on corporations can be properly understood. In this chapter we have used two contemporary empirical cases to underpin the proposition that regulation develops as a regulatory field. We have particularly noted in our empirical cases how a multitude of actors interact to form regulations, and how these interactions inform both the regulators and those being regulated in reciprocal processes. This, in turn, leads to the forming of common meaning systems and activities, and to the creation of new relationships and further organizing.

By conceptualizing regulations and regulators as a regulatory field, we are able to better understand the complex interplay of actors, meanings and actions that make up contemporary regulation. Three things in particular are highlighted.

First, regulators and regulations are dependent on, and closely interrelated with, the development of a particular field. This means that we need to see regulations in a particular area or setting as interrelated, and recognize the sometimes multiple institutional contexts in which regulatory processes and actors are embedded. We have particularly recognized the interrelation between national and transnational institutional contexts and arenas, suggesting that these are mutually constitutive for regulatory actions. Such embeddedness shapes both activities and meaning within the field.

Second, we emphasize the relationship among various regulators, as well as among regulators and those being regulated, and how these relationships are structured and develop over time to mold a regulatory outcome. These relations are reciprocal, shaping both regulators and those being regulated, as interests, roles and responsibilities develop in interactions. Such reciprocity furthermore means that it is difficult to clearly distinguish individual regulations and their impact—as these come to form regulatory knots of interdependent regulations and regulators—entailing complications regarding who is to be held responsible for such regulatory efforts.

Third, we point to the need to see regulation as a process that takes shape over time and in complex interactions among a large set of actors. In such processes, relations become increasingly organized and structured, contributing to field development and change as well as to further regulations and revised regulatory relations and processes.

With the concept of regulatory field, we wish to particularly emphasize the regulators and the regulatory relations that develop among groups or sets of actors. By doing so, we single out the role of a varied set of organizations, including corporations, in contemporary regulatory processes, stressing the constitutive and important function of regulations for the developing field of governance influencing contemporary organizations. As noted in Chapter 2, organizations and actors such as investors, the media and CSO may take many roles in the governing of corporations, thus comprising important elements in the wider field of governance. In this chapter, however, we suggest that many of these actors, in specific situations, also take on a significant role in regulation. Thus we suggest that one way that the different governing relations discussed in this volume are interrelated is through regulations and regulatory processes.

References

Annan, K., 1999, "Help the Third World Help Itself," *Wall Street Journal*, November 29, 1999.

Ayres, I. and Braithwaite, J., 1992, *Responsive Regulation*, Oxford: Oxford University Press.

Bache, I. and Flinders, M., 2004, *Multi-level Governance*, Oxford: Oxford University Press.

Baldwin, R., 2008, "Regulation Lite: The Rise of Emissions Trading," *Regulation and Governance*, 2(2): 193–215.

Baldwin, R. and Cave, M., 1999, *Understanding Regulation: Theory, Strategy and Practice*, Oxford: Oxford University Press.

Beck, N. and Walgenbach, P., 2002, "The Institutionalization of the Quality Management Approach in Germany," in: Sahlin-Andersson, K. and Engwall, L. (eds.),

The Expansion of Management Knowledge: Carriers, Flows and Sources, Stanford: Stanford University Press, pp. 145–174.
Bendell, J. and Visser, W., 2003, "World Review April—June 2003: A Synopsis of the Key Strategic Developments in Corporate Responsibility Around the Globe Over the Last Quarter," *Journal of Corporate Citizenship*, 3(11): 5–19.
Boli, J. and Thomas, G., 1999, *Constructing World Culture*, Stanford, CA: Stanford University Press.
Braithwaite, J., 2008, *Regulatory Capitalism: How It Works, Ideas for Making It Better*, Cheltenham: Edward Elgar.
Braithwaite, J. and Drahos, P., 2000, *Global Business Regulation*, Cambridge: Cambridge University Press.
Braun, M., 2009, "The Evolution of Emissions Trading in the European Union: The Role of Policy Networks, Knowledge and Policy Entrepreneurs," *Accounting, Organizations and Society*, 34(3–4): 469–487.
Brunsson, N., Jacobsson, B. and Associates, 2000, *A World of Standards*, Oxford: Oxford University Press.
Brunsson, N., Rasche, A. and Seidl, D., 2012, "The Dynamics of Standardization: Three Perspectives on Standards in Organization Studies," *Organization Studies*, 33(5–6): 613–632.
Buhr, K., 2008, *Bringing Aviation into the EU Emissions Trading Scheme: Institutional Entrepreneurship at Windows of Opportunity*, Doctoral Dissertation No. 140 from the Department of Business Studies, Uppsala: Uppsala University.
Coen, D., 1998, "The European Business Interest and the Nation State: Large-firm Lobbying in the European Union and Member States," *Journal of Public Policy*, 18(1): 75–100.
Cutler, A. C., Haufler, V. and Porters, T., 1999, *Private Authority and International Affairs*, New York: State University of New York Press.
DiMaggio, P. J., 1983, "State Expansion and Organizational Fields," in: Hall, R. H. and Quinn, R. E. (eds.), *Organizational Theory and Public Policy*, Beverly Hills, CA: Sage, pp. 142–172.
DiMaggio, P. J., 1987, "Classification in Art," *American Sociological Review*, 52(4): 440–455.
DiMaggio, P. J., 1991, "Constructing an Organizational Field as a Professional Project: U.S. Art Museums, 1920–1940," in: Powell, W. W. and DiMaggio, P. J. (eds.), *The New Institutionalism in Organizational Analysis*, Chicago: University of Chicago Press, pp. 267–292.
DiMaggio, P. J. and Powell, W. W., 1983, "The Iron Cage Revisited: Institutional Isomorphism and Collective Rationality in Organizational Fields," *American Sociological Review*, 48(2): 147–160.
Djelic, M.-L. and Quack, S. (eds.), 2003, *Globalization and Institutions*, Cheltenham: Edward Elgar.
Djelic, M.-L. and Sahlin-Andersson, K. (eds.), 2006a, *Transnational Governance: Institutional Dynamics of Regulation*, Cambridge: Cambridge University Press.
Djelic, M.-L. and Sahlin-Andersson, K., 2006b, "Introduction: A World of Governance: The Rise of Transnational Regulation," in: Djelic, M.-L. and Sahlin-Andersson, K. (eds.), *Transnational Governance: Institutional Dynamics of Regulation*, Cambridge: Cambridge University Press, pp. 1–28.
Eberhard-Harribey, L., 2006, "Corporate Social Responsibility as a New Paradigm in the European Policy: How CSR Comes to Legitimate the European Regulatory Process," *Corporate Governance*, 6(4): 358–368.

European Commission, 2001, "Environment 2010: Our Future, Our Choice—The Sixth Environment Action Programme," COM (2001) 31–1 <http://ec.europa.eu/environment/air/pdf/6eapbooklet_en.pdf> accessed August 10, 2017.

European Commission, 2005a, "Reducing the Climate Impact of Aviation: Report on the Public Consultation, March–May 2005" <https://ec.europa.eu/clima/sites/clima/files/transport/aviation/docs/report_publ_cons_en.pdf>accessed on May 12, 2017.

European Commission, 2005b, "Reducing the Climate Change Impact of Aviation," COM (2005) 459 Final <http://ec.europa.eu/transparency/regdoc/rep/1/2005/EN/1-2005-459-EN-F1-1.Pdf> accessed on May 30, 2017.

European Commission, 2006a, "Implementing the Partnership for Growth and Jobs: Making Europe a Pole of Excellence on Corporate Social Responsibility," COM (2006)136 Final <http://eur-lex.europa.eu/LexUriServ/LexUriServ.do?uri=COM:2006:0136:FIN:en:PDF> accessed May 17, 2017.

European Commission, 2006b, "European Transparency Initiative, Green Paper" <http://europa.eu/documents/comm/green_papers/pdf/com2006_194_en.pdf> accessed on May 10, 2017.

European Commission, 2007, "Follow-up to the Green Paper 'European Transparency Initiative," COM (2007) 127 Final <http://eur-lex.europa.eu/legal-content/EN/TXT/PDF/?uri=CELEX:52007DC0127&from=EN> accessed on May 17, 2017.

Finnemore, M. and Sikkink, K., 1998, "International Norm Dynamics and Political Change," *International Organization*, 52(4): 887–917.

GES-invest, 2017, "Portfolio Screening and Analysis" <www.ges-invest.com> accessed on May 12, 2017.

Golub, J. (ed.), 1998, *New Instruments for Environmental Policy Within the EU*, London and New York: Routledge.

Green Cowles, M., 2003, "Non-state Actors and False Dichotomies: Reviewing IR/IPE Approaches to European Integration," *Journal of European Public Policy*, 10(1): 102–120.

Greenwood, J., 2003, *Interest Representation in the European Union*, Basingstoke: Palgrave Macmillan.

Greenwood, R., Suddaby, R. and Hinings, C. R., 2002, "Theorizing Change: The Role of Professional Associations in the Transformation of Institutionalized Fields," *Academy of Management Journal*, 45(1): 58–80.

Gulbrandsen, L. H., 2010, *Transnational Environmental Governance*, Cheltenham: Edward Elgar.

Haas, P., 1992, "Introduction: Epistemic Communities and International Policy Coordination," *International Organization*, 46(1): 1–35.

Hedmo, T., Sahlin-Andersson, K. and Wedlin, L., 2006, "The Emergence of a European Regulatory Field of Management Education," in: Djelic, M.-L. and Sahlin-Andersson, K. (eds.), *Transnational Governance: Institutional Dynamics of Regulation*, Cambridge: Cambridge University Press, pp. 308–328.

Hirst, P. and Thompson, G., 1996, *Globalization in Question: The International Economies and the Possibilities of Governance*, Cambridge: Cambridge University Press.

Hoffmann, S., 1982, "Reflections on the Nation-State in Western Europe Today," *Journal of Common Market Studies*, 21(1–2): 21–37.

Holm, H.-H. and Sørensen, G., 1995, *Whose World Order?: Uneven Globalization and the End of the Cold War*, Boulder, CO: Westview Press.

Holton, R., 1998, *Globalization and the Nation-State*, New York: Macmillan.

Jacobsson, B., 2006, "Regulated Regulators: Global Trends of State Transformation," in: Djelic, M.-L. and Sahlin-Andersson, K. (eds.), *Transnational Governance: Institutional Dynamics of Regulation*, Cambridge: Cambridge University Press, pp. 205–224.

Jacobsson, B. and Sahlin-Andersson, K., 2006, "Dynamics of Soft Regulations," in: Djelic, M.-L. and Sahlin-Andersson, K. (eds.), *Transnational Governance: Institutional Dynamics of Regulation*, Cambridge: Cambridge University Press, pp. 247–265.

Jenkins, R., 2001, *Corporate Codes of Conduct: Self-Regulation in a Global Economy*, Technology, Business and Society Programme Paper Number 2, April 2001, Geneva: United Nations Research Institute for Social Development <www.unrisd.org/80256B3C005BCCF9/(httpAuxPages)/E3B3E78BAB9A886F80256B5E00344278/$file/jenkins.pdf> accessed on August 10, 2017.

Jordan, A., Rudiger, K. G., Wurzel, Z. and Anthony, R., 2003, *New Instruments of Environmental Governance: National Experiences or Prospects*, London: Routledge.

Jutterström, M., 2004, *Att påverka beslut—företag i EUs regelsättande* (Influencing Decisions: Companies in the Rule-Making of the European Union), Doctoral Dissertation from the Stockholm School of Economics, Stockholm: EFI.

Katzenstein, P., Keohane, R. and Krasner, S., 1998, "International Organization and the Study of World Politics," *International Organization*, 52(4): 645–685.

Keck, M. and Sikkink, K., 1998, *Activists Beyond Borders: Advocacy Networks in International Politics*, Ithaca, NY: Cornell University Press.

Kirton, J. J. and Trebilcock, M. J., 2004, *Hard Choices, Soft Law: Voluntary Standards in Global Trade, Environment and Social Governance*, Aldershot: Ashgate.

Kohler-Koch, B. and Eising, R., 1999, *The Transformation of Governance in the European Union*, London: Routledge.

Kolk, A. and van Tulder, R., 2002, "The Effectiveness of Self-regulation: Corporate Codes of Conduct and Child Labour," *European Management Journal*, 20(3): 260–271.

Leblebici, H., Salancik, G. R., Copay, A. and King, T., 1991, "Institutional Change and the Transformation of Interorganizational Fields: An Organizational History of the U.S. Radio Broadcasting Industry," *Administrative Science Quarterly*, 36(3): 333–363.

Levi-Faur, D. and Jordana, J. (eds.), 2005, "The Rise of Regulatory Capitalism: The Global Diffusion of a New World Order," *The ANNALS of the American Academy of Political and Social Sciences*, 598(1): 12–32.

MacKenzie, D., 2009, "Making Things the Same: Gases, Emission Rights and the Politics of Carbon Markets," *Accounting, Organizations and Society*, 34(3–4): 440–455.

March, J. G. and Olsen, J. P., 1984, "The New Institutionalism: Organizational Factors in Political Life," *American Political Science Review*, 78(3): 734–749.

Marcussen, M., 2004, "OECD Governance Through Soft Law," in: Mörth, U. (ed.), *Soft Law in Governance and Regulation*, Cheltenham: Edward Elgar, 103–126.

Marks, G., 1993, "Structural Policy and Multilevel Governance in the EC," in: Cafruny, A. W. and Rosenthal, G. G. (eds.), *The State of the European Community Vol.2: The Maastrich Debates and Beyond*, Boulder: Lynne Rienner, pp. 391–410.

Marks, G., Hooghe, L. and Blank, K., 1996, "European Integration From the 1980s: State-Centric vs. Multilevel Governance," *Journal of Common Market Studies*, 34(3): 341–378.

Marsh, D. (ed.), 1998, *Comparing Policy Networks*, Buckingham: Open University Press.

Mazey, S. and Richardson, J. (eds.), 1993a, *Lobbying in the European Community*, Oxford: Oxford University Press.

Mazey, S. and Richardson, J., 1993b, "Introduction: Transference of Power, Decision Rules, and Rules of the Game," in: Mazey, S. and Richardson, J. (eds.), *Lobbying in the European Community*, Oxford: Oxford University Press, pp. 3–26.

Mazey, S. and Richardson, J., 2006, "Interest Groups and EU Policy-making," in: Richardson, J. (ed.), *European Union: Power and Policy-making*, New York: Routledge, pp. 239–260.

Milward, A. S., 1999, *The European Rescue of the Nation-State*, London: Taylor & Francis.

Ministry of Foreign Affairs, 2002, "Gemensamt ansvar: Sveriges politik för global utveckling" (Joint Responsibilty: Sweden's Policy for Global Development), Government Bill 2002/03:122 <www.regeringen.se/49b734/contentassets/877bf84550a243cca631222e984d3d81/gemensamt-ansvar-sveriges-politik-for-global-utveckling> accessed on May 29, 2017.

Moravcisk, A., 1993, "Preferences and Power in the European Community: A Liberal Intergovernmental Approach," *Journal of Common Market Studies*, 31(4): 473–524.

Mörth, U. (ed.), 2004, *Soft Law in Governance and Regulation*, Cheltenham: Edgar Elgar.

Oberthür, S. and Roche Kelly, C., 2008, "EU Leadership in International Climate Policy: Achievements, and Challenges," *The International Spectator*, 43(3): 35–50.

Official Journal of the European Union, January 13, 2009, "Directive 2008/101/EC of the European Parliament and of the Council, of 19 November 2008, Amending Directive 2003/87/EC so as to Include Aviation Activities in the Scheme for Greenhouse Gas Emission Allowance Trading within the Community" <http://eur-lex.europa.eu/legal-content/EN/TXT/?uri=OJ:L:2009:008:TOC> accessed on May 29, 2017.

Power, M., 1997, *The Audit Society: Rituals of Verification*, Oxford: Oxford University Press.

Power, M., 2007, "Corporate Governance, Reputation and Environmental Risk," *Environment and Planning C: Government and Policy*, 25(1): 90–97.

Pulver, S., 2004, *Power in the Public Sphere: The Battle Between Oil Companies and Environmental Groups in UN Climate Change Negotiations 1991–2003*, Dissertation Submitted in Partial Satisfaction of the Requirements for a Doctor of Philosophy in Sociology in the Graduate Division of the University of California, Berkeley, Fall 2004.

Rosenau, J. and Czempiel, E.-O. (eds.), 1992, *Governance Without Government: Order and Change in World Politics*, Cambridge: Cambridge University Press.

Ruef, M. and Scott, W. R., 1998, "A Multidimensional Model of Organizational Legitimacy: Hospital Survival in Changing Institutional Environments," *Administrative Science Quarterly*, 43(4): 877–904.

Sahlin-Andersson, K., 2004, "Emergent Cross-Sectional Soft Regulations: Dynamics at Play in the Global Compact Initiative," in: Mörth, U. (ed.), *Soft Law in Governance and Regulation*, Cheltenham: Edward Elgar, pp. 129–153.

Sahlin-Andersson, K., 2006, "Corporate Social Responsibility: A Trend and a Movement, But of What and for What?" *Corporate Governance*, 6(5): 595–608.

Sahlin-Andersson, K. and Sevón, G., 2003, "Imitation and Identification as Performatives," in: Czarniawska, B. and Sevón, G. (eds.), *The Northern Lights: Organization Theory in Scandinavia*, Malmö: Liber, pp. 249–265.

Schneiberg, M. and Bartley, T., 2008, "Organizations, Regulation, and Economic Behavior: Regulatory Dynamics and Forms From the Nineteenth to Twenty-First Century," *Annual Review of Law and Social Science*, 4: 31–61.

Stone, D., 1996, *Capturing the Political Imagination: Think Tanks and the Policy Process*, London: Frank Cass.

Stone Sweet, A., Sandholtz, W. and Fligstein, N. (eds.), 2001, *The Institutionalization of Europe*, Oxford: Oxford University Press.

Svallfors, S., 2017, "Knowing the Game: Motivations and Skills Among Partisan Policy Professionals," *Journal of Professions and Organization*, 4(1): 55–69.

Torfing, J., Peters, G., Pierre, J. and Sørensen, E., 2012, *Interactive Governance*, Oxford: Oxford University Press.

United Nations, 2005, "Global Compact Governance Framework" <www.unglobalcompact.org> accessed on May 17, 2017.

United Nations, 2008a, "Resolution Adopted by the General Assembly 62/211: Towards Global Partnerships" (A/RES/62/211) <www.unglobalcompact.org/docs/about_the_gc/government_support/A-62-211.pdf> accessed on August 10, 2017.

United Nations, 2008b, "Corporate Citizenship in the World Economy: United Nations Global Compact" <www.unglobalcompact.org/docs/news_events/8.1/GC_brochure-_FINAL.pdf> accessed on August 21, 2009.

United Nations, 2008c, "630 Companies Delisted as Part of Integrity Measures," June 25, 2008 <www.csrwire.com/press_releases/21646-United-Nations-Global-Compact-630-Companies-Delisted-as-Part-of-Integrity-Measures> accessed on August 10, 2017.

United Nations, 2009a, "UN Global Compact Participants" <www.-unglobalcompact.org/ParticipantsAndStakeholders/index.html> accessed on August 21, 2009.

United Nations, 2009b, "Global Compact Governance" <www.-unglobalcompact.org/AboutTheGC/stages_of_development.html> accessed on August 21, 2009.

United Nations, 2009c, "The Corporate Commitment" <www.unglobal-compact.org/HowToParticipate/Business_Participation/index.html> accessed on December 12, 2009.

United Nations, 2009d, "Communicating Progress" <www.unglobal-compact.org/COP/> accessed on December 12, 2009.

United Nations, 2010, "Global Compact International Yearbook 2010," <http://international-yearbook.com/editions/> accessed on May 10, 2017.

United Nations, 2017a, "The Ten Principles of the UN Global Compact" <www.unglobalcompact.org/AboutTheGC/TheTenPrinciples/index.html> accessed on May 10, 2017.

United Nations, 2017b, "Our Participants" <www.unglobalcompact.org/what-is-gc/participants> accessed on May 10, 2017.

Utting, P., 2002, "Regulating Businesses via Multi-stakeholder Initiatives: A Preliminary Assessment," in: The United Nations Research Institute for Social Development (UNRISD) (ed.), *Voluntary Approaches to Corporate Social Responsibility: Readings and a Resource Guide*, Geneva: UNRISD, pp. 61–130.

Wallace, H. and Young, A. (eds.), 1997, *Participation and Policy-Making in the European Union*, Oxford: Clarendon.

Wallström, M., 2003, *Climate Change and Aviation*, Speech by Ms. Margot Wallström, European Commissioner for the Environment, European Commission, BAA Climate Change and Aviation Conference, 13 October 2003, London.

Washington, M., 2004, "Field Approaches to Institutional Change: The Evolution of the National Collegiate Athletic Association 1906–1995," *Organization Studies*, 25(3): 393–414.

Windell, K., 2006, *Corporate Social Responsibility Under Construction: Ideas, Translations, and Institutional Change*, Doctoral Dissertation No. 123 from the Department of Business Studies, Uppsala: Uppsala University.

Woll, C. and Artigas, A., 2007, "When Trade Liberalization Turns Into Regulatory Reform: The Impact on Business—Government Relations in International Trade Politics," *Regulation and Governance*, 1(2): 121–138.

4 Market Actors

Jaan Grünberg and Ingemund Hägg

Introduction

In recent decades, the amount of capital allocated to cross-border equity investments increased dramatically until the 2008 financial crisis. Then it dropped, but a few years later started to increase again (McKinsey & Company 2011). Globalization of ownership has presented investors with a number of challenges. In response to the market, they have to find proper solutions in their relation to the field of governance. As argued in Chapter 2 (see Table 2.1 and the comments around it), we should expect to find mimetic behavior in response to market signals.

The underlying topic of this chapter is thus the classic governance relation between investors and corporations and the changes that have occurred in this relation during the past few decades. Using the theoretical framework outlined in Chapter 2, we will analyze the processes taking place in the field of governance.

First, we turn to the processes that are in action in large global enterprises. We show that, in contrast to the traditional principal-agency model, the investors in the field of governance are not monoliths. On the basis of an empirical study, we have identified three major types of investors: (1) cross-border investors, (2) national block-holders and (3) national retail shareholders. In relation to these groups, corporations develop different kinds of relationships in response to the practice in the field.

Second, we show how corporations interact with investors through two types of structured governance interactions—namely, the road show and the annual general meeting. The road show is particularly oriented toward actors on the international capital market, while most of the participants in the annual general meetings are national retail shareholders. For these interactions, specialized organizational boundary-spanning units and intermediaries in the form of investor relations consultancies and investment banks play important roles.

Third, we show how a field of global corporate governance is developing, often beyond the reach of national jurisdictions and ownership structures. Through studies of corporate governance codes, global corporate governance organizations and intermediaries, such as proxy advisory services and rating institutes, we demonstrate how mechanisms for the articulation of investor opinions have been created, which in turn reinforces imitation in the field.

From Absentee Owners to Investor Activists

For a long time the classical problem of corporate governance was identified as the distance or disconnection between owners and corporations. This is captured in well-known terms such as *absentee ownership* (Veblen 1923) or *the separation of ownership and control* (Berle and Means 1932). However, it has been shown that the corporate governance structures in Continental Europe, and other parts of the world, are rather characterized by concentrated ownership and dominating owners, with the consequence that a separation between owners and managers is not as evident as in the United States (e.g., La Porta, Lopez-de-Silanes and Shleifer 1999).

The US context has also changed over the last few decades, however. The key development, which also includes the United Kingdom, has been the growth of the shareholder-activism movements. There are several issues that have been brought to the research agenda by the rise of shareholder activism, such as the motives for this activism, what companies get targeted and the effects of activism (see Denes, Karpoff and McWilliams 2017 for a review). As far as the latter are concerned, they are debated considerably and seem to vary over time.

The organizational responses of corporations have received less attention than the activities on the investor side, but there are important exceptions. Seminal was the work by Michael Useem (1993, 1996). In *Executive Defense* (1993), based on several case studies, he pointed to the gradually increasing importance of investor relations in aligning shareholders, that is, the proactive influencing of shareholders, for example, by trying to alter their assessment of the company (so called re-education) or by trying to impact the mix of shareholders. But the very character of interaction also changed. Useem noted in a later work (1996: 169):

> Investors and executives seek informative dialogue in place of proxy battle. They opt for dispassionate alliance over heated struggle, for quiet collaboration over defensive resistance.

Through a study of a large sample, Rao and Sivakumar (1999) have pointed to the influence of forces external to the company in spreading the practice of investor relations (IR) units. In particular, they show how the pressure of both analysts and activists coerced the adoption of units, but they also demonstrate that interlocking directorates work toward the diffusion of IR units, which they interpret as a mimetic form of adoption. There are thus important processes at play in the field of governance.

There is a growing body of knowledge of interaction practices. Here, Roberts et al. (2006) provide a review of published research on company-management interactions and find that very little has been done to understand such interactions. They offer evidence from their own study of private meetings between investors, drawing on interviews with finance directors and investor relations (IR) managers from 13 FTSE 100 companies in the United Kingdom. Private meetings are shown to be seen as important and as having disciplinary rather than informational effects. The meetings enable managers to speak on behalf of investors, and shareholder value rhetoric becomes natural for the managers. Similarly, Tengblad (2004) has observed such dialogues between Swedish CEOs and investor representatives and concludes that executives strive for alignment with market participant expectations.

The practice of dialogues has a long tradition in many European countries and has now also become institutionalized, which is underscored by the way such interactions have become part of the self-regulatory discourse (see the next section in this chapter). Examples include the guidelines for companies listed on the London Stock Exchange that devote considerable space to the subject of creating dialogues, or the Danish corporate governance code, which recommends an "ongoing dialogue between the company and its shareholders" (*Recommendations on Corporate Governance* 2014: Section 1.1.1), which can be achieved by an IR strategy.

Three Groups of Owners

An Empirical Study

Against the aforementioned background, we have performed an empirical study of the interactions between corporate executives and investors in the first half of the first decade of the twenty-first century. These studies included interviews with chairmen of corporate boards, chief executive officers and investor relation executives in six large Swedish publicly traded corporations (four of them multinationals) regarding their contacts with investors. Some interviews were conducted in English, but in most of them, we used Swedish. In the latter cases, the quotations that follow are our translations into English.

Our study means that we have studied the investors from the perspective of the corporations, which is not only fruitful but also has the advantage that it avoids the difficulties of accessing investors. Another feature of our study is that the evidence we provide is based on a number of Swedish corporations. Nevertheless, there are several reasons that some general conclusions can be drawn on the basis of this information. First of all, the relatively open attitude of Swedish top managers to management research has provided a unique opportunity to access and thus cover sensitive issues, thereby making it possible to identify examples of relevant situations and processes. Second, due to the small domestic market, Swedish industry has long been internationalized and has therefore been linked to international developments in corporate governance. Third, the Swedish case is particularly interesting, since it used to display a traditional continental corporate governance system, with concentrated ownership. With the increasing flows of cross-border equity capital, business corporations now have to accommodate both national and international owners. Therefore, although national systems still display distinguishing characteristics—e.g., labor co-determination on German and Swedish boards—international investors are to an increasing extent becoming significant counterparts. We would therefore claim that the Swedish case—although it contains some special features like differentiated voting power of shares—provides valuable evidence of relations and interactions that are not unique to Sweden, but can be found in many other countries.

Our data demonstrates how corporations interact through interpersonal relations with investors as an important and complex part of corporate top management. Among the forces driving this complexity, we find the changing composition of investors, increasing regulation of interactions and an increasing number of issues that are brought to bear on such relationships (cf. Chapter 3).

Our interviews showed that corporations handle their contacts with investors by means of segmentation into different kinds of owners. We identified three types of owners: (1) cross-border investors, (2) national block-holders and (3) national retail shareholders.

Cross-Border Investors: Routinized Interaction Patterns

The internationalization of financial markets and the subsequent rise of cross-border investors in most countries have implied that corporations increasingly build relations to such actors. For Sweden, the level of their ownership of the largest corporations had thus reached roughly 40 percent of market value at the end of 2016 (Vilenius 2017). At the same time, it should be noted that there are a number of Swedish corporations with a long history of foreign ownership, like the telecommunications company Ericsson. Relations to foreign investors have been built through the extensive travel of top executives like CEOs, CFOs and IR executives. As will be shown more in detail next, this is often formally framed as part of road shows. However, a basic hurdle for companies to enter into dialogues with international investors is that their identity is not always clear. Several companies therefore commission studies with IR consultancies in order to find out who their owners are, for example, through studies of US 13F filings.

The context of international investors entails a large number of contacts for these corporations. One of the IR executives gave us the following image:

> We have thousands of different institutions investing, about 2,400 funds. So you can imagine there are a couple of thousand portfolio managers

> that we have to know. . . . There are about seventy different sell-side firms covering [our company] on equity.

What also adds to the complexity is the high mobility of persons in the financial sector. Consider the financial analysts (sell-side) with whom primarily IR executives build relations. One of the IR executives reported how the analysts covering his firm had moved around in a couple of months:

> The guy from Merrill Lynch moved over to Morgan Stanley, . . . , the Morgan Stanley guy moved to J. P. Morgan who picked up coverage of [our company], a new person came into Merrill Lynch who used to work at Salomon, Smith, and Barney . . . and all this happened in five months, so all the people were the same, [but] the companies different.

Handling these numerous relations is the main task of the IR function, but structuring and disclosing information are also involved. This means that the IR function to a large extent involves gathering and compiling information in order to make it widely available. However, according to our interviewees, in spanning the corporate boundary it is also important "to pull as much information as possible, not only about [the] company, but also about what the competitors are doing [and] what the competitors are saying." In this great web of relations, the IR executives try to build personal relationships. One of the IR executives told us:

> I bring what I call an account management philosophy, and that is [that] you have to make contact and build a basic relationship, at least so that they know your face and voice, and then you can do the rest of the business via e-mail and telephone calls. So that requires a certain amount of face-to-face time.

In order to allocate the time invested in relation building efficiently, the executives try to understand which investors are potential long-term owners. Hedge funds, with their often short investment horizons, are generally seen as a waste of time.

A major reason that interviewees mentioned for companies to enter into dialogues with the international investors is the wish to stimulate interest in the share, thereby increasing both the liquidity and the price. Another benefit mentioned is the fact that the dialogues may be constructive and that investor voices offer valuable feedback on firm performance and give an approximation of investor sentiments. In the words of one CEO:

> These chaps are the brightest students who have worked in the City or Wall Street, very knowledgeable. . . . You learn something, that's what's exciting about it. I find that these contacts mean added value [although]

> our owners are so terribly capitalistic, they want their returns . . . nothing else matters.

In a similar way, an IR executive stressed the importance of bringing back opinions from investors to management:

> The large shareholders all [voice their opinion]. They will say "we really don't think you should do this" or "we really like it that you're doing this." [The CEO and CFO] need to know there are two [shareholders] that would like to see the dividend raised or that there are [another] two that would like us to buy back more shares . . . Being London-based they don't understand why Swedish companies don't buy back more shares and issue more options . . . The UK and New York have a totally different way of thinking.

Arrangements to engage with the international capital markets are expensive and time consuming. The smallest company that we studied had therefore decided not to seek capital in foreign markets since they were still able to generate sufficient funds in Sweden.

In spite of all the aforementioned activities that CEOs and IR executives get involved in, the chairmen's view was often that international investors were absent or silent and sometimes seen as primarily an audience to whom to "sell the share."

National Block-Holders: Traditional Ties

Even if the internationalization of financial markets has implied changes in ownership structures, national ownership structures still reflect the heritage of many national corporate governance systems. One aspects of this, in Sweden as in most countries outside of the Anglo-Saxon world, is the presence of a number of business groups. In addition to these, Swedish national block-holders include the state pension funds as well as a number of private mutual funds and pension funds. Although these national block-holders are the smallest category of owners in terms of numbers, for most companies, they are the strongest owners in terms of voting power—in many cases underpinned by the presence of the aforementioned dual class shares.

Investment companies often have long-term relations with corporations, often based on personal relationships. In the Swedish case important owner groups—such as those headed by the Wallenberg family (through the investment company Investor and the Wallenberg foundations) or Handelsbanken (through the investment company Industrivärden and foundations associated with the bank)—have for several decades held controlling stakes in major corporations, such as ABB, Ericsson, SCA and Volvo. In such groups, dialogues between owners, directors, and managers have been a natural feature, with owners involved in strategy and seeking industrial synergies between their various holdings (see, for example, Lindgren 1994: 171–174). These owners generally have strong representation on company boards.

In maintaining the corporate relationship to the block-holders, the chairman of the board plays a key role. One aspect of the relationships is their informality. The chairmen we interviewed spoke about their contacts with the large owners as something that is both continuous and spontaneous. In these interactions, the roles of the principal and the agent differ for different issues, that is, the investor could sometimes be the agent and the chairman the principal. In other words, the relationship is a mutual interaction without clear roles.

The relationships are not always limited to the particular corporation at hand; rather they are intermingled with governance relationship in other firms as well as with relationships of a social kind, such as sailing regattas or moose hunting. The tightly knit social networks are further seen as providing a form of social control. One of our informants exemplifies this by saying that it would be impossible to build a multimillion-dollar mansion without anyone noticing, implying that this may curb improper behavior.

Considering the tightly knit Swedish network, the role of nationality does not seem to have played out its role despite the globalization of financial markets. One of the chairmen we spoke to said, "We have a Swedish culture in this company and as long as we can find competent Swedish directors [we will not change this and] as long as the company is doing well, few demands are raised." Another chairman has the experience that international investors will be "surprised" if they are approached in governance matters. Still another sees the location of the head office in Sweden as essential since "this is where we have our ownership, and it is here that we need a good relationship with institutions and A shareholders [i.e., shareholders holding stock with multiple votes]." An international investor we spoke to pointed out that among domestic shareholders there is often a common understanding and a propensity not to challenge company management:

> The concern or interest of foreign shareholders does trigger action on the part of the boards. Whereas when it is just domestic shareholders [expressing concerns], management [just] says "You are . . . getting excited about nothing." It is bizarre because the domestic shareholders are usually going to be large holders of the stock and in effect more influential since they can hassle you there.

The relations to the block-holders can be of importance for broader concerns than those immediately tied to corporate governance. One of the IR executives we interviewed saw the communication from Swedish institutions as key to the understanding of broader sentiments in society with bearing on the firm, particularly when it came to understanding how issues would be valued in the mass media. However, the importance of understanding this is not merely a concern for the relations to other investors; the perception of corporate image in the media is also tied to the company being a very large employer in Sweden and its standing in relation to regulators. The characteristics of your owners are also part of building a corporate image. One CEO pointed out how certain owners may be seen as "marks of quality": "If AP3 [one of the Swedish state pension funds] steps in it is seen as a high grade."

The issues that are dealt with in the contact with national block-holders are often related to preparations for board meetings. Among recurring issues, we find the election of directors and remuneration. Many of the chairmen make it clear that they do not deal with other kinds of investor contacts, which they see as part of daily operations that should be dealt with by the CEO or the IR department. The attitude to IR work is ambivalent; many of the chairmen speak about it as an often too time-consuming task.

There is substantial contact with the major shareholders also in preparing for the meetings of the board of directors. The process of preparing the annual general meeting is becoming increasingly formalized. The key element in this change was the gradual introduction, from the early 1990s, of nomination committees, which in 2005 became a requirement through the Swedish Code of Corporate Governance (see further in the following section). The consequence is a structured and more transparent element to the selection of directors to the board. However, it has also entailed some unintended consequences: the nomination committees now provide an arena where broader governance issues and company strategies can be discussed.

National Retail Investors

A third group of investors are the national retail investors, that is, small private domestic shareholders, which in Sweden can be counted in hundreds of thousands, if not in millions, for the largest corporations. However, these great numbers do not correspond to the amount of interaction that the companies under study have with such shareholders. In only one of the companies were retail investors seen as one of the main tasks of the IR department. The interaction with retail investors is generally not seen as an important task for chairmen and CEOs. Instead, in most of the corporations where we undertook interviews, it is primarily corporate communication departments that deal with information to retail investors. The direct contacts are few. They are concentrated in the annual general meeting, where the retail investors form a majority of the audience, and in presentations given to savings clubs. Other interactions are sporadic. Some of our interviewees mention telephone calls from retail investors or letters from dissatisfied retail shareholders: "So, when you get calls from small shareholders you need to be polite and courteous and try to answer the questions as politely as possible" as one IR executive told us.

Nevertheless, cooperation among and organizations of retail shareholders can give them power. Interest organizations for retail shareholders have therefore emerged in many countries. In Sweden, for example, considerable influence is exerted by the Swedish Shareholders' Association (*Sveriges Aktiesparares Riksförbund*)—an interest organization for retail shareholders. Founded in 1966, in recent years it has maintained a membership of around 70,000. It provides its members with information and advice about investments in shares and also participates in lobbying and consultation processes. One of the high-profile activities of the association is to attend annual general meetings. Representatives of the association thus regularly attend some 500 such meetings, and they are often interviewed in media for their opinions on governance arrangements in the companies. As a result, the company representatives we interviewed often mentioned the association and its representatives as a virtually permanent feature of the annual general meetings. Nonetheless, retail investors are not so much seen as a source of capital or a governing principal, that is, a group that should be handled by IR officers. Rather they are seen as an audience whose opinions need to be managed with communication strategies.

Specialization and Integration

The picture that emerges from the aforementioned is thus one of specialization in handling a particular kind of relation in a specific setting. This specialization is the result of the characteristics and demands of particular owner categories (e.g., cross-border investors) and the capabilities of the firms. The companies were similar in the manner in which they organized their interaction with investors. However, across the companies we find considerable variation in the extent to which these specialized functions cooperate. The lynchpin is the CEO, but whether or not the chairman and IR function cooperate differs. Companies that were in the process of raising new capital displayed a higher degree of cooperation among the three functions.

Structured Governance Interactions: Road Shows and Annual General Meetings

In the discussion about the three types of investors, two types of structured governance interactions were mentioned. One, which is limited primarily to international investors, is *the road show*, meaning presentations of the company to specific audiences. Another, directed toward all three owner groups, but particularly attracting the national retail investors, is *the annual general meeting*—that is, the meetings to which all shareholders are called upon to make decisions on board composition, executive compensation programs, dividends, etc. These two activities are recurring and follow strongly institutionalized norms for interaction. For both kinds of activity, it is important to pay attention to direct relations as well as indirect relations through intermediaries.

Road Shows

Representatives of large corporations routinely travel to investor meetings in large financial centers. From the corporate point of view, these activities involve both highly standardized presentations and interactions. In addition, they afford the company with the opportunity for constructive dialogue with important international investors. In arranging these kinds of activities, IR executives show their forte. Those we spoke to were all proud schedulers of meetings as well as avid travelers. The IR executives may road show alone, but a corporate executive, such as the CEO or the CFO, often participates. In special cases, for example in connection with the issue of new equity, the chairman may also be present. In meeting new investors, a general rule is to send IR officers for a first meeting to brief the analyst or fund manager on the basic company information. Once the investor knows the company better, meetings with the CEO or the CFO may follow.

Although the road shows follow predictable itineraries (for example, with New York, Boston and London being visited most quarters of the year) and standardized forms for interaction (presentations, Q & A sessions and face-to-face meetings), they involve extensive preparations. A first part of the preparations has to do with standardizing the information to be given. This may be an "investor kit," which includes PowerPoint presentations and basic company information or a "briefing book" that contains background information that executives can use if they are asked difficult questions. One IR executive thus described the preparations for the road shows as studying for an exam; you have to learn the whole contents of all the reports. According to one CEO, answers are prepared in advance and rehearsed in order to cover all possible questions that could come up in meetings with investors. Such preparations all aim to ensure a confident and consistent performance during these events, which in the words of one IR executive is a "grilling." He depicted a meeting with the American investor Fidelity in the following way:

> I've got five people on the other side of the table. You've got one analyst, you've got the head fund manager, you've got other fund managers who all have holdings in Fidelity funds. For an hour and a half they will grill me on every single point . . . It's like a hearing . . . They will ask me questions and I say, "I can't provide you with that information; however, here are the pieces we have provided." Boom, Boom. "Now you can make your decision on that."

A second part of the preparations concerns efforts to understand what the current investor sentiments and concerns are. In view of the large number of international investors, this is quite a daunting task. One way to manage this is to engage one of the many consulting firms, such as Citigate Dewe Rogerson to conduct surveys before road shows. However, these are costly, and IR executives told us how they try to balance the cost of conducting such surveys with the benefits they may provide.

A third important part of preparations involves a decision on using an intermediary to set up meetings with investors and analysts. These arrangements are often made by investment banks. When it comes to choosing what bank to use, there is general agreement that a company should rotate the organizer of road shows. One IR executive explains the motives for such rotation as fairness and avoidance of becoming tied to and identified with a particular broker. In selecting a partner, he requires the broker to have done research on the company and to have traded enough in the share to be interesting to the institutions. However, he also mentioned that the recommendations made by analysts have an influence; if an analyst has a sell recommendation that the company disagrees with, then it is a problem:

> [Since] we strive for a value that is as high as possible and then it is difficult to go on tour with a broker who has taken a view of the company as uninteresting or mismanaged.

After meetings with investors, the companies strive to get feedback from them. The brokerage houses that arranged the road shows are expected to provide this "within a week, if they want to go out with me again," according to an IR executive interviewed. And, he added, "I require that they call up all the people that I met with and ask them [for their opinions]."

The most striking part of the accounts about road shows that we collected concerned the character of the meetings. In part, they are shaped by the great number of meetings; some mentioned having 17 meetings in one day, and in part by the repetitious character of the interaction. With such a fundamental structure, it is quite a challenge to maintain interpersonal exchanges that build lasting relations. In the words of one chairman:

> You have to meet the demand that you should give everyone the same information. Then you can't add and take away [as you please]. So you need to be disciplined in order not to get sick and tired of yourself and start to add something in order to make it a little more exciting, which is easy to do when you're into your twenty-fifth interview.

The chairman pointed to the need for a watchdog that "ensures that you stay close to the script," and he also points out that it takes a large measure of training and discipline to stay cool. There is a tension between a predictably calm façade and emotional outbursts. We also heard this from a CEO when he told us about how he was confronted by questions about the possibility that he was going to leave his position:

> So, there are a lot of rhetorical questions . . . that you try to answer as amiably as possible. But sometimes you just can't cope and then there

> is a risk that you will say something that shows what you really think about the issue and then there is a risk that you're classified as arrogant.

Interactions are described as going through standard motions, but this is generated not only by routine but also from the ambition to disclose information fairly and equally. One of the IR executives told us about the fine balance between "what you can say and not when you get questions":

> It is a situation where you have knowledge but can't communicate it. You can call it concealing or presenting half-lies or whatever, but you do end up with these ethical considerations. . . . I think it is the most difficult part of this job.

Another executive told us, "You have to have a split brain in this business, because there is the information that is provided, and then there is the information for two months out of every three that you have but nobody else has."

Taken together, the aforementioned evidence demonstrates that road shows imply interactions with cross-border investors that are carefully scripted according to well-established norms. Routines and standardized information constitute significant parts of these scripts. For the selection of relevant audiences, surveys by consultancies are important, while rigorous rehearsals are used in order to keep company actors to the script during the performances. In terms of the mode of interaction, road shows bear a clear resemblance to examinations with the prospective investors as examiners and executives as examinees.

Annual General Meetings

Annual general meetings are complex events that involve potential interactions with international investors, block-holders and retail shareholders. Planning such events involves matters of a technical legal character, matters dealing with governance and matters dealing with corporate image.

In the corporate governance debate, the meetings have been the subject of much discussion. For institutional shareholders the exercise of influence of authority at these meetings entails substantial amounts of work. In the Anglo-Saxon markets, in particular the rise of investment advisory services, governance issues are therefore often sub-contracted to intermediaries.

From the perspective of corporations, there are two broad processes that unfold with bearing on relations to owners. There is one chain of events that involves large owners and revolves around the nomination of candidates for election to the board of directors and the remuneration of top management. As mentioned earlier, these matters are directly concerned with preparing the decisions of the annual general meeting.

The other chain of events deals with the presentation and image-enhancing function of the meeting. One of the CEOs told us how he sets the theme for the meeting and gave as an example that his message for the last meeting had been a "back to basics." The CEO however doubted whether the annual general meeting really is a concern for all owners. He said,

> I think the most significant thing there is . . . is to understand who are in the audience. It is not the big owners. . . . Look at who comes, it is the small shareholders, the pensioners, the press and a good deal of it is aimed at the employees.

Making the annual general meeting a festivity is something that one chairman saw as important. He described one of the recent such meetings as having had

> very much of a hallelujah feel and having been very familiar. [When the issue of] directors' fees came up I called out: "aren't there any higher bids, that's way too low." Makes it easy-going. Not like a funeral in a church.

Several interviewees described the process of preparing the CEO's speech as involving cooperation between the CEO and the chairman. For example, one CEO said that he would not say anything startling without having spoken to his chairman and major shareholders. In another company, the chairman and CEO circulate drafts of their speeches to each other and involved IR in their preparations as well.

An IR executive characterized the annual general meeting in the following way:

> Generally, it is a forum for a company to air its views and it's a forum for other parties to air their views so those can be made in public . . . and people can report on them. That is what it has become. . . . The real reason for an annual meeting has been diminished so much by corporate communications.

In the view of the corporate officers, we interviewed, the presence of international investors, either directly or indirectly, was insignificant. However, they pointed out that, when they were present, they often created confusion since they did not understand the Swedish system. One chairman recalls an annual general meeting where a proposal to amend the articles of association was on the agenda:

> An attorney suddenly gets up [and says] "I vote against" [and the chairman replies] "I see. Why?" [and the attorney replies] "Well, I don't know." And he was representing some funds out in California and had received instructions from a representative that no changes to the statutes were to be approved.

The limited involvement of the international investors is also underscored by the low propensity of IR executives to participate in these meetings. Some of them saw their role as waiting by the phone ready to take calls from international investors if any should come.

The symbolic aspect of the annual general meetings is significant. The meetings present opportunities to "manage meaning" through means such as speeches, décor, and succession ceremonies. Yet, in parallel to this, significant governance matters such as executive compensation and director elections unfold.

Specialization in Different Contexts

A generalization of the aforementioned through the identification of ideal types provides us with variations between the three investor groups in terms of arenas, investor role models and executive role models (Table 4.1). For the cross-border investors, the road shows constitute the main arena for their interaction with corporations. These imply that investors act as examiners and executives are examinees. For national block-holders, on the other hand, the board is an important arena, and the role models of investors and executives are to a large extent as principals and agents, respectively, although with a reciprocal influence in the relationship. For retail investors, finally, the annual general meeting is the main arena and their role model is guest, while that of executives is host.

In addition to the identification of these ideal types, an important conclusion from the evidence presented earlier is that interaction with investors is not handled solely by one specific corporate unit. Rather, we find that there is organizational specialization of interaction between the chairman of the board, the CEO, the CFO and the IR function. This is an illustration of Thompson's argument that boundary-spanning units are created for homogeneous segments of the environment (Thompson 1967: 66–67). However, this does not mean that the company has created "perfect buffers" against such a segment. We believe that the function of the boundary-spanning unit also lies in its ability to channel and concentrate contextual pressures and demands into the firm.

Table 4.1 Relationships Between Corporations and Three Groups of Investors

Investor Group	*Arena*	*Investor Role Model*	*Executive Role Model*
Cross-Border Investors	Road Shows	Examiner	Examinee
National Block-Holders	Board	Principal	Agent
Retail Investors	Annual General Meeting	Guest	Host

Our interviews also show that companies are able to act "multi-contextually"—that is, to deal with several distinct segments of the field of governance. There are a number of questions concerning this multi-contextuality that need to be addressed, in particular the way in which the internal relations between the boundary-spanning units are handled. Our studies indicate variation across companies in the extent that the units cooperate, and attention should be paid to what forces drive such integration.

We have also found that in some activities there is considerable routinization of interaction. This routinization is related to the complexity of the environment in terms of numbers of investors and is most evident in interactions between the company and cross-border investors.

In addition to direct interaction, there are considerable amounts of indirect interactions between companies and investors through various forms of intermediaries. This use of intermediaries seems to be most prolific in interactions that are both highly specialized and routinized. It appears that intermediaries are best suited to solve problems related to the external perception of the corporate image.

Taken together, these observations provide us with an understanding of how boundary-spanning units are organized and played out vis-à-vis investors. In cases where long-term personal relations can be built, companies operate through direct contacts, but where the number of relations is large and complex we see how more structured, formalized and routinized mechanisms come into play. This is clearly evidenced by the contacts with international investors. Thus the organization and practice of some boundary-spanning units rely on classic uncertainty-reducing mechanisms. Nevertheless, companies need to implement boundary-spanning units that are in accordance with accepted norms in the particular segment they are buffering, for example the structure and practices surrounding road shows. Thereby the boundary-spanning units come to have a double function, in part the intended buffering, but at the same time also bringing the company more into alignment with the very environment that it is supposedly buffering itself from.

The Articulation of Corporate Governance Ideas

Until now, we have focused on the relationships between individual corporations and their investors. However, as pointed out in Chapter 1, the field of corporate governance also includes a number of other relationships to actors in the field of governance. Of these, we will here particularly focus on actors and relationships that are involved in creating and signaling role models. They range from the creation of self-regulation to organizations that function as intermediaries that exploit the need for global monitoring control. We will demonstrate how this implies an articulation of governance ideas and practices by focusing on: (1) corporate governance codes, (2) global organizations and networks and (3) rating institutes and proxy advisory services. They represent three types of articulation, respectively—namely, articulation through codification, through socialization and through standardization.

Articulation Through Codification: Corporate Governance Codes

As pointed out in the previous chapters, the past few decades have seen an increasing proliferation of self-regulation and a rise in the number of regulating actors (Braithwaite, Coglianese and Levi-Faur 2007). This has been particularly reinforced by the globalization of financial markets, a process that appears to have been even more strengthened by the financial turbulence from 2008 and onwards. In the governance area we have, for example, seen the development of ever more international accounting standards, particularly manifested in the International Financial Reporting Standards (IFRS) developed by the International Accounting Standards Board (IASB) and the concentration of the accounting profession into the Big Four global accounting firms: EY, KPMG, PwC and Deloitte (cf., e.g., Botzem and Quack 2006).

One particular kind of regulation is constituted by corporate governance codes. They are an especially interesting feature as they attempt to regulate large parts of the corporate governance process (Cuomo, Mallin and Zattoni 2016). Such codes have been adopted in one form or another since the early 1990s in most developed economies. Usually they are self-regulatory instruments that deal with issues of accountability, transparency and disclosure. This development is driven in part by needs to improve the efficiency of national corporate governance systems, sometimes in the wake of corporate scandals, but also in part by a need to enhance the legitimacy of these systems (Aguilera and Cuervo-Cazurra 2004). A central part of the legitimacy argument in non-Anglo-Saxon economies has been that international investors have a poor understanding of the specifics of individual economies, such as the German system with corporations both having a supervisory board (*Aufsichtsrat*) and a management board (*Vorstand*). As a result, corporate governance codes have been introduced in order to attract global capital in a process of changes in regulation and the construction of financial markets. These codes in turn have resulted in a standardization of the conduct of corporate governance bodies such as boards, auditors and annual general meetings.

Codes often build on a comply-or-explain principle—that is, a company has to give explanations of, and most often, reasons for non-compliance. The arrangements for this differs between countries: In Germany, studies of compliance and non-compliance are done yearly by the commission that manages the code (Werder and Bartz 2014), while in the United Kingdom, compliance studies are done by accounting firms. The efficiency of code self-regulation has been debated. Some find no effects on company performance (e.g., Nowak, Rott and Mahr 2004; de Jong et al. 2005). Others claim that company behavior is affected positively (Aguilera and Cuervo-Cazurra 2004). Those holding the latter position argue that deficiencies in legal systems can be remedied and that there are legitimation effects.

Corporate governance codes more or less define corporate governance as "the system by which companies are directed and controlled" (Cadbury Report 1992: 15). Codes have often been included as parts of listing rules for stock exchanges and thus become compulsory for companies wanting to be listed or to remain listed. In Germany, there is thus a legal requirement that the German code be met. Sometimes the initiators of codes have been corporate élites and sometimes organizations like stock exchanges. Various interests have thus influenced the codes adopted.

As shown by Aguilera and Cuervo-Cazurra (2004), the reasons for implementing the codes differ across countries. Nevertheless, there are many similarities in the arguments that are given for the implementation of codes. A common assertion is that codes may be a tool for countries to be successful in the competition for foreign capital. As such, they build on a faith in regulation to build legitimacy for national systems of governance.

Corporate governance codes are self-regulatory texts, and in most cases, they are tied to organizations that oversee their development and implementation. Such organizations may have very different status ranging from government commissions (Germany), financial supervisory agencies (Spain), independent regulators (the United Kingdom), to bodies set up by the business community (Sweden). Thus, although codes are not organizations, their development shows that they are launched by organizations, and they structure norms about good governance in a reasonably coherent manner. A number of transnational organizations, such as the European Union (EU) and the OECD, have also set up corporate governance frameworks that provide the standards for what is seen as good governance.

Codes develop in the intersection between national governance regimes and global investments and regulation. They can thus be conceptualized as a form of bridge that builds legitimacy in national economies for global ideas about corporate governance. At the same time, they are attempts at building legitimacy for national systems of corporate governance in the global context.

Articulation Through Socialization: Global Organizations and Networks

Investors have long organized themselves in their home country. Examples are the Council of Institutional Investors in the United States, *das Deutsches Aktieninstitut* in Germany, and the Institutional Shareholders Committee (up to 2014) and Investor Forum (from 2014) in the United Kingdom. However, faced with the challenges of global investments, investors have also found it appropriate to organize themselves internationally. From the 1990s and onwards, numerous transnational organizations have thus been created to deal with corporate governance issues. Many of them were founded around the new millennium, but the actors that they organize differ. We will illustrate these kind organizations with two kinds of collaboration regarding international corporate governance. The first, the International Corporate Governance Network (ICGN), has national investor organizations as its members, while the other, European Corporate Governance Institute (ECGI), is mainly oriented toward academics doing research on corporate governance issues. Obviously, they differ in membership and orientation, thereby illustrating how the views on proper corporate governance appear from a number of different sources.

ICGN: Investors Organizing Themselves

The ICGN was founded in 1995 as a response to needs felt by investors to communicate across boundaries. As mentioned earlier, at the time of foundation, national investor and corporate organizations had been established in many countries. It was therefore possible to gather representatives of such organizations. A meeting, attracting representatives from almost 50 investor organizations, was held in 1995 in Washington, DC, on the initiative of the US organization the Council for Institutional Investors. Since this first meeting, ICGN has gradually grown into an established permanent organization. Its activities include annual conferences and lobbying to influence policy decisions on corporate governance. The strategic goals of the network imply that the organization is involved in three processes that may shape developments in the field of governance in three ways (ICGN 2016: 2):

- *Influence policy* by providing a single source of international experience and best practice for standard setters through commentary, engagement and guidance;
- *Connect peers* by facilitating engagement between investors, companies and other stakeholders at international meetings; and
- *Inform dialogue* by enhancing the professionalism of good governance and stewardship practices through education and publications.

The annual conferences, which are held in cities all around the world, have speakers from the top levels of governments and business. In terms of topics covered the panels at the ICGN London 2015 meeting provide a good illustration (ICGN 2015):

- Global governance reform: progression or regression?
- Financial market regulation: time for a holistic review?
- Inside the boardroom black box.
- The changing face of ownership in a new world order.
- Global capital market reform: pipe dream or achievable reality?
- The board of the future: will it be fit for purpose?

The network has a number of committees specializing in various areas of corporate governance. These include committees for auditing and accounting practices, corporate governance principles and cross-border voting practices. As for the auditing committee, its primary purpose is representation of ICGN members in relation to relevant bodies, such as regulators, governments and international bodies, in corporate governance issues. It is particularly focused on the development of accounting and auditing practices in the interest of international investors. This means that it is involved in reviews of proposals from at the IASB and the Financial Accounting Standards Board and other regulatory bodies.

The output from committee work is published on the network's website. The documents are often representations of the network's views on corporate governance matters to various policy instances such as the EU, the US Securities and Exchange Commission (SEC) and the IASB (see ICGN 2017).

The ICGN is thus an important interest organization for international investors. Through its activities, members are connected, and decision-makers and the general public are influenced to the advantage of the international corporate community. Similar roles are played by many other similar international organizations in the global field of corporate governance.

ECGI: Academics Organizing

While our first case, ICGN, constitutes an organization of investors, our second case, the ECGI, has its origin among academics. Founded in 2002, it had been preceded by a more informal network of scholars: the European Corporate Governance Network. The purpose of ECGI is to provide a platform for interaction between academics, regulators and business in relation to corporate governance issues in order to promote best practice. In terms of the academics, ECGI particularly encourages interdisciplinary work between scholars from economics, law, finance and management (see ECGI 2017). However, ECGI has also non-academic members, individuals as well as institutions. Yet, in terms of the board, academics are in the majority: of the 11 directors, 6 are academic members and 5 are non-academics.

Hence, just like ICGN, ECGI is involved in organizing actors in the field of governance. However, it differs by being focused on connecting academic researchers to practitioners in the field. Through research reports and conferences, governance ideas and practices are critically examined. Thus it is a manifestation of how the field force of scientization (Drori and Meyer 2006) becomes manifest in the context of investing. In this way, academic research may have a certain influence on corporate governance practice.

Organizing and Scientization

The ICGN and the ECGI demonstrate well how different actors in the field of investors find it important to create standards within corporate governance.

These efforts are linked to the globalization of financial markets. Investors seek to develop international agreements in order to facilitate international financial activities as well as to prevent legal regulation by striving to create soft regulations. Academic researchers have likewise found an interest in exchanging ideas and research results among themselves and with practitioners and policy makers in an expanding field. These interactions are in part made possible through the interactions of the type of organizations that we discussed earlier. In such interactions, the agendas of both researchers and policy makers are set and developed. This is a demonstration of how both organizing and scientization interact in the field of governance.

It is also quite natural that policy makers have been active to create organizations around corporate governance both among themselves and for investors. It is also evident from the aforementioned that the different organizations are interlinked to a great extent and that they together constitute significant actors for the standardization of corporate governance practices.

The creation of formal investor organization further facilitates coordinated action and also functions as a clear representation of interest or, in Neil Fligstein's terms, "a description of the real social relations of domination that exist in a particular market" (Fligstein 2001: 35). These tendencies are the outlines of an idea of control for global investments. This conception in turn is one of high organizational complexity. Yet the pattern is not confined to the corporate relations with market actors such as investors, but recurs, as we argued in Chapter 2, to regulators and scrutinizers.

Articulation Through Standardization: Rating Institutes and Proxy Advisory Services

A significant aspect of the changing social structure of global investments is rationalization. In these processes, *rating institutes* and *proxy voting services* are significant for institutional investors in their handling of global portfolios. These companies are not disconnected from other organizations in the field of governance; rather, the services they provide build on the ideas about good corporate governance that have developed in the field. It is possible that by using these ideas they are also in some ways part of formulating and developing such ideas. They are important for the rationalization of corporate governance in a global context. Both provide pressures for corporations to comply with standards created through a successive process of soft regulation. Being neither investors nor policy makers, they constitute significant intermediaries.

Rating Institutes

Rating institutes have a long history in the financial industry. Leading rating institutes trace their origins to the nineteenth and early twentieth centuries. Presently three rating institutes dominate the market: Moody's (founded in 1909), Standard & Poor's (with origins from 1860), and Fitch Ratings (founded in 1914). Together, these three rating institutes account for 95 percent of the US market (Eckstein 2017: 9)—a circumstance that gives them considerable power through their ratings of corporations, public organizations and even nation states.

However, since the financial crisis 2008, external credit ratings have been called into question because of serious failures. Questions of regulating the industry have been and still are topics both in the United States and within the EU (see the following section also for regulation of proxy advisors). In the United States, several measures have been taken to increase the transparency of the industry: the Credit Rating Agency Reform Act of 2006, the Dodd-Frank Act in 2010 and new rules for credit rating agencies from the SEC in 2014 (Securities and Exchange Commission 2014). On the other side of the Atlantic, the EU is trying to evaluate the credit rating market and have discussed alternatives to external credit ratings, the need for more competition in that market and the feasibility of a European credit rating agency (European Commission 2016). Thus the whole issue of the credit rating is in flux.

A new feature in the rating industry is that rating institutes have started to include measures of governance in their ratings (Louizi and Kammoun 2016). In this way they are meeting a demand from institutional investors, who, according to Newell and Wilson (2002: 21), are open to paying a premium for companies adopting the best corporate governance practices. The obvious logic behind this is that companies with good governance are less risky. What aspects of corporate governance are seen as relevant to assess differ across rating companies. For instance, Morgan Stanley Capital International (MSCI) rates standards of corporate governance through indicators such as (1) independence and diversity of board of directors, (2) ownership and control structure of the company, (3) accounting practices and (4) auditor opinions. The resulting measure of corporate governance is then used to discount the security's financial quality score, and the indicators are published by MSCI ESG Research as part of MSCI ESG Governance Metrics Research (MSCI 2017).

The last few decades have seen the emergence of an industry of rating institutes focusing on corporate behavior in a wider sense: this is the Environment, Social and Governance (ESG) industry (Avetisyan and Ferrary 2013). Originally consisting of a number of small companies, over time, as demonstrated by Avetisyan and Hockerts (2017), the industry has undergone consolidation. In this process, the aforementioned MSCI has been a leading actor. In terms of ESG ratings it calculates the MSCI Global Socially Responsible Indexes (MSCI 2016), which identify companies offering products "with high negative social or environmental impact," such as alcohol, gambling, tobacco, military weapons, civilian firearms, nuclear power, adult entertainment, and genetically modified organisms." These indexes also aim at identifying companies that score high on ESG criteria. It is still too early to determine the impact of these social responsibility indexes, since the ESG industry is new and changing. Doubts have also been expressed whether it will really be possible to put ESG in focus in comparison with other rating elements (Avetisyan and Hockerts 2017).

Needless to say, corporate governance ratings provide an extremely condensed view of corporate governance. As such, it is an example of how belief in structured and statistical reductions of complex political and economic features can be meaningfully used as a basis for decisions and classification. It also illustrates how regulatory structures such as corporate governance codes and principles issued by various organizations are translated into standard-like issues.

Proxy Voting Services

As already pointed out earlier, annual general meetings of shareholders have been the subject of much discussion in the corporate governance debate. For institutional shareholders the exercise of influence of authority at these meetings entails substantial amounts of work. Therefore, in the Anglo-Saxon markets in particular, the rise of investment advisory services provides a procedure for subcontracting governance to intermediaries.

In the United States, two proxy voting services dominate: Institutional Shareholder Services (ISS) and Glass Lewis, which, according to Eckstein (2017: 13), account for 97 percent of the industry. Of these, the ISS, founded in 1985, has thousands of clients with estimated equity assets in the trillions of dollars. Until April 2014, it was owned by MSCI (see the earlier discussion) and was then acquired by Vestar Capital Partners, an American private equity firm (ISS 2014).

ISS reports that it offers coverage of about 40,000 annual general meetings in 117 countries annually, making voting recommendations thereby assisting "the financial community to manage governance risk for the benefit of shareholders" (ISS 2017). An example from 2016 is that ISS, at the annual general meeting 2016 of the Swedish commercial bank Swedbank, voted against the granting of discharge for the chairman of the board and the president (Hägerstrand and Rex 2016).

The second major player, Glass Lewis, founded in 2003, is owned by the Ontario Teachers' Pension Plan Board and the Alberta Investment Management Corporation. It claims to cover more than 200,000 meetings annually in 100 countries, to have more than 1,200 clients with total assets of USD 35 trillion, and to have a focus on "providing corporate governance solutions that deliver transparency and efficiency to investment, operations and compliance teams" (Glass Lewis 2017a). Among recent stands taken by Glass Lewis mention can be made of the recommendation that an executive officer should not be member of more than two company boards and that the other directors should not have a total of more than five such posts (Glass Lewis 2017b).

In addition to the two global players mentioned, other organizations provide comparable services in various countries. For instance, in the United Kingdom, the Pensions and Life Time Savings Association (until 2015 known as the National Association of Pension Funds, NAPF), issues voting recommendations. In Sweden, the Nordic Investor Services was established in 2002 for the same purpose. Similar examples could be given for other countries. All in all, this means that a number of organizations formulate, pool and mediate ownership influence. An issue that has been raised in relation to them is that the number of such organizations is limited and that there is therefore a risk of excessive concentration of influence. Over the years, this has led to the consideration of regulating the proxy advice industry. In the United States, this circumstance prompted the Government Accountability Office (GAO) to instigate an investigation of proxy voting services a few years ago due to a concern that the "industry suffers from significant conflicts of interest and a lack of competition and that these firms have a disproportionate influence on proxy voting" (GAO 2007: 2). A bill, the Corporate Governance Reform and Transparency Act of 2016, was put before the US Congress, and was approved by the House Financial Services Committee in October 2016. It included a number of measures, including the registration of proxy advisors with the US SEC.

Also in Europe, the activities of proxy advisors have been debated. In contrast to the United States, this has so far not led to any hard law but rather to self-regulation. In Europe, the European Securities and Markets Authority (ESMA) thus published a discussion paper in 2012 in order to express its position regarding proxy advisors. In this paper, the organization acknowledges that institutional investors may have legitimate reasons to use the services of proxy advisors. However, it also expressed its awareness of the concerns of market participants regarding the strong influence of proxy advisors on the voting at annual general meetings (ESMA 2012).

The discussion paper led to a consultation where the ESMA issued a report concluding that the industry should not be regulated, but where the organization wished to encourage self-regulation and therefore issued a set of principles for such a purpose (ESMA 2013). This call for self-regulation was heeded by a group of industry actors that included ISS and Glass Lewis, which in 2014 issued a document entitled *Best Practice Principles for Providers of Shareholder Voting Research & Analysis* (Best Practices Principles Group 2014). At the end of 2015, ESMA published its follow-up report on the development of the *Best Practice Principles for Providers of Shareholder Voting Research and Analysis* (ESMA 2015). This report assessed activities of proxy advisory firms during 2015 and expressed that the industry seemed to move in the right direction, although there was still "room for improvement in certain areas" (ESMA 2015: 22).

As far as the proxy advisory services are concerned, they demonstrate that the field of governance provides a space for entrepreneurial actors. These act as intermediaries offering and developing services to international investors. However, in the same way as the proxy advisory service firms act as scrutinizers of corporations, they are themselves subject to counter-forces, as they tend to become too powerful, with many large investors delegating voting rights to them. As noted earlier in relation to our interviews, their representatives sometimes may not even know why they are taking a certain stand.

Codification, Socialization and Standardization

In this section, we have provided further evidence of the increasingly global character of corporate governance. We have shown how organizations develop as intermediaries and have traced both changes in regulation as well as in concrete behavior and relational patterns that are played out in corporate governance processes. Taken together, these observations show that new forms of self-regulation and the way that institutional investors are organizing have led to the articulation of national as well as transnational concerns across the governance field.

First, we have seen many examples of *articulation through codification* in the form of statements in codes for what is seen as proper governance or appropriate managerial actions (regarding disclosure, for example), the policy documents of organizations and the consultation papers that organizations in the field of governance produce. Overall this suggests that what end up as regulatory processes (be it hard or soft regulation) lead up not only to the production of rules but also to interactions and discussions about concepts and models for governance. The three mechanisms for regulation all serve to make explicit ideas and agendas of what is proper corporate governance; as such, they can be devices for raising the legitimacy of an actor's views of governance. The evidence we have provided also shows that the different organizations in varying degrees refer to each other as partners, and the activities of others are recognized. To some extent, there are also personal ties, such as in board interlocks. The empirical evidence indicates that the arenas provided by the organization tie the different actors together and allow them to draw on each other's legitimacy. For example, the role of academics and research suggest how the institutional force of scientization is active in the field of governance.

Second, we have shown that important means to launch and disseminate governance are meetings, conferences and networks that the organizations in the governance field arrange, something we label *articulation through socialization*. This enables actors to build personal networks as well as a cognitive agreement on what proper corporate governance consists of.

The third mechanism for the articulation of governance that we have pointed to is *articulation through standardization*, particularly manifested by the standards of rating or proxy advisory services. The explicit nature of this form of articulation is likely to provide the means for investors to coordinate actions with each other on various issues as well as a reduction of uncertainty about governance concerns for corporations, which will enable them to strategically respond to the actions.

Conclusions

Our analysis of corporations, investors and intermediaries has shown the organizational and field-wide processes of market actors that are active in corporate governance. When comparing organizing on the company level and on the field level, similarities are found in the way that corporate governance is becoming *routinized* and *standardized*. On the company level, routinization and standardization are most evident in how companies organize their contacts with international investors. On the field level, they are reflected in the diffusion of corporate governance codes, international organizations, rating agencies and proxy voting services. This occurs by means of processes that we have denoted as articulation through codification, socialization and standardization, respectively.

On the field level, our research has indeed underlined that global investors are very important in shaping corporate governance in action. This is consistent with observations by theorists of globalization and the global society, for instance Beck (2008), who has pointed out that cosmopolitanization has stimulated the building of bridges between actors. For these bridges to function there needs to be legitimacy for the ideas and the forms of social interaction that the bridges involve. And, from Beck's perspective, international investors and multinational corporations are forerunners in this process of cosmopolitanization as they embrace the possibilities of global activity and by "developing and using the productivity of diversity" (Beck 2008: 797).

This discussion on the bridging of corporate governance interests is not completely new, however. Changes in ordering have been a prominent theme in corporate governance discussions throughout history. At the beginning of the last century, Rudolf Hilferding (1910) coined the term "organized capitalism" to describe the integration of finance capital in networks of banks, other financiers, and corporations. It was a particularly apt description of some of the bank-dominated economies in Europe until the end of the post-war era. Changes in the global economy, like the deregulation of capital markets, the increasing internationalization of product markets and production, as well as changes in industrial relations, seemed to break up some of that organization. The thesis of "disorganization" was therefore launched by Lash and Urry (1987), who proposed that traditionally organized capitalist societies were undergoing changes both on the top (international capital markets) and bottom levels of society (less inclination to participate in mass organizations). Their work is imbued with a sense of bewilderment at how "national economies are increasingly out of control" (Lash and Urry 1987: 309). The developments we have reported point to an ongoing reorganization of capitalism on a global scale. The many organizations that are active in the field of governance are a potent force for a re-establishment of categories, concepts and regulations that are coercive, mimetic and normative.

However, despite the cosmopolitanization of investor contacts, corporations are still able to maintain contacts that lie outside the rationalized and standardized bridges. Earlier, we have shown how the relations to traditional Swedish investors are upheld and carried out in great informality. Again, this is evidence of the capacity of corporations to act multi-contextually. It also underscores that even though there are field processes that push for a substantial global integration, there are also mechanisms in action that enable segmentation or loose coupling.

In a nutshell, this chapter has presented evidence how investors in the field of governance are part of multiple processes of high organizational complexity. This pattern is not confined to the relations of corporations with investors but involves, as the chapter demonstrates, different kinds of market and public sector actors. It recurs, as the following two chapters will show, also in the relations to NGOs and the media.

References

Aguilera, R. and Cuervo-Cazurra, R., 2004, "Codes of Good Governance Worldwide: What Is the Trigger?" *Organization Studies*, 25(3): 415–443.

Avetisyan, E. and Ferrary, M., 2013, "Dynamics of Stakeholders' Implications in the Institutionalization of the CSR Field in France and in the United States," *Journal of Business Ethics*, 115(1): 115–133.

Avetisyan, E. and Hockerts, K., 2017, "The Consolidation of the ESG Rating Industry as an Enactment of Institutional Regression," *Business Strategy and the Environment*, 26(3): 316–330.

Beck, U., 2008, "Reframing Power in the Globalized World," *Organization Studies*, 29(5): 793–804.

Berle, A. A. Jr. and Means, G. C., 1932, *The Modern Corporation and Private Property*, New York: MacMillan.

Best Practices Principles Group, 2014, *Best Practice Principles for Providers of Shareholder Voting Research & Analysis* <http://bppgrp.info/wp-content/uploads/2014/03/BPP-ShareholderVoting-Research-2014.pdf> accessed on July 10, 2017.

Botzem, S. and Quack, S., 2006, "Contested Rules and Shifting Boundaries: International Standard-setting in Accounting," in: Djelic, M.-L. and Sahlin-Andersson, K. (eds.), *Transnational Governance: Institutional Dynamics of Regulation*, Cambridge: Cambridge University Press, pp. 266–286.

Braithwaite, J., Coglianese, C. and Levi-Faur, D., 2007, "Can Regulation and Governance Make a Difference?," *Regulation & Governance*, 1(1): 1–7.

Cadbury Report, 1 December 1992, *Report of the Committee on the Financial Aspects of Corporate Governance*, London: Gee.

Cuomo, F., Mallin, C. and Zattoni, A., 2016, "Corporate Governance Codes: A Review and Research Agenda," *Corporate Governance: An International Review*, 24(3): 222–241.

de Jong, A., DeJong, D. V., Mertens, G. and Wasley, G. E., 2005, "The Role of Self-regulation in Corporate Governance: Evidence and Implications From the Netherlands," *Journal of Corporate Finance*, 11(3): 473–503.

Denes, M. R., Karpoff, J. M. and McWilliams, V. B., 2017, "Thirty Years of Shareholder Activism: A Survey of Empirical Research," *Journal of Corporate Finance*, 44(4): 405–424.

Drori, G. S. and Meyer, J. W., 2006, "Scientization: Making a World Safe for Organizing," in: Djelic, M.-L. and Sahlin-Andersson, K. (eds.), *Transnational Governance: Institutional Dynamics of Regulation*, Cambridge: Cambridge University Press, pp. 31–52.

ECGI, 2017, "European Corporate Governance Institute" <www.ecgi.org> accessed on July 10, 2017.

Eckstein, A., 2017, "Skin in the Game for Credit Rating Agencies and Proxy Advisors: Reality Meets Theory," *Harvard Business Law Review* <https://papers.ssrn.com/sol3/papers.cfm?abstract_id=2756033> accessed on July 10, 2017.

ESMA, 2012, *An Overview of the Proxy Advisory Industry: Considerations on Possible Policy Options*, ESMA 2012/212, Paris: European Securities and Markets Authority <www.esma.europa.eu/sites/default/files/library/2015/11/2012-212.pdf> accessed on July 10, 2017.

ESMA, 2013, *Feedback Statement on the Consultation Regarding the Role of the Proxy Advisory Industry*, ESMA 2013–84, Paris: European Securities and Markets Authority <www.esma.europa.eu/sites/default/files/library/2015/11/2013-84.pdf> accessed on July 10, 2017.

ESMA, 2015, *Follow-up on the Development of the Best Practice Principles for Providers of Shareholder Voting Research and Analysis*, ESMA 2015/1887, Paris: European Securities and Markets Authority <www.esma.europa.eu/sites/default/files/library/2015-1887.pdf> accessed on July 10, 2017.

European Commission, 2016, *Report from the Commission to the European Parliament and the Council on Alternative Tools to External Credit Ratings, the State of the Credit Rating Market, Competition and Governance in the Credit Rating Industry, the State of the Structured Finance Instruments Rating Market and on the Feasibility of a European Credit Rating Agency*, COM, 2016, 664 Final, Brussels: European Commission <https://ec.europa.eu/transparency/regdoc/rep/1/2016/EN/1-2016-664-EN-F1-1.PDF> accessed on August 10, 2017.

Fligstein, N., 2001, *The Architecture of Markets*, Princeton, NJ: Princeton University Press.

GAO, 2007, *Corporate Shareholder Meetings: Issues Relating to Firms that Advise Institutional Investors on Proxy Voting*, GAO-07-765, Washington, DC: United States Government Accountability Office.

Glass Lewis, 2017a, "About Glass Lewis" <www.glasslewis.com/> accessed July 11, 2017.

Glass Lewis, 2017b, "2017 Proxy Paper Guidelines. An Overview of the Glass Lewis Approach to Proxy Advice: United States" <www.glasslewis.com/wp-content/uploads/2016/11/Guidelines_US.pdf> accessed on July 11, 2017.

Hägerstrand, A. and Rex, M., 2016, "Utländska ägare vill straffa Sundström" (Foreign Owners Want to Punish Sundström), *Dagens industri*, March 31, 2016 <www.di.se/artiklar/2016/3/31/utlandska-agare-vill-straffa-sundstrom/> accessed on August 10, 2017.

Hilferding, R., 1910, *Das Finanzkapital: Eine Studie über die jüngste Entwicklung des Kapitalismus*, Wien: Verlag der Wiener Volksbuchhandel Ignaz Brand.

ICGN, 2015, "ICGN London 2015 Transcript" <www.icgn.org/icgn-london-2015-transcript> accessed on July 10, 2017.

ICGN, 2016, "ICGN Annual Review 2016 & Progress to June 2017" <http://icgn.flpbks.com/icgn_2016-2017_annual_review/> accessed on July 10, 2017.

ICGN, 2017, "Latest News" <www.icgn.org> accessed on July 10, 2017.

ISS, 2014, "Vestar Capital Partners Completes Acquisition of Institutional Shareholder Services" <www.issgovernance.com/vestar-capital-partners-completes-acquisition-of-institutional-shareholder-services/> accessed on July 11, 2017.

ISS, 2017, <www.issgovernance.com/about/about-iss/> accessed July 10, 2017.

La Porta, R., Lopez-de-Silanes, F. and Shleifer, A., 1999, "Corporate Ownership Around the World," *Journal of Finance*, 54(2): 471–517.

Lash, S. and Urry, J., 1987, *The End of Organized Capitalism*, Cambridge: Polity.

Lindgren, H., 1994, *Aktivt ägande: Investor under växlande konjunkturer* (Active Ownership: Investor During Changing Business Cycles), Stockholm: EHF.

Louizi, A. and Kammoun, R., 2016, "Evaluation of Corporate Governance Systems by Credit Rating Agencies," *Journal of Management and Governance*, 20(2): 363–385.

McKinsey & Company, 2011, *Mapping Global Capital Markets 2011*, Report, McKinsey & Company <www.mckinsey.com/industries/private-equity-and-principal-investors/our-insights/mapping-global-capital-markets-2011> accessed on July 10, 2017.

MSCI, 2016, "MSCI Global Socially Responsible Indexes Methodology" <www.msci.com/eqb/methodology/meth_docs/MSCI_Global_SRI_Methodology_May_2016.pdf> accessed on July 11, 2017.

MSCI, 2017, "MSCI Governance-Quality Indexes, Methodology," June 2017 www.msci.com/eqb/methodology/meth_docs/MSCI_Governance-Quality_Indexes_Methodology_June2017.pdf> accessed on July 10, 2017.

Newell, R. and Wilson, G., 2002, "A Premium for Good Governance," *The McKinsey Quarterly*, 40(3): 20–23.

Nowak, E., Rott, R. and Mahr, T. G., 2004, *Does Self-regulation Work in a Civil Law Country?: An Empirical Analysis of the Declaration of Conformity to the German Corporate Governance Code*, Unpublished Paper from the University of Lugano.

Rao, H. and Sivakumar, K., 1999, "Institutional Sources of Boundary-Spanning Structures: The Establishment of Investor Relations Departments in the Fortune 500 Industrials," *Organization Science*, 10(1): 27–42.

Recommendations on Corporate Governance, 2014, Copenhagen: Committee on Corporate Governance <https://corporategovernance.dk/sites/default/files/recommendations-ebs-12401-rapport-selskabsledelse-uk-5k-nov-2014.pdf> accessed on July 10, 2017.

Roberts, J., Sanderson, P., Barker, R. and Hendry, J., 2006, "In the Mirror of the Market: The Disciplinary Effects of Company/Fund Manager Meetings," *Accounting, Organizations and Society*, 31(3): 277–294.

Securities and Exchange Commission, 2014, *Nationally Recognized Statistical Rating Organizations*, 17 CFR Parts 232, 240, 249, and 249b, Release No. 34–72936; File No. S7–18–11, RIN 3235-AL15, Washington, DC: Securities and Exchange Commission <www.sec.gov/rules/final/2014/34-72936.pdf> accessed on July 11, 2017.

Tengblad, S., 2004, "Expectations of Alignment: Examining the Link Between Financial Markets and Managerial Work," *Organization Studies*, 25(4): 583–606.

Thompson, J. D., 1967, *Organizations in Action*, New York: McGraw-Hill.

Useem, M., 1993, *Executive Defense: Shareholder Power and Corporate Reorganization*, Cambridge, MA: Harvard University Press.

Useem, M., 1996, *Investor Capitalism: How Money Managers Are Changing the Face of Corporate America*, New York: Basic Books.

Veblen, T., 1923, *Absentee Ownership and Business Enterprise in Recent Times: The Case of America*, New York: Allen & Unwin.

Vilenius, M., 2017, "Det utländska kapitalet har hittat tillbaka till svenska aktier och satt turboeffekt på Stockholmsbörsen" (The Foreign Capital Has Found Its Way Back to Swedish Shares and Had a Turbo Effect on the Stockholm Stock Exchange), *Dagens Industri*, January 26, 2017 <www.di.se/nyheter/mikael-vilenius-de-hetaste-svenska-aktierna/> accessed on July 10, 2017.

Werder, A. V. and Bartz, J., 2014, "Corporate Governance Report 2014," *Der Betrieb*, 67(17): 905–914.

5 Scrutinizers: NGOs

Magnus Frostenson, Laurence Romani and Karolina Windell

Introduction

Although questions about the purpose of the firm, the consequences and legitimate scope of corporate action, and the prerequisites for management in general do not belong to the day-to-day issues in business, it seems likely that the pressure on corporations to answer such questions has become ever stronger in the last few decades. This is a reality that is not confined to internal organizational aspects of corporate life, but rather is largely formulated by external constituents (Sahlin-Andersson 2006; Windell 2006; Grafström, Göthberg and Windell 2015). These constituents are eager to confront corporations, holding them accountable not only for abiding by laws and providing consumers with decent products but also for external effects of corporate activity with regard to human well-being and social and environmental responsibility. The ability to handle such confrontations seems to become increasingly more important for corporations, not least in order to obtain and maintain moral legitimacy (Dowling and Pfeffer 1975; Pfeffer 1978; Pfeffer and Salancik 1978; Suchman 1995).

In line with the overall framework of this book presented in Chapter 2, we argue that organizations are embedded in a field of governance that conditions their scope of action, their way of thinking, and their mandate to operate. In this chapter, we will demonstrate how scrutinizers in the form of non-governmental organizations (NGOs) are embedded in the institutional context of corporations to such a degree that modern governance must seriously take their ideas into account. A mutual, and sometimes multilateral, construction of actors has become an essential aspect of corporate life. The views of scrutinizers (for example, NGOs) are organized and articulated in such a distinct way that they are now a vital concern for corporations to handle and react to. An implication of this is that a number of patterns exist that call for the structuring of meaning. Different kinds of relationships exist between NGOs and corporations and different strategies are adopted by corporations and NGOs vis-à-vis each other.

The chapter will show by means of empirical evidence how social movement ideas, actions and activities are important for modern corporations to address, as they are a salient aspect of the field of governance. Various modes of interaction between NGOs and corporations will be highlighted. The main data sources are interviews with representatives of NGOs, other information from these organizations (particularly published on web pages) and literature.

In the following, we first discuss the emergence of NGOs and their roles in modern society. Then we present a framework with three interactional modes, illustrated by empirical evidence in a subsequent section. A final section provides conclusions related to the questions and framework presented in Chapter 2.

NGOs in the Field of Governance

Normative organizations have gradually assumed an increasingly important role in society and have come to influence corporate life (Teegen, Doh and Vachani 2004). Such organizations can be defined as coalescing around common ideas, needs or causes, collectively mobilizing common interests. Several of them have raised awareness about issues related to corporate behavior and social responsibility: Oxfam International, Fairtrade Labelling Organizations International, Friends of the Earth, Christian Aid, the International Council of Human Rights Policy, Human Rights Watch, Sweatshop Watch and CorpWatch, to mention a few historical examples (Arnold and Bowie 2003). Organizations of this kind represent different areas of interest and their methods of working and organizing differ as well. In previous research, it has been noted that they can exist for advocacy purposes, serving as the voice of those whose voices are not well heard, in an attempt to influence key decision makers, or they can be operational, like the Red Cross, providing other groups with goods and services (Teegen, Doh and Vachani 2004).

In the literature, normative organizations are usually mentioned as NGOs or civil society organizations (CSO), thereby referring to organizations that present no connection (in the form of ownership, agenda, etc.) to governmental or nation-state organizations. This is therefore a very general term that covers a wide range of local or international organizations. However, in practice, the term is often used to refer to organizations whose raison d'être is in the pursuit of a religious, humanitarian or environmental ideological standpoint and social movement organizations—that is, complex or formal organizations that identify their goals with the preferences of a social movement or counter-movement and work actively to implement those goals (McCarthy and Zald 1977; Lounsbury 2005). In practice, normative organizations are thus usually labeled NGOs, despite the fact that not all normative organizations are NGOs.

It should be noted that definitions of what constitutes an NGO are contested (Vakil 1997). Reinalda (1999) defines NGOs as private organizations pursuing public political missions, rather than profit. At the same time, financial profit can in fact be combined with humanitarian or environmental concerns. For example, many microfinance institutions, while delivering micro credit to disfavored populations, combine the humanitarian goal of fighting poverty by providing microfinancing at very low interest rates with the goal of financial profit to ensure the sustainability of their own enterprise.

For the purpose of this chapter, we will use a more detailed definition—based on Hudson and Bielefeld (1997) and Lindenberg and Bryant (2001)—that views normative organizations as organizations that

1. Exhibit value-based rationality, often with ideological components.
2. Are voluntary in the sense that they are created, maintained and terminated on the basis of voluntary decisions and initiatives by members or a board of directors.
3. Are not allowed to distribute profits to persons in their individual capacities.
4. Provide useful (in some specified legal sense) goods or services, thereby serving a specified public purpose.

For example, Greenpeace, a well-known normative organization, was founded by private individuals in 1971 to prevent the United States from carrying out a second nuclear test in Alaska. Currently, Greenpeace is an international organization that had a total income close to EUR 350 million in 2015 (Greenpeace International Annual Report 2015: 28). It defines itself as an independent global campaigning organization that acts to change attitudes and behavior, to protect and conserve the environment, and to promote peace. In the past, it has contributed to the image of normative organizations as "troublemakers" by its various campaigns against states and large corporations. Today, the organization emphasizes peaceful non-violent direct action and cooperation, and, for example, has helped make the multinational companies Hewlett-Packard, Apple and Sony Ericsson abandon the use of dangerous chemicals in their electronic production processes.

As we can see from the examples of mission—or, alternatively, purpose or charter—statements exhibited in Table 5.1, the objectives of the various normative organizations are often stated in ethical terms, such as justice and rights, implying that the organizations act in a moralized context with clear missions to fulfill:

- to help create lasting solutions to the injustice of poverty (Oxfam);
- to force the solutions which are essential to a green and peaceful future (Greenpeace);
- [to provide] assistance to populations in distress, to victims of natural or man-made disasters and to victims of armed conflict (Médecins Sans frontières); and
- to inspire, encourage, facilitate and promote at all times all forms of humanitarian activities (International Federation of Red Cross and Red Crescent Societies).

Table 5.1 Examples of Mission and Purpose Statements of Normative Organizations

Our purpose is to help create lasting solutions to the injustice of poverty. We are part of a global movement for change, empowering people to create a future that is secure, just, and free from poverty (Oxfam 2017).
Greenpeace is an independent campaigning organisation, which uses non-violent, creative confrontation to expose global environmental problems, and to force the solutions which are essential to a green and peaceful future (Greenpeace 2017).
Médecins Sans Frontières provides assistance to populations in distress, to victims of natural or man-made disasters and to victims of armed conflict. They do so irrespective of race, religion, creed or political convictions. Médecins Sans Frontières observes neutrality and impartiality in the name of universal medical ethics and the right to humanitarian assistance and claims full and unhindered freedom in the exercise of its functions. Members undertake to respect their professional code of ethics and maintain complete independence from all political, economic or religious powers. As volunteers, members understand the risks and dangers of the missions they carry out and make no claim for themselves or their assigns for any form of compensation other than that which the association might be able to afford them (MSF 2017).
International Federation of Red Cross and Red Crescent Societies: To inspire, encourage, facilitate and promote at all times all forms of humanitarian activities by National Societies, with a view to preventing and alleviating human suffering, and thereby contributing to the maintenance and promotion of human dignity and peace in the world (IFRC 2017).

Their international outreach is also evident, as is their will to emphasize independence from the state or governments. Essentially, targets are social in nature. Normative organizations are thus active in a context involving multifaceted relationships where problematic social issues may arise for a number of reasons, including bad policies, unethical business and natural disasters, to mention just a few.

NGOs and Corporations

It seems fair to say that the corporate landscape of today is circumscribed by norms that condition the position of contemporary corporations. In the last decade or so, phenomena such as globalization, increased interest in corporate social responsibility (CSR) and the debate on climate change have fueled a new framework for understanding the role of the corporation. One of the forces behind this is a form of moral rationalization (Boli 2006). Normative organizations are active in celebrating and certifying virtue and virtuousness in global society in the sense that they scrutinize, rank, criticize or (perhaps more rarely) laud corporate activities against a background of norms and ideals.

The role of normative organizations is multifaceted, however. Their image as non-profit organizations, whose members act on ideological grounds, often as critics of large corporations, is a strong enduring one, even though it does not reflect the diversity of goals and forms that they can exhibit.

Partly contradicting this traditional image is the development of corporate relationships with normative organizations in recent years. They have not only increased in number but also changed their character in many cases (Teegen, Doh and Vachani 2004; De Geer, Borglund and Frostenson 2009). Corporations no longer automatically fend off criticism and claims stemming from normative organizations, but seem to embrace and respond to them. Cooperation and collaboration are gaining footage at the expense of distance and hostility (Chandler 2009). In addition, in some cases, the ideas of civil society underpin overarching regulation that corporations cannot disregard if they want to maintain their legitimacy or license to operate in society (De Geer 2002).

The aforementioned reasoning leads to the identification of basically three modes of organizing relationships between corporations and normative organizations (Table 5.2). In a traditional account, the activism of normative organizations takes the shape of *critique* in words and deeds against corporations (second row in Table 5.2). Such activism can be pursued individually but is frequently channeled through networks of normative organizations (de Bakker 2012). Historically, activism, whether in the form of confrontation or civic engagement (de Bakker et al. 2013) has prompted defensive reactions from corporations. This has to do with the fact that the normative organizations are kept at arm's length, being seen as less relevant actors from a corporate point of view. Corporate (re)action can be seen as a process building on the company's independence from external actors.

Common interests are the rationale of the next level in the relationship between corporations and the normative organizations (third row in Table 5.2). It is *dialogue*-oriented and implies collaboration on the premise of common interests and an insight from a corporate point of view that collaboration with normative organizations is a step toward being accepted as a speaking partner in the socio-political discourse. We see that corporations today engage in stakeholder dialogues. In the same manner, some normative organizations seek dialogue with corporations in order to influence their behavior.

On the third level (fourth row in Table 5.2), corporations realize that it is not merely a matter of their activities benefiting from a dialogue with normative organizations; it also dawns upon them that they cannot dodge the presence of civil society interests in their own corporate structural context. In this mode, normative organizations become part of the *norm*

Table 5.2 Interactional Modes Between NGOs and Corporations

Interactional mode	*Relationship*	*Corporate action*
Critique	Independence	Reaction
Dialogue	Common interests	Collaboration
Norm setting	Dependence	Compliance

setting of corporate behavior, and corporations become dependent and have to comply.

Importantly, the interactional modes, which constitute ideal types, are chosen by normative organizations, reflecting how they can best achieve their goals (de Bakker 2012; de Bakker et al. 2013). The mode used can be expected to change over time. However, this does not imply a simple path from critique via dialogue to norm setting. As with other activities and relationships within the field, different activities exist simultaneously in the field. One and the same normative organization may thus be involved in all three modes of interaction at the same time. And, as will be shown in our examples that follow, the sequence of interactional modes is not necessarily one-directional. No deterministic path makes relationships develop from critique to dialogue to norm setting. For example, dialogue orientation can revert to critique as relations develop.

Due to the expanded space for normative organizations to exert their influence (Sahlin-Andersson 2006), the power, legitimacy and urgency of their interests have most likely increased (Mitchell, Agle and Wood 1997). The reasons for this can be discussed. We might suggest that the realization of an inability to tackle worldwide issues like poverty, diseases, and economic crises has contributed to a joint acceptance of the need to involve business in development aid, for example (Sahlin-Andersson 2006). The lack of super-national structures and entities for handling issues related to globalization also plays a part as well as an increasing interest in general responsibility issues.

The different interactional modes reflect different approaches of normative organizations. The modes oriented toward dialogue and norm setting reflect acceptance of the relevance of the ideas in a business context. Since the turn of the century, such acceptance seems to have been gaining ground. One reason for this may have been the negative attitude of corporations to coercive governance (Frostenson and Borglund 2006; Grafström, Göthberg and Windell 2015). Soft regulation has channeled ideas that corporations, whether they like it or not, have found it appropriate to adopt. By doing so, corporations profile themselves with regard to normative ideas.

It should also be noted that corporations are also facing indirect pressure from normative organizations, as the establishment of funds with social, environmental and ethical concerns has added to the pressure on corporations to acknowledge social concerns in their business operations. In this way, new opportunities have opened up for investors, ethical analysts, etc. to influence corporations to take a greater interest in the human rights and environmental protection aspects of their business operations.

The number of funds with social, environmental, and ethical concerns—socially responsible investments (SRI)—has grown rapidly, although not always with homogeneous selection criteria. According to a report from the accounting firm KPMG (2013), 1,775 responsible investment funds existed in Europe at the end of 2012, managing total assets of EUR 237.9 billion. Socially responsible investors—apart from traditional positive and negative screening of companies—have begun to implement a proactive method of influencing corporations that do not fulfill criteria of responsibility. They actively seek dialogues with these companies in order to demand change, sometimes using the media as a channel of pressure for those that refuse to engage in discussion, publishing articles on corporate misbehavior or instigating shareholder activism (Windell 2006; Sjöström 2009). In concert with this development, various indices of SRI have been established. They can be compared with a traditional market index that follows the price movements of a fund by following the price from its inception. There are several indices of SRI throughout the world with varying criteria for including corporations in their funds. The Dow Jones Sustainability Index and FTSE4Good are two of the better-known ones (Sjöström 2009).

The three interactional modes discussed earlier also take on their character through the approaches of normative organizations toward corporations. The different approaches—critique, dialogue, and norm setting—do not preclude each other (see, e.g., Domask 2003 on the protection of world forests). Rather, they often exist as parallel relational modes within the field of governance. As mentioned earlier, even one and the same normative organization can exhibit different kinds of relationships with different actors in its multifaceted relationships with the surrounding environment, sometimes even with one and the same actor in the field. In this chapter, however, they will be illustrated through various case studies (see Table 5.3): Clean Clothes for critique, Amnesty for dialogue and the International Standards Organization (ISO), the Global Reporting Initiative (GRI) and the Principles for Responsible Investment (PRI) for norm setting.

Table 5.3 The Empirical Cases of This Chapter

Interactional Mode	*Cases*	*Sources*
Critique	Clean Clothes	Burns and Spar (2002) Zadek (2004) Windell (2006) Micheletti and Stolle (2007) Micheletti and Stolle (2008) Boström and Garsten (2008) Doorey (2011)
Dialogue	Amnesty	Windell (2006) Tomson (2008)
Norm Setting	International Standards Organization (ISO) Global Reporting Initiative (GRI) Principles for Responsible Investment (PRI)	Windell (2006) Tamm-Hallström (2008) Frostenson, Helin and Sandström (2015) Majoch, Hoepner and Hebb (2017)

Critique

Introduction

In recent decades, normative organizations have become better organized and increasingly specialized, improving their chances of influencing corporate behavior (Teegen, Doh and Vachani 2004). One group of them specializes in scrutinizing corporate activities, primarily their operations in developing countries and their influence on human lives. Their aim is to influence corporations directly through campaigns and boycotts and more indirectly through the mobilization of other actors such as the media or consumers (Windell 2006; Balsiger 2010). There are numerous examples of direct actions by normative organizations to influence organization policies, investments or modes of production. For decades, such organizations have gained a legitimate and influential role with the use of controversy. Direct actions include systematic pressure on organizations, for instance, to divest from South Africa in the early 1980s. There are many examples of corporations and industries that have been criticized and scrutinized over the past ten years. Reports of corporate misconduct have provided the foundation for news stories published in the dailies. In particular, normative organizations have accused corporations that have outsourced their production to developing countries of using local suppliers or producers that violate human rights and labor rights. These corporations are frequently singled out as being irresponsible in their undertakings in developing countries. Normative organizations that scrutinize corporations monitor corporate operations in countries where there is a risk of the corporation misusing or mistreating workers or influencing the local community in a negative way. These organizations publish reports on their websites or distribute them through diverse media channels, making them available to other interested organizations. Such actors—other normative organizations, consumers, ethical analysts, social investors and the media, etc.—thereby become informed about business operations throughout the world, and can use this information to exert pressure on corporations. In this respect, scrutinizing normative organizations constitute part of a chain of actors that may ultimately have an impact on the way corporations conduct their businesses (Arnold and Bowie 2003; Windell 2006).

During the 1990s, normative organizations began to demand that corporations communicate and disclose their impact, not only upon the environment but also upon the human lives in the communities where they operate (Windell 2006; Sjöström 2009). Protests have been directed toward various corporations, but some industries were more likely to find themselves under scrutiny. In addition to the aforementioned corporations or industries with operations in developing countries, such actions have been particularly directed toward corporations with internationally known brands and industries producing hazardous goods. For instance, several clothing retailers have been scrutinized and criticized regarding their production conditions. Normative organizations in this area—CorpWatch, Human Rights Watch and Sweatshop Watch, etc.—have networks around the world. These organizations are primarily concerned with such social issues as labor and production, but they also attend to environmental issues or to particular industries with practices that are considered unethical.

Boycotts have also proven to be a frequently used method by different normative organizations (de Bakker et al. 2013). For example, the boycott of the multinational corporation Nestlé for its sales of infant products in developing countries was launched by the British organization War on Want in 1974 (Sethi 1994). The years of polemical attacks it created not only had a considerable impact on Nestlé's corporate image but also contributed to the elaboration of the International Code of Marketing of Breast-milk Substitutes (1981). In 1984, Nestlé signed this code, and the boycott was officially suspended. The oil company Shell is another example of a corporation that has become the target of massive protests and boycotts. In 1995, Shell conferred with technical and environmental experts on the most environmentally friendly and economical way of disposing of the Brent Spar oil rig (see, e.g., Grolin 1998). The result of the investigation was a plan to sink the oil rig in the North Atlantic—a decision approved by the UK government. Nevertheless, Shell was attacked by activists and sharply criticized by a number of normative organizations (particularly Greenpeace), by the media and by consumers. The result was boycotts and negative publicity. After a few months of mounting protests, Shell reconsidered and decided to dismantle Brent Spar and dispose of it in the form of a new ferry terminal near Stavanger, Norway. However, the publicity contributed to decreasing sales and a damaged reputation for Shell. In these protests against Shell, normative organizations played a critical role, not only by spreading information through their own channels but also by drawing media attention to the issue (Bowie and Dunfee 2002). In the spring of 2010, the turn had come to Shell's competitor BP to manage an environmental catastrophe. The enormous damage of the Deepwater Horizon incident had repercussions on the entire company (see, e.g., Lin-Hi and Blumberg 2011).

Denunciations of modes of production connected to child labor have also hit companies, such as Walmart and many international sportswear brands, leading to important losses in sales. They reacted with the elaboration of codes that included specific prohibitions on child labor and new criteria for selecting manufacturers and suppliers. For example, Reebok International Ltd., Levi Strauss and IKEA developed such codes between 1992 and 1998. The case of Nike is yet another illustration of the power that normative organizations can exert on corporations and corporate governance in general. The repeated public attacks by the organization Clean Clothes on Nike and Nike-related manufacturers have progressively led Nike to make changes linked to its policy regarding manufacturing sites and its position on CSR. We will use this case to explore the critical and activist approach of NGOs in greater depth.

Clean Clothes

In the mid-1990s, the old term "sweatshops" came into use again when reports started to spread about the abusive working conditions of workers in factories in developing countries producing clothes and sportswear for the North American market (Micheletti and Stolle 2007; Micheletti and Stolle 2008). Burns and Spar (2002) explain that reports suggested exploitation of young women in factories resembling prisons, insufficient payment, as well as verbal and physical abuse of workers among Nike's suppliers (and also among other sportswear brands, like Reebok). These reports were written by individuals (e.g., Jeff Ballinger in Indonesia) and became known to the public through the press. In July 1993, CBS broadcasted the interview of Indonesian workers earning 19 cents an hour in Nike's supply chain. In 1996, *Life* magazine reported on child labor in Pakistan, publishing a picture of a 12-year-old boy stitching a Nike soccer ball. In 1997, the Doonesbury comic strip devoted a full week to Nike's labor issues (Burns and Spar 2002; Micheletti and Stolle 2007). The media coverage of the working conditions for workers in Nike's supply chain had put serious pressure on Nike, but the company had not undertaken radical changes in its activities; rather, it used auditing and reporting to deal with the issues.

Activism organized by normative organizations changed the situation. Students at the University of North Carolina at Chapel Hill, the University of Michigan and the University of California, Irvine, began to question the affiliations of their universities with Nike for campus attire. North American students progressively got organized in United Students Against Sweatshops (USAS 2017, Micheletti and Stolle 2008). In July 1999, over 200 students gathered in Washington, DC, for the second Sweat-Free Campus Conference. USAS organized the expansion of its campaign and worked to create an alternative to the Fair Labor Association (FLA), which was an association of normative organizations and corporations with the aim of fighting sweatshops with voluntary company monitoring (Micheletti and Stolle 2008). The FLA was viewed by many as window dressing to hide exploitation.

In September 1999, a public address was made in the name of Clean Clothes to Nike's CEO Philip Knight conjointly by normative organizations and academic researchers, to denounce the working conditions of many Nike-related manufacturers, especially in China, Indonesia, Vietnam and El Salvador (see Table 5.4).

The letter reveals interesting aspects of thoughts that lie behind activist approaches, for example, demands for accountability, disrespect for words without deeds, as well as a denunciation of the reduction of general ethical and societal problems to organizational ones ("Nike turns its back on workers," etc.). Moreover, the letter illustrates the active role of normative organizations in collecting information from sources other than corporations themselves.

For example, it was reported that the Hong Kong Christian Industrial Committee and the Asia Monitor Resource Centre interviewed workers

Table 5.4 Excerpts From the Open Letter to Philip Knight

Wednesday, 22 September 1999

An open letter to Philip Knight, CEO of Nike Inc., from human rights organizations, unions and academic researchers concerned about the human rights of workers. . . .

Dear Mr. Knight,

Almost a year and a half ago you made a speech to the US National Press Club announcing a series of measures to improve conditions in your suppliers' factories. Many of us concerned about these issues hoped that this announcement might signal a change in Nike's corporate heart. We hoped that the attitude to the human rights of workers who make your products might have moved from cynicism, denial and concealment towards a commitment to respect, openness and accountability.

Seventeen months later these hopes have proved false. Workers in your suppliers' factories continue to be overworked and subject to abusive management practices. Workers who tell journalists the truth about conditions in their factories or try to organize unions to defend their rights continue to be systematically humiliated and then dismissed.

Wages in Nike's suppliers' factories remain unconscionably low. In Indonesia employees of your clothing suppliers are being expected to work in excess of 65 hours a week and yet are struggling to survive on less than $US1 a day. Research by the Interfaith Centre for Corporate Responsibility last year indicated that a worker earning the minimum wage in a Nike factory in Vietnam must work for ten hours just to earn enough to buy one kilogram of chicken.

Nike remains complicit in this exploitation. Your company continues to source products from totalitarian states where workers' human rights, including their right to form unions, are brutally repressed. If corporations choose to source their products from such places they have a huge responsibility to work actively to promote positive change. Instead Nike refuses even to make public statements calling for greater respect for human rights in these countries.

Worse, *Nike turns its back on workers* who are punished or dismissed for speaking out about the conditions in their factories. This not only punishes those workers, it sends a clear message to others that they must keep silent or else lose their jobs. It is hard to avoid the conclusion that Nike is determined to do all it can to conceal conditions in its suppliers' factories and to maintain the status quo in which workers producing Nike's products are powerless to assert their rights and afraid to reveal the conditions under which they work.

Source: Clean Clothes (1999a). Italics added.

from the Nike contractor, Sam Yang Vietnam Co. The workers indicated that their wages were inadequate to cover their living expenses and that they were unable to save and at times they had to borrow money from their families. They also said that workers who were late or "did something wrong" were penalized by deductions from their wages and were sometimes struck by their supervisors—usually with bare hands but occasionally with rods. The workers told of one case where a worker had been hospitalized after receiving a beating from a supervisor. Against this background, the public address urged Nike to take action (Table 5.5) (Clean Clothes 1999a).

The text in Table 5.5 shows that the normative organizations expected action as well as transparent processes. In particular, there was a call for a systematic approach that is "credible, rigorous, transparent and publicly accountable." The role that Nike was urged to play went far beyond a traditional idea of just "doing business." The company was supposed to create a system for organizing relationships and standards among its suppliers. The letter from the normative organizations led to a response from the CEO Philip H. Knight (Table 5.6).

The response of Nike is remarkable on two points. First, it presents the problem in terms of communication, with numerous references to a "dialogue" that needs to be established between the corporation and the normative organizations. This dialogue is suggested to take place within the framework of Nike's CSR program, and stresses the stakes of owners/manufacturers and workers. In other words, the ethical problem perceived by the normative organizations regarding the exploitation of workers is

Table 5.5 Examples of Actions Called for by the Authors of the Letter

We call on you to bring about a real change of heart at Nike. Despite endless promises and an eight year campaign against your company we are still waiting for you to put in place *a credible, rigorous, transparent and publicly accountable system* for checking labour standards in your suppliers' factories, involving individuals and organizations committed to earning the trust of workers. We urge you to do so as soon as possible. The following actions are also required in order to demonstrate that Nike is attempting, in good faith, to end this exploitation:

—In Vietnam, . . . at the Sam Yang factory, put an end to the use of violence to punish workers. . . . Guarantee that any workers producing Nike goods who have the courage to speak out about conditions in their factories will be protected from discrimination and dismissal.
—In Indonesia, . . . ensure that the Indonesian military leave the PT Nikomas factory and are never called to any of your suppliers' factories to pressure workers to accept particular wages or conditions. Ensure that all your suppliers in Indonesia and other parts of the world respect the right of workers to organize unions. . . .
—In China, make public statements calling on the Chinese government to allow workers to exercise their right to freedom of association in factories producing for Nike and other companies. Ensure that unions and human rights groups are allowed access to your suppliers' factories in China and other parts of the world to talk to workers about their rights and to provide training and any other support requested by workers. . . .
—Regularly publish a list of the addresses and orders from each of your suppliers' factories, so that any concerned person can travel to any of those factories and find out from workers what conditions are like.

We strongly urge you to take these steps. Until workers producing Nike products are allowed the freedom to tell the world about the conditions they are working under and the right to join together in unions and negotiate for their own welfare, your suppliers' factories will remain sweatshops and Nike will continue to attract the condemnation of the international human rights community.

Source: Clean Clothes (1999a). Italics added.

Table 5.6 Excerpt From Nike's Answer

October 5th, 1999

To all the signatories of the Clean Clothes Campaign's open letter:

Thank you for your letter. . . . I could go into a long list of all of the things we have done over the past 17 months to continuously improve living and working conditions for the 500,000 workers in our subcontracting factories. Instead, our director for labor practices Dusty Kidd will provide an update and address the specifics in the letter attached.

The current state of communications between us—in which your organizations and supporters continue attacking Nike based on an unchanging list of past incidents and Nike offering answers which you clearly find unsatisfactory—is simply not advancing our understanding of global labor practices or the ways in which we are each working to improve them. We are searching for ways to better communicate with a large NGO community of varying interests and perspectives. . . .

We are now an active participant in the Global Alliance for Workers and Communities . . ., strongly support the Fair Labor Association as it begins its work and continue to execute independent monitoring pilot projects with the goal of developing a comprehensive system.

We have spent time engaged in dialogue with workers and NGOs trying to build bridges so we can be more effective in improving the lives and working conditions of Nike contract workers. . . .

I ask you to propose a process to us for dialogue in which we ALL have a stake and common goal—improving how we deal with the issues around global manufacturing. . . . I have directed Maria Eitel, our vice president of corporate responsibility, to work with a core team of individuals you designate as representative of your collective interests. We are open to everyone's concerns but it is simply impossible for us to sustain a dialogue with so many interested organizations and individuals. The only precondition we want to put on that dialogue is that it includes workers and owner/manufacturers so those who are most affected have a voice and important role in the process. . . .

I hope—and I ask of you—that from this point on we can establish a process for talking together about this effort and its results.

Sincerely,

Philip H. Knight

Source: Clean Clothes (1999b).

addressed in terms of communication and what seems to be the necessity to find a compromise. Second, Nike stresses its support for the FLA, an association that is criticized by both USAS and other normative organizations, since, in their view, the FLA permits corporations to continue their practices of exploitation.

During the summer of 1999, USAS was working on the development of an alternative to the FLA in order to allow independent monitoring of suppliers' factories (Doorey 2011). This involved the public disclosure of the names of the factories used, which was also requested by the international letter addressed to Nike. Publishing a list of its manufacturers was strongly rejected by Nike on the basis of arguments concerning the company's competitiveness. As the founding conference of the Worker Rights Consortium (WRC)—an organization with similar objectives as the FLA but without the possibility of corporate membership—approached, in April 2000, Nike CEO Philip H. Knight, the company withdrew a promised USD 30 million donation to the University of Oregon and pulled out of negotiations for a USD 22 million exclusive licensing contract with the University of Michigan after they joined the WRC (see Klein 2000; Doorey 2011). This was remarkable, since USAS was not the only association concerned with the working conditions in Nike's suppliers. Normative organizations such as Oxfam (in particular Oxfam's NikeWatch) and the Clean Clothes Campaign were also serving as watchdogs for the practices in use at garment factories around the world (Klein 2000).

Nike's tactic made national headlines, and the price of its shares fell from USD 76.375 in 1997 to USD 26.563 in 2000 (Morgan 2007: 466). During the following year, additional campaigns were organized against Nike and the working conditions at Nike's contractors. Examples of what was denounced were the denial of female workers' freedom of association at a Mexico-sited manufacturer in August 2001 and the physical abuse these women endured. However, when the factory was forced to allow the right to its workers to form unions, Nike withdrew its contract (Burns and Spar 2002).

As a corollary to the repeated denunciations of working conditions at Nike's suppliers in developing countries, Nike's views of its CSR evolved (see, e.g., Boström and Garsten 2008: 4). Over the years, Nike's attitudes and commitment to issues related to sustainability changed. In 2000, the company thus disclosed a list of collegiate factories, that is, the production sites of campus apparel for the North American market. In 2005, Nike revealed its first list of more than 700 active Nike factories and now updates it twice a year (Doorey 2011). As a result, in 2006, 2007 and 2008 Nike was included on Fortune's list of "100 Best Companies to Work For." Likewise, Nike's ranking on the "100 Best Corporate Citizens" List published by *CRO Magazine* rose from No. 31 in 2005, No. 13 in 2006, to No. 3 in 2007. Later on, for supply chain management and transparency, Nike implemented a medal-based rating system of their factories in 2011, following a Sourcing & Manufacturing Sustainability Index (SMSI) as a tool for control and transparency for its entire supply chain. In this way, it enables normative organizations to independently investigate working conditions in Nike-related factories. Nike's changed position with regard to transparency has been unmistakable. If they first thought revealing their suppliers' and factories' names would hamper their competitiveness, they later admitted that this change was welcomed by their suppliers and did not reduce their competitive advantage (Doorey 2011). In 2017, the company is committed to being a leader in sustainable innovation (Nike 2017).

The Nike case offers many insights for understanding the relationships between various actors involved in a common field. Zadek (2004) underscores that the choice of Nike as a target by normative organizations was strategic. The working conditions of employees in the Nike supply chain were similar to those at other important enterprises in the garment industry, but the focus on Nike allowed the organizations to reach a key and influential actor in the field. Targeting Nike meant exerting coercive pressure on a key player, with the hope that other actors in the field (e.g., Adidas, Redbook) would follow Nike's actions. The choice of Nike was clearly justified by the belief that other actors would fall in line.

An additional element that is underlined in the Nike case is the fact that the actors are local but also exert international influence. For example, the students' association USAS is a local North American player, as is the Hong Kong Christian Industrial Committee, which denounced the working conditions among Nike-related garment manufacturers. However, their impact on the whole international Nike group was critical. Furthermore, the Nike case underlines the fact that the actors of a given field interact. This is a clear case of normative organizations providing the media with opinions, interpretations and evaluations of a company. Normative organizations and media acted jointly in terms of both the public accusations made against the CEO Philip H. Knight and the exertion of pressure on the company. For example, the denouncing of working conditions was followed up by the media, and the broadcast in early 2000 of a documentary in the United Kingdom on working conditions in Nike's supply chain added to the burden of previous pressures and reports of their poor performance in respecting labor standards (Burns and Spar 2002).

Most importantly, the impact that the normative organizations and media actors have had on Nike is critical both for Nike and for the field. Early on, Nike adopted an attitude of denial, in brief pleading that this was not their responsibility or that the other actors were doing exactly the same things. Then, through the 1990s, Nike's strategy changed to one of compliance, allowing external audits and considering issues of working conditions as legitimate. Moreover, other actors in the field followed a similar path. However, the previous example of the altercation between Philip H. Knight and the normative organizations, and additional pressure from the media, mark a turning point in Nike's strategy. It decided to change from compliance to an active integration of the issue into its core managerial practices (see Zadek 2004). A team was instructed to investigate why the company was continually failing to effectively comply with its own labor code, despite its dedicated department of CSR. The outcome of the investigation underscored internal management problems of coordination between Nike's departments that led to reproducing bad working conditions in its supply chain. In sum, the pressure exerted by external actors like the normative organizations led to a restructuring of Nike's management processes, and, a specific role being played by Nike in its field. Nike transformed this experience into a competitive advantage by taking the position of a potential norm-setter in terms of transparency (Doorey 2011) and the importance it assigns to CSR.

Dialogue

Introduction

Normative organizations also seek to influence corporate behavior by encouraging corporations to take different kinds of preventive measures for safeguarding human rights and certain values within the field of business. From a strategic point of view, normative organizations do not necessarily resort to activism or appeal to overarching regulation through various frameworks. Rather, they prefer to work in collaboration. This means entering into dialogue with corporations, providing them with advice on how to put their social concerns into action. These normative organizations work with corporations on the basis of common interests.

The consultative work of these normative organizations is similar to the work of many consultants, in the sense that they engage in dialogues with corporations, and sometimes with other stakeholders, informing them about various aspects of human rights issues and social responsibility. Together with corporations, the normative organizations seek to provide solutions to such problems and to develop action plans. The prerequisites for this seem to be common interests and a willingness to collaborate with business on the basis of a conviction of the important role of business as a facilitator or at least a legitimate and important actor in terms of human rights issues or other concerns. Often, the more consultative role of normative organizations follows a local or national anchoring of operations—that is, cooperation is facilitated by the relative geographical proximity of the normative organization and the corporation, where the former can be seen as a speaking partner for the corporation to gain more knowledge and advice with regard to business issues in distant countries (Windell 2006; Tomson 2008). We will demonstrate this mode of action with Amnesty International.

Amnesty International

Amnesty International reflects several aspects of the consultative role that some normative organizations have come to play. Being a worldwide organization working for human rights, it epitomizes the idealistic approach of the field. In recent years, however, an increasing interest in corporate activities and the relationship between such activities and general human rights issues has been manifest. The story that Amnesty tells bears witness to concerns over the effects of modern business in the context of globalization (for example on its homepage). The unprecedented power and influence of corporations today warrant special attention to issues related to business and human rights, in particular since societies where corporations have been operating have not necessarily benefited from this. Normative organization must be active, it is claimed, since few effective mechanisms exist that prevent corporate human rights abuses or hold companies accountable for possible infringements. Governmental action and power do not necessarily suffice when it comes to corporate activities, it is claimed, and voluntary codes and initiatives fail to eliminate abuses of fundamental rights.

The overarching aim of Amnesty is to establish global standards on business and human rights along with stronger legal frameworks on different levels to hold companies to account for their impact on human rights worldwide. When calling for corporate accountability, Amnesty specifically mentions some necessities (see Amnesty 2017a):

- Prevention: all companies should be required by law to take steps to identify, prevent and address human rights abuses (known as due diligence).
- Accountability: companies must be held to account for abuses they commit.
- Remedy: people whose rights have been abused by companies must be able to access justice and effective remedy.
- Protect rights beyond borders: companies operate across borders, so the law must also operate across borders to protect people's rights.

Given this background, it is important to note that local chapters of Amnesty International tackle the issue of corporate accountability differently. While more traditional activism, such as shareholder activism, still plays an important role, other local approaches are more consultative and collaborative in character.

For example, on American soil, shareholder activism in support of human rights concerns in business stands on Amnesty's agenda (see, for example, Billenness 2016). Such activism can be direct (buying stocks in a certain corporation and using it to file resolutions) or indirect (engaging other concerned and more powerful shareholders like pension funds, unions and other institutions to take action in support of measures to safeguard human rights). Stock ownership opens up for a range of opportunities, such as filing shareholder resolutions. Amnesty International USA has used its shareholder ownership to press companies toward implementing human rights policies. The organization has also made inquiries and pushed for changes with regard to alleged human rights abuses. This has been done through different activities such as writing letters and filing shareholder resolutions for annual meetings, for example, with Chevron and Dow Chemical. Resolutions do not necessarily have to win majority approval at the annual general meetings to make an impact. Merely filing them may shed light on issues that the corporation, as a consequence, decides to deal with in one way or another (Sjöström 2009).

Looking at Amnesty activities around the globe, collaborative and consultative approaches seem to have played an important role (Chandler 2009; Lin-Hi and Blumberg 2011; de Bakker 2012). However, this is not to say that a dialogue orientation implies a path of no return to a more critical approach, or that a kind of coexistence of both approaches is not possible. In Scandinavia, examples can be found in Sweden and Denmark.

The idea that Amnesty should work with corporations and human rights issues in a consultative way was introduced into the organizations by new members that had their background in the business world (Tomson 2008). They brought with them new practices, networks and financial means from their earlier experience. Consequently, a specialized group within Amnesty was founded: the Swedish Amnesty Business Group (ABG). In contrast to other organizations that wish to maintain their independence and remain in opposition to corporations (Thorsell and Abrahamsson 2003), ABG was established in order to engage in debates with corporations and to give them advice on handling human rights issues (Sjöström 2009). This approach is not unique to Scandinavia. The first ABG was in fact instigated in the United Kingdom in 1991, with the goal of creating greater awareness of human rights issues in business and to induce companies and business people to use their influence to work for improvements in human rights (Tomson 2008; Chandler 2009). Business groups were later introduced in several other countries. These local organizations were chaired by former business leaders whose main goal was to establish dialogues with corporations around human rights issues.

One concrete example of how the Swedish ABG developed its dialogue approach was through its Business Forum (see, for example, GP 2005). Guided by an ambition to assist corporations in honoring human rights, the ABG created the forum to serve as a platform for information and education with regard to corporate responsibility. Joining the forum was a possibility for corporations that wanted to work together with the ABG in order to deepen the respect for human rights in their operations. Through dialogue, either between the ABG and individual companies or through activities involving several companies, the forum participants got access to information, education and exchange of experiences. The contribution of the ABG concerned specific knowledge on how human rights can be respected and exercised in concrete business situations as well as specific knowledge of country or business-specific characteristics concerning human rights. In certain cases, the ABG could contribute external specialist resources through its network.

Business Forum conferences were held two or three times a year. These meetings built upon the ABG recommendations on human rights and contained, for example, risk and business-specific analyses as well as education on human rights and independent monitoring. For each participating corporation, consultations were held each year regarding work and progress with regard to human rights. In holding consultations, the ABG sought to provide constructive support for the corporation involving concrete confidential recommendations. For participating firms, the ABG also assisted with informants, advisors and education aimed at specific employee groups. In return, a membership fee and respect for the independent role of the ABG were expected.

Interestingly, the Business Forum lost its importance within the ABG over the years and the organization reverted to a more critical approach. The position of the ABG became more explicitly formulated as primarily being oriented toward activism, lobbying and debating. Furthermore, albeit more downplayed, ABG wants to be a meeting point for people interested in CSR issues, and providing a competence resource is part of the organization's work. In other words, such activities are no longer directly aimed at corporations; the dialogue approach has lost its significance, mainly owing to new priorities within the organization. To be a critical voice has become central (Amnesty 2017 b) where the organization calls for "activists" to join the organization). However, nothing says that this will be the final position of the ABG. The case shows that prioritizations and preferences of how and whether to interact with companies develop and change over time.

Notably, a dialogue approach was taken by the Danish Amnesty Business Forum (ABF), established as a platform for Danish corporations wishing to work actively to safeguard human rights (see, for example, Berlingske Business 2007). The target group of the ABF was Danish corporations with operations in developing countries. The ABF tried to stimulate corporate policy making in the field of human rights and make companies take on responsibility wherever they operate. This involved consequence analyses of corporate activities, education, implementing management systems, reporting, and supply chain control. By joining the ABF, corporations could gain access to Amnesty reports and research, get a contact person at the ABF, participate in seminars, engage in exchange and round table discussions with other members. Dialogue meetings were also held. The dialogue approach has been upheld over the years, though in slightly different forums. In 2017, the Danish branch of Amnesty was a member of a state-run dialogue forum for corporate responsibility and growth called *Dialogforum for Samfundsansvar og Vækst* (Dialogue Forum for Social Responsibility and Growth; see Amnesty DK 2017), that supports corporations' work with responsibility. A striking feature of the Danish case is that the dialogue approach *coexists* with a more critical and activist approach toward companies, at least in the sense that the Danish Amnesty works actively with, for example, documenting human rights abuses in business.

The Amnesty case shows that the interface between normative organizations and corporations can be understood in terms of both collaboration and activism. As noted by Chandler (2009), the more consultative role suggests common interests with regard to vital issues such as human rights. In this case, civil society ideas are not in opposition to the corporate understanding of the contextual framework of business. Rather, they can be seen as informative to business, expressing a normative content that is in agreement with corporate ideas of how business should be carried out. Basic ideas of rules that should be obeyed do not undermine business, but create a field on which the game can be played on just and reasonable terms. The structure of a normative organization like Amnesty also facilitates the collaborative approach. On the local level, as evidenced in the Scandinavian examples, relative proximity facilitates the realization of common interests through joint forums and activities. However, the multifaceted structure also implies that divergent paths can be chosen, for example dialogue orientation in one place and collaboration in another. Obviously, as the Danish case suggests, there is no sharp line between a critical and a dialogue-oriented approach (see also de Bakker 2012). But whatever the case, Amnesty evinces features that go beyond the merely critical interaction mode through its initiatives that recognize business as a speaking partner.

Norm Setting

Introduction

As became clear in Chapter 3, the development of soft regulation has been intensive in recent years. Many regulative initiatives have been taken within a wider context of corporate responsibility (Jutterström 2006). A plethora of normative frameworks, guidelines, governance codes, codes of conduct, compacts and other arrangements have emerged on national and supernational levels. The number of regulative frameworks began to escalate in the 1970s, and expanded rapidly in the mid-1990s, and in the first decade of the twenty-first century, more than 100 CSR standards existed (Jutterström 2006: 8). Although other organizations have been involved, approximately half of the standards launched in the decade around the turn of the century were instigated by normative organizations situated in Europe (Jutterström 2006 : 7). The 1970s saw the inauguration of several initiatives to regulate corporate operations in developing countries. In 1972, the International Chamber of Commerce (ICC) launched guidelines for international investment; in 1975, the OECD guidelines for multinational corporations were established; and a few years later, in 1977, the International Labour Organization (ILO) developed its convention on labor standards. Frameworks like these are steadily updated as new issues and challenges emerge. In contrast to the initiatives instigated in the 1970s, the new wave of corporate behavior control and the advocating of social responsibility in the 1990s emerged from the industrial countries (Jenkins 2001). As a rule, the frameworks developed from around the new millennium and onwards have addressed different aspects of social responsibility in corporate activities, that is, not only environmental issues. Whereas some of them served to outline how corporations should behave in developing countries or how they should treat their suppliers, others were addressing the integration of CSR in corporations. Yet others provided guidelines for CSR reporting. Some of these later initiatives were the Fair Trade Labelling Organization, formed in 1980; AccountAbility (AA1000), established in 1995; Social Accountability (SA 8000), started in 1997; and the GRI, launched in 1997. Two years later, a number of other guidelines were launched: Social Accountability

International and the Global Sullivan Principles, for example. A later initiative is the engagement of the ISO that launched its standard for social responsibility, called ISO 26000, in 2010 (see ISO 2017a).

Fransen and Kolk (2007) note that normative organizations tend to support rather strict guidelines and policies. However, they cannot ensure the implementation of their standards. Such standards, addressing CSR are, for example, WRC (1999), No Dirty Gold Golden Rules (2004), INGO Accountability (2006) (see Kolk, van Tulder and Welters 1999). Another type of activity of normative organizations is their participation in the development of multi-stakeholder standards, which have recently gained in importance. Standards are developed through the joint work of normative organizations, corporations, consumer groups, labor organizations and sometimes governments. According to Fransen and Kolk (2007), these standards tend to leverage the strengths of other types of standards. For instance, multi-stakeholder standards tend to be precise and specific and use methods to monitor their implementations similar to the ones used by standards from business associations (therefore being strong on implementation). Examples of multi-stakeholder standards are Ethical Trading Initiative (1998), Kimberley Process Certification Scheme (2002), and Common Code for the Coffee Community (2004) (Fransen and Kolk 2007).

The standards and principles that will be highlighted in the remaining parts of this section share the underlying idea of creating a common set of norms for how business should be undertaken in an increasingly globalized world. Three different solutions developed through direct participation of normative organizations will be highlighted. They are, in turn, (1) the ISO 26000 standard for social responsibility, (2) the GRI guidelines for sustainability reporting and (3) the PRI, developed as an investor initiative in partnership with the UN Environment Programme Finance Initiative and the UN Global Compact, but in close collaboration with stakeholders from different fields of society. These three approaches are different in character but can all be seen as ways to impose, from a normative vantage point, ideas to influence the corporate context in terms of defining the role and accountability of corporations in modern society. Still, they can be understood as frameworks with different purposes: guiding and standardizing the responsibility range of corporate and organizational action (ISO 26000), offering a transparency framework for visualizing corporate responsibility (GRI) and providing a corporate governance framework defining fundamental ownership principles for institutional investors.

The ISO 26000 Standard for Social Responsibility

Consisting of more than 160 national standards institutes, the ISO (the International Organization for Standardization) considers itself a network nonprofit organization that constitutes a link between the public and private sectors, even though many national institutes are part of the governmental structures (ISO 2017b).

The focal areas of ISO, notably technical and environmental standards, have been developed into standards through processes characterized by negotiation and consensus. Pinpointing social responsibility as an area for standardization suggests, as in the case of other standards, an interest and a recognized need to create common basic definitions, working methods and evaluation practices for the sake of simplification and practicality. However, as the rhetoric of the ISO 26000 standard suggests (see ISO 2017c), simplification and practicality walk hand in hand with normative ideas about the role and behavior of business in society. The action sphere of corporations is circumscribed by pressure to operate in a socially responsible manner, pressure that is mounted by normative organizations, customers, governments, associations and the public at large. At the same time, the factual claim that social responsibility in accordance with basic norms of right and wrong is in the interest of companies and organizations aiming at long-term profitability is constantly present in the rhetoric of ISO 26000. Credibility is a must, one can infer, and is reached through paying heed to central behavioral principles that include transparency with regard to corporate activities.

At ISO, initial concerns about the need for a standard for social responsibility grew along with the general interest in issues concerning consumer policy and corporate responsibility at the turn of the millennium (see, e.g., Tamm-Hallström 2008). After the ISO multi-stakeholder conference on social responsibility in 2004, which positively treated the topic of launching a social responsibility standard, a working group was set up to develop a standard for social responsibility. ISO 26000 is a multi-stakeholder initiative, formally spearheaded by the Swedish Standards Institute and the Brazilian Association of Technical Standards, consisting of experts from developed and developing countries, governments, industry, labor, normative organizations, consumer organizations and others, for example, research. These stakeholder categories were consciously chosen to create balanced representation in the working groups (ISO 2017c).

The principles build on strongly normative ideas (Tamm Hallström 2008). For example, a normative organization like Consumers International, a global membership organization consisting of a wide range of independent consumer organizations, took part in the development of ISO 26000. Consumers International forward consumer interests within the ISO context of social responsibility of organizations (Consumer International 2017). This implies advocating consumer-related issues as a part of the core content of social responsibility along with social, environmental, human rights and labor issues. In line with this reasoning, corporations and organizations must devote themselves to fair treatment of consumers, adopting safety responsibility for products and services as well as providing possibilities of consuming in a sustainable manner. Unfair marketing or contractual practices should also be avoided. At the heart of asserting consumer interests lies a conviction of the possibility and moral legitimacy of using purchasing power as an incentive to reward socially responsible practices.

ISO 26000 is a guidance standard, not a set of requirements or a standard intended for third party certification. The guidance, rather than control or coercive, approach signals that abstract components like voluntarism and commitment strongly underpin the standard, just like consensus thinking and approval by a recognized body consisting of representatives of the different stakeholders of the process.

Understanding social responsibility as a wider term than CSR signifies a conviction of the need for other organizations and governmental agencies also to show in public that they work in accordance with consistent norms in a societal context (cf. Higgins and Tamm Hallström 2007). Such norms reflect a more profound wish to incorporate the entire value chain of business activities into a normative evaluation framework. ISO 26000 identifies environmentally harmful production, child labor, dangerous working conditions and other inhumane conditions as examples that contradict a basic normative understanding of what business should be allowed to generate or be positioned within.

ISO 26000 is meant to be a distillation of the meaning of social responsibility as understood by international expertise. Its complementary character and consistency with UN and ILO standards are emphasized (ISO 2017a). This means that the ISO principles focus on normative foundations, namely: (1) formulate terms and definitions, (2) identify the general responsibility context of organizations, (3) offer concrete guidelines on social responsibility subjects or issues and (4) guide the implementation of the principles. It is thus a project that introduces norms into the field of governance through norm setting.

The Global Reporting Initiative

While ISO 26000 can be seen as an appeal to managers of corporations and organizations to conform to basic standards of social responsibility, instruments of control and governance have been developed to promote conformity to socially established norms of right and wrong. Civil society in general and normative organizations in particular can be said to have had an influence on this development. The existence and history of the GRI, today the organization providing the most widely used standard for sustainability reporting illustrates this.

The main idea of the GRI, a non-profit organization based in Amsterdam, is to help businesses, governments and other organizations understand and communicate the impact of business on a number of critical sustainability issues. The GRI bolsters the idea of making reporting on economic, environmental and social performance just as mainstream as financial reporting. The GRI spells out principles and indicators that organizations can use to measure and report economic, environmental and social performance.

The core of the reporting framework is the guidelines of the organization. These guidelines have appeared in different forms over the years. In 2016, GRI launched its GRI Standards, constituting a fifth generation of reporting guidelines (GRI 2016).

According to the GRI website, reports of more than 10,000 organizations are featured in its public database. The majority of these reports have been prepared according to the guidelines of GRI, accounting for performance in the area of economic, social and environmental impact on society. The GRI works closely together with an active multi-stakeholder network to ensure the continuous relevancy and applicability of its guidelines. The formal governance bodies of the GRI include representatives of hundreds of different stakeholders from business, civil society, labor and professional institutions (GRI 2017a).

A brief overview of the historical roots of the GRI underlines the importance of normative ideas finding their ways into the realities of corporations. The GRI can be traced back to the Boston-based, non-profit organizations the Coalition for Environmentally Responsible Economies (Ceres) and the Tellus Institute. In the 1990s, Ceres, a network of investors, environmental organizations, and other public interest groups focusing on sustainability issues, elaborated a framework for environmental reporting as a means to ensure that corporations followed the Ceres principles for responsible environmental conduct (GRI 2017b). Such an initiative reflects the organization's mission to integrate sustainability into capital markets for the health of the planet and its people. To accomplish this, the organization aspires to leverage the collective power of investors and other major stakeholders.

After poor reception of the reporting framework in the United States, international outreach was determined to be a way to spread and develop the framework (GRI 2017b). In the late 1990s, the GRI project was launched, involving staffing, fundraising and network development, alongside the appointment of a GRI steering committee. A global platform for the GRI was created, partnering with the United Nations Environmental Programme. In 2000, the first sustainability reporting guidelines were released, with some 50 organizations completing sustainability reports based on the guidelines. In 2001, a decision was taken to separate GRI from Ceres, making it an independent institution. The following year the GRI Institution was publicly inaugurated at the United Nations in New York City and relocated to Amsterdam, becoming independent of Ceres. That year the second generation of the guidelines were released, followed by a third generation in 2006, a fourth in 2013 and a fifth in 2016 (see GRI 2016). The frequent updates and changes of the guidelines reflect new developments and demands to adapt to a changing environment with new issues coming up. The introduction of the GRI Standards signals a will to establish a flexible structure, with three overarching standards and a large number of ancillary standards that can be changed without having to release a completely new generation of guidelines.

A basic idea of the GRI is that performance in areas other than the purely financial can be visualized and reported. Sustainability reporting, the GRI asserts, is the practice of measuring, disclosing and being accountable to internal and external stakeholders for organizational performance toward the goal of sustainable development. The 2016 GRI Standards contain, as noted previously, three overarching standards and a number of ancillary standards relating to economic, environmental and social performance (including human rights, labor practices and decent work, society and product responsibility), for which management approaches to material topics of sustainability are also to be reported (GRI 2016). Underlying norms that dictate a given understanding of responsible management can be found among the topics covered in the standards. For example, going into the category of labor practices and decent work, we find core indicators like percentage of employees covered by collective bargaining agreements (representative ideal), percentage of total workforce represented in formal joint management, worker health and safety committees (participative ideal), and breakdown of employees per category according to gender, age group, minority group membership (diversity ideal) and ratio of basic salaries of men to women by employee category (gender equality ideal).

The Principles for Responsible Investment

The UN initiated creation of the Principles for Responsible Investment (PRI) can be characterized as a cooperative best-practice attempt to provide the world's largest institutional investors with an operative framework for handling Environmental, Social and Governance (ESG) issues (see, e.g., Lydenberg and Sinclair 2009; Majoch, Hoepner and Hebb 2017). The PRI initiative aims at helping investors to integrate ESG concerns into investment decisions and ownership practices. A central idea is that ESG concerns are central for the long-term performance of investment portfolios (PRI 2017a).

The joint process of developing the principles started in 2005 when an Investor Group representing 20 institutional investors from twelve countries accepted ownership of the principles that were officially announced in 2006. During the process, a 70-person multi-stakeholder group of experts representing the investment industry, intergovernmental and governmental organizations, civil society and academia assisted the Investor Group (PRI 2017a).

Essentially, the principles involve a commitment from investors to adopt certain fundamentals related to ESG, worded in the following way (PRI 2017a, see also Majoch, Hoepner and Hebb 2017):

1. We will incorporate ESG issues into investment analysis and decision-making processes.
2. We will be active owners and incorporate ESG issues into our ownership policies and practices.

3. We will seek appropriate disclosure on ESG issues from the entities in which we invest.
4. We will promote acceptance and implementation of the Principles within the investment industry.
5. We will work together to enhance our effectiveness in implementing the Principles.
6. We will each report on our activities and progress toward implementing the Principles.

Under these general principles, a number of possible actions are suggested. Examples include asking financial analysts and other service providers to integrate ESG factors into research and analysis, filing shareholder resolutions consistent with long-term ESG considerations, and requesting standardized reporting on ESG issues using tools such as the GRI.

The principles are voluntary, building on aspiration and without absolute performance benchmarks. No compulsory fee is required from signatories, although a voluntary fee is encouraged to help the work of the secretariat. In general, signatories are actors on the financial markets with long investment horizons and diversified portfolios. It should be noted that the principles are open to asset owners, investment managers and professional service partners—all of whom are eligible as signatories—that express support for them. In early 2017, nearly 2,000 signatories are recorded on the PRI website (PRI 2017b). Signing the principles implies a declaration of support for top-level management of the investors. The rationale behind the principles is not only to contribute to long-term financial performance and to lower risk but also to reconcile the objectives of institutional investors with society at large. No contradiction is found here, since it is claimed that ESG issues tend to be relevant for the long-term performance of portfolios (PRI 2017a). Among signatories there are a substantial number of asset owners such as Munich Reinsurance Company, Swiss Re Ltd., CalPERS and the Norwegian Government Pension Fund (Norway and Global); investment managers representing companies such as HSBC Group Investment Businesses, JP Morgan Asset Management and Daiwa Asset Management Co. Ltd.; and service providers, for example BNP Paribas Securities Services and Morningstar, Inc., to mention just a few (PRI 2017a).

To support implementation of the principles a number of arrangements have been made available. In 2017, PRI has established a governance instrument of particular interest for governance, a proxy vote declaration system (cf. Chapter 4). Through this system, investors can voluntarily declare in public how they intend to vote on shareholder resolutions concerning ESG issues that have been filed or co-filed by PRI signatories (PRI 2017c). Such an arrangement mirrors increasing demands from signatories for greater transparency in proxy voting. Knowing how investors exercise their influence is of interest. Making proxy voting public increases information on how signatories work, and it visualizes investor expectations on managers and corporations. The proxy vote declaration system is channeled through the PRI Collaboration Platform, which is a forum that allows signatories to pool and share resources and information and to enhance their influence on ESG issues (PRI 2017d). In other words, PRI provides a forum or communication channel concerning activities and measures taken in order to promote responsible business. Through such arrangements, the PRI becomes a coordinated instrument for influencing corporations with regard to behavior, policies or systematic conditions (PRI 2017d). Basically, through making individual signatory proposals of how to act with regard to certain corporations or situations public, an arena is created where other signatories can be inspired to undertake the same actions. Coordination is facilitated. Through such arrangements, the burden of having to individually monitor an impracticably large number of corporations can be overcome, as can the weakness of single-actor pressure against corporations in ESG issues. Few international investors have the power and legitimacy to individually affect corporate ESG policies.

Communication is also provided through other electronic channels. This means that signatories get an opportunity to find information around responsible investment issues and approaches taken by leading signatories. Special attention is also paid to investment in emerging markets and developing countries. Supporting institutional investors in these markets to better understand ESG issues is a matter of concern. In addition, coordination of shareholder engagement by PRI signatories with global and local companies operating in developing countries is encouraged (PRI 2017e). Identifying and addressing systematic constraints to responsible investment in these markets is central).

Unlike some forms of socially responsible investment, the PRI does not suggest screening procedures to exclude investment in certain corporations (cf., e.g., Schwartz 2003). Instead, a policy of dialogue with companies is suggested. The principles promote a perhaps more general approach to asset ownership, implying a fundamental normative idea that investment activities as such should be infused with a special meme of responsibility.

What is striking about investor concerns expressed in PRI is the fact that institutional investors accept it as their responsibility to influence both corporate activities and responsibilities and to urge other investors to do likewise. The astounding aspect of this is the fundamental change in the general assumption of what constitutes shareholder interests. Thus, a function of corporate governance systems is not only to increase efficiency but also to ensure the legitimacy of a certain system (Aguilera and Cuervo-Cazurra 2004; Chapter 4). The principles suggest that institutional shareholders have the motivation and interest to actively take part in the creation of a sustainable and financially viable economy. This perspective is striking. While corporate activities have been the focus of the partly normative organization-driven CSR movement, demanding responsible action with regard to stakeholders affected by corporate activities, the PRI movement adopts a normative framework from an ownership position, thereby undermining the refuge of corporations to claim that CSR is acceptable only if it increases long-run shareholder value. With PRI, institutional shareholders take the initiative themselves to spell out what is really in their interest.

Conclusions

In this chapter, we have discussed the role of normative organizations in corporate governance. We have argued that these organizations are embedded in the institutional context of corporations to such an extent that it is impossible for the modern corporation to ignore their existence and ideas. The chapter underpins our claim that the field of governance is composed of various relationships. In line with the framework presented in Chapter 2, we note that there is a multilateral construction of organizations and interests within the field.

Our empirical studies have led us to identify three ideal types of interaction modes between normative organizations and corporations (Table 5.1). They range from critique to dialogue, and ultimately to norm setting. The relationships can be reactive (seen from the perspective of the corporation), collaborative, or oriented toward the compliance of the corporation. Having this model as a vantage point, it is possible to infer some findings from our empirical examples—Nike and Amnesty, as well as ISO, GRI and PRI—that further support our approach to corporate governance (Table 5.7).

First, the relationships that characterize the field support the idea that for a multinational corporation it is more or less impossible to act in isolation from norms and ideas of communities on a global scale. As the Clean Clothes case demonstrates (second row in Table 5.7), a reactive approach is quite possible to adopt. However, owing to the mutuality of the relationships, it is not possible to escape the norms and ideas that shape the logic of the field. Firms are embedded in a global context. Their doings and dealings are strongly dependent on the logic of the field, which means that their understanding and adaptation to the contextual framework of the corporation is necessary for survival. Communities and normative organizations act as whistle-blowers who are likely to be successful particularly as they are backed up by the media.

Second, common interests do exist in a field of governance where different actors compete not only for ideational acceptance but also for recognition as

Table 5.7 Summing Up Our Findings

Interactional Mode	*Relationship*	*Corporate Action*	*Example*	*Role of Communities*
Critique	Independence	Reaction	Clean Clothes	Whistle-blowers
Dialogue	Common Interests	Collaboration	Amnesty	Consultants
Norm Setting	Dependence	Compliance	ISO, GRI, PRI	Regulators

speaking partners (third row in Table 5.7). From the perspective of normative organizations, collaborative action has proven to be a promising means of diffusing knowledge, good practice and responsible behavior. In other words, using this mode, normative organizations choose not to approach businesses with hostility, but to create common ground for best possible effects. This is shown in our ABG case (which also points to flexibility and the possibility of normative organizations reverting to activist positions). In this mode, communities and normative organizations operate like consultants.

Third, we claim that the field of governance is structured, ordered and organized. We suggest that there is a strong tendency to structure and organize the field through different means of norm setting (fourth row of Table 5.7). As this chapter shows, this activity can vary substantially in its focus. Frameworks for standardization (ISO 6000), transparency (GRI) and governance (PRI) are all aspects of corporate reality today. It seems clear that communities not only contribute to norms but also take on an active role in creating them. In so doing, communities and their normative organizations act like regulators.

An implication of the aforementioned is that communities and their normative organizations should no longer be seen as a separate entity distant from the activities of corporations but as an integral part of a wider governance framework of the corporation of today. The recognition of normative organizations in the field of governance is a mutual, intertwined, and complex process involving different kinds of relationships between corporations and communities as well as different strategies adopted by corporations and normative organizations in their mutual coexistence. Governance issues are best understood not in isolation from environmental and social issues but in connection with these concerns. Corporations have realized that the prerequisites for running a business and for managerial work in general are conditioned by the position of the firm in relationship to external expectations on the corporation. This is something completely different than merely obeying laws and behaving in a formally correct way. As the creators of the ISO 26000 standard explicitly suggest, dynamism, voluntarism, development orientation, consensus, openness, positive commitment and, above all, a bottom-up perspective rather than a top-down approach seem to be part of the normative logic that communities and their normative organizations contribute. Even if such components do not stand in contradistinction to legislation, they represent quite another awareness-raising mental construct than simply being obliged to comply with legislation.

References

Aguilera, R. and Cuervo-Cazurra, R., 2004, "Codes of Good Governance World-wide: What Is the Trigger?" *Organization Studies*, 25(3): 415–443.

Amnesty, 2017a, "What We Do" <www.amnesty.org/en/what-we-do/corporate-accountability> accessed on August 7, 2017.

Amnesty, 2017b, "Gör något för de mänskliga rättigheterna!" (Do Something for the Human Rights) <www.amnesty.se/engagera-dig/bli-aktivist/> accessed on August 8, 2017.

Amnesty DK, 2017, "Økonomi og samfundsansvar" (Economy and Societal Responsibility) <http://amnesty.dk/emner/fattigdom/oekonomi-og-samfundsansvar> accessed on August 8, 2017.

Arnold, D. G. and Bowie, N. E., 2003, "Sweatshops and Respects for Persons," *Business Ethics Quarterly*, 13(2): 221–242.

Balsiger, P., 2010, "Making Political Consumers: The Tactical Action Repertoire of a Campaign for Clean Clothes," *Social Movement Studies*, 9(3): 311–329.

Berlingske Business, 2007, "Arla melder sig under Amnestys faner" (Arla Enters under the Amnesty Banner) <www.business.dk/foedevarer/arla-melder-sig-under-amnestys-faner> accessed on August 8, 2017.

Billenness, S., 2016, "Amnesty International: Shareholder Activist," <http://blog.amnestyusa.org/uncategorized/amnesty-international-shareholder-activist/> accessed on September 25, 2017.

Boli, J., 2006, "The Rationalization of Virtue and Virtuosity in World Society," in: Djelic, M.-L. and Sahlin-Andersson, K. (eds.), *Transnational Governance: Institutional Dynamics of Regulation*, Cambridge: Cambridge University Press, pp. 95–118.

Boström, M. and Garsten, C., 2008, "Organizing for Accountability," in: Boström, M. and Garsten, C. (eds.), *Organizing Transnational Accountability: Mobilization, Tools, Challenges*, Cheltenham: Edward Elgar, pp. 1–26.

Bowie, N. E. and Dunfee, T. W., 2002, "Confronting Morality in Markets," *Journal of Business Ethics*, 38(4): 381–393.

Burns, J. and Spar, D., 2002, *Hitting the Wall: Nike and International Labor Practices*, Harvard: Harvard Business School, Case 9-700-047.

Chandler, G., 2009, "The Amnesty International UK Business Group: Putting Human Rights on the Corporate Agenda," *Journal of Corporate Citizenship*, 9(33): 29–34.

Clean Clothes, 1999a, "Letter to Philip Knight" <https://archive.cleanclothes.org/news/4-companies/956-an-open-letter-to-phillip-knight-ceo-of-nike-inc.html> accessed on March 29, 2017.

Clean Clothes, 1999b, "Answer to All the Signatories of the Clean Clothes Campaign's Open Letter" <https://archive.cleanclothes.org/news/1016.html> accessed on March 29, 2017.

Consumer International, 2017 <www.consumersinternational.org/what-we-do/consumer-protection/sustainable-consumption/consumer-information-for-sustainable-consumption/> accessed on August 8, 2017.

de Bakker, F. G. A., 2012, "Exploring Networks of Activism on Corporate Social Responsibility: Suggestions for a Research Agenda," *Creativity & Innovative Management*, 21(2): 212–223.

de Bakker, F. G. A., den Hond, F., King, B. and Weber, K., 2013, "Social Movements, Civil Society and Corporations: Taking Stock and Looking Ahead," *Organization Studies*, 34(5–6): 573–593.

De Geer, H., 2002, "Business and Society," in: Zsolnai, L. (ed.), *Ethics in the Economy: Handbook of Business Ethics*, Oxford: Peter Lang, pp. 59–80.

De Geer, H., Borglund, T. and Frostenson, M., 2009, "Reconciling CSR With the Role of the Corporation in Welfare States: The Problematic Swedish Example," *Journal of Business Ethics*, 89(Supplement 3): 269–283.

Domask, J., 2003, "From Boycotts to Global Partnership: NGOs, the Private Sector, and the Struggle to Protect the World's Forests," in: Doh, J. P. and Teegen, H.

(eds.), *Globalization and NGOs: Transforming Business, Government, and Society*, Westport, CT: Praeger, pp. 157–185.

Doorey, D. L., 2011, "The Transparent Supply Chain: From Resistance to Implementation at Nike and Levi Strauss," *Journal of Business Ethics*, 103(4): 587–603.

Dowling, J. B. and Pfeffer, J., 1975, "Organizational Legitimacy: Social Values and Organizational Behavior," *Pacific Sociological Review*, 18(1): 122–136.

Fransen, L. W. and Kolk, A., 2007, "Global Rule-Setting for Business: A Critical Analysis of Multi-Stakeholder Standards," *Organization*, 14(5): 667–684.

Frostenson, M. and Borglund, T., 2006, *Företagens sociala ansvar och den svenska modellen* (The Social Responsibility of Firms and the Swedish Model), SEIPS Report 2006:9, Stockholm: SIEPS.

Frostenson, M., Helin, S. and Sandström, J., 2015, *Hållbarhetsredovisning: Grunder, praktik och funktion* (Sustainability Reporting: Foundations, Practice and Function), 2nd ed., Malmö: Liber.

GP, 2005, "Stora företag kan göra mycket" (Large Corporation Can Do Many Things) <www.gp.se/nyheter/sverige/stora-f%C3%B6retag-kan-g%C3%B6ra-mycket-1.1220812> accessed on August 8, 2017.

Grafström, M., Göthberg, P. and Windell, K., 2015, *CSR: Företagsansvar i förändring* (CSR: Corporate Responsibility in Flux), 2nd ed., Malmö: Liber.

Greenpeace, 2017, "Our Core Values" <www.greenpeace.org/international/en/about/our-core-values/> accessed on August 8, 2017.

Greenpeace International Annual Report, 2015 <www.greenpeace.org/international/Global/international/publications/greenpeace/2016/2015-Annual-Report-Web.pdf> accessed on February 23, 2017.

GRI, 2016, *GRI 101: Foundation 2016*, Amsterdam: Global Reporting Initiative <www.globalreporting.org/standards/media/1036/gri-101-foundation-2016.pdf> accessed on August 10, 2017.

GRI, 2017a, "About GRI" <www.globalreporting.org/Information/about-gri/Pages/default.aspx> accessed August 10, 2017.

GRI, 2017b, "GRI's History" <www.globalreporting.org/information/about-gri/gri-history/Pages/GRI's%20history.aspx> accessed on August 8, 2017.

Grolin, J., 1998, "Corporate Legitimacy in the Risk Society: The Case of Brent Spar," *Business Strategy and the Environment*, 7(4): 213–222.

Higgins, W. and Tamm Hallström, K., 2007, "Standardization, Globalization and Rationalities of Government," *Organization*, 14(5): 685–704.

Hudson, B. A. and Bielefeld, W., 1997, "Structures of Multinational Nonprofit Organizations," *Nonprofit Leadership and Management*, 8(1): 31–49.

IFRC, 2017, "Our Vision and Mission" <www.ifrc.org/en/who-we-are/vision-and-mission/> accessed on August 7, 2017.

ISO, 2017a, "ISO 26000 – Social Responsibility" <www.iso.org/iso-26000-social-responsibility.html> accessed on August 8, 2017.

ISO, 2017b, "About ISO" <www.iso.org/about-us.html> accessed on August 8, 2017.

ISO, 2017c, "Guidance on Social Responsibility" <www.iso.org/obp/ui/#iso:std:iso:26000:ed-1:v1:en:sec:A> accessed on August 8, 2017.

Jenkins, R., 2001, *Corporate Codes of Conduct: Self-Regulation in a Global Economy*, Technology, Business and Society Programme Paper Number 2, April 2001, Geneva: United Nations Research Institute for Social Development <www.unrisd.org/80256B3C005BCCF9/(httpAuxPages)/E3B3E78BAB9A886F80256B5E00344278/$file/jenkins.pdf> accessed on August 10, 2017.

Jutterström, M., 2006, "Corporate Social Responsibility: The Supply Side of CSR-standards," *Score Working Paper 2006–2*, Stockholm.

Klein, N., 2000, *No Logo*, London: Flamingo.

Kolk, A., van Tulder, R. and Welters, C., 1999, "International Codes of Conduct and Corporate Social Responsibility: Can Transnational Corporations Regulate Themselves?" *Transnational Corporations*, 8(1): 143–180.

KPMG, 2013, *European Responsible Investment Fund Survey 2013*, Luxemburg: KPMG.

Lindenberg, M. and Bryant, C., 2001, *Going Global: Transforming Relief and Development NGOs*, Bloomfield, IN: Kumarian Press.

Lin-Hi, N. and Blumberg, I., 2011, "The Relationship Between Corporate Governance, Global Governance, and Sustainable Profits: Lessons Learned From BP," *Corporate Governance: The International Journal of Business in Society*, 11(5): 571–584.

Lounsbury, M., 2005, "Institutional Variation in the Evolution of Social Movements: Competing Logics and the Spread of Recycling Advocacy Groups," in: Davis, G. F., McAdam, D., Scott, W. R. and Zald, M. N. (eds.), *Social Movements and Organization Theory*, Cambridge: Cambridge University Press, pp. 73–95.

Lydenberg, S. and Sinclair, G., 2009, "Mainstream or Daydream?: The Future for Responsible Investing," *Journal of Corporate Citizenship*, 9(33): 47–67.

Majoch, A. A. A., Hoepner, A. G. F. and Hebb, T., 2017, "Sources of Stakeholder Salience in the Responsible Investment Movement: Why Do Investors Sign the Principles for Responsible Investment?" *Journal of Business Ethics*, 140(4): 723–741.

McCarthy, J. D. and Zald, M. N., 1977, "Resource Mobilization and Social Movements: A Partial Theory," *American Journal of Sociology*, 82(6): 1212–1241.

Micheletti, M. and Stolle, D., 2007, "Mobilizing Consumers to Take Responsibility for Global Social Justice," *The Annals of the American Academy of Political and Social Science*, 611(1): 157–175.

Micheletti, M. and Stolle, D., 2008, "Fashioning Social Justice Through Political Consumerism, Capitalism, and the Internet," *Cultural Studies*, 22(5): 749–769.

Mitchell, R. K., Agle, B. R. and Wood, D. J., 1997, "Toward a Theory of Stakeholder Identification and Salience: Defining the Principle of Who and What Really Counts," *Academy of Management Review*, 22(4): 853–886.

Morgan, G., 2007, "Globalization and Organizations," in: Knights, D. and Willmott, H. (eds.), *Introducing Organizational Behaviour and Management*, London: Thomson, pp. 440–479.

MSF, 2017, "About MSF" <www.msfaccess.org/content/about-msf> accessed on August 8, 2017.

Nike, 2017, "Sustainable Performance Innovation" <www.nike.com/us/en_us/c/sustainability> accessed on August 8, 2017.

Oxfam, 2017, "Our Purpose and Beliefs" <www.oxfam.org/en/our-purpose-and-beliefs> accessed on August 8, 2017.

Pfeffer, J., 1978, *Organizational Design*, Arlington Heights, IL: AHM Publishing Corporation.

Pfeffer, J. and Salancik, G. R., 1978, *The External Control of Organizations*, New York: Harper and Row.

PRI, 2017a, "About the PRI" <www.unpri.org/about> accessed on August 8, 2017.

PRI, 2017b, "Signatory Directory" <www.unpri.org/directory/> accessed on August 8, 2017.

PRI, 2017c, "PRI Launches Proxy Voting Declaration System" <www.unpri.org/press-releases/pri-launches-proxy-voting-declaration-system> accessed on August 8, 2017.

PRI, 2017d, "Collaboration Platform" <www.unpri.org/about/pri-teams/esg-engagements/collaboration-platform> accessed on August 8, 2017.

PRI, 2017e, "Global Networks and Outreach"<www.unpri.org/about/pri-teams/global-networks-and-outreach> accessed on August 8, 2017.

Reinalda, B., 1999, "NGO Influence on International and Transnational Politics," in: Arts, B. and Van Roozendaal, G. (eds.), *The Influence of Non-Governmental Organizations on International and Transnational Politics*, Nijmegen: Nijmegen University Press, pp. 7–13.

Sahlin-Andersson, K., 2006, "Corporate Social Responsibility: A Trend and a Movement, But of What and for What?" *Corporate Governance*, 6(5): 595–608.

Schwartz, M., 2003, "The 'Ethics' of Ethical Investing," *Journal of Business Ethics*, 43(3): 195–214.

Sethi, S. P., 1994, *Multinational Corporations and the Impact of Public Advocacy on Corporate: Nestlé and the Infant Formula Controversy*, Amsterdam: Kluwer.

Sjöström, E., 2009, *Shareholder Influence on Corporate Social Responsibility*, Stockholm: EFI.

Suchman, M. C., 1995, "Managing Legitimacy: Strategic and Institutional Approaches," *Academy of Management Review*, 20(3): 571–610.

Tamm-Hallström, K., 2008, "ISO Expands Its Business Into Social Responsibility (SR)," in: Boström, M. and Garsten, C. (eds.), *Organizing Transnational Accountability: Mobilization, Tools, Challenges*, Cheltenham: Edward Elgar, pp. 46–60.

Teegen, H., Doh, J. P. and Vachani, S., 2004, "The Importance of Nongovernmental Organizations (NGOs) in Global Governance and Value Creation: An International Business Research Agenda," *Journal of International Business Studies*, 35(6): 463–483.

Thorsell, J. and Abrahamsson, H., 2003, "Att ställa företag till svars" (Making Firms Responsible), in: Magnusson, Å. (ed.), *Det globala ansvaret: Sjutton röster om internationellt företagande och etik* (The Global Responsibility: Seventeen Voices on International Business and Ethics), Stockholm: Ekerlids, pp. 180–197.

Tomson, K., 2008, *Amnesty in Translation: Ideas, Interests and Organizational Change*, Doctoral dissertation from the School of Business, Stockholm: University of Stockholm.

USAS, 2017, "About" <http://usas.org/about> accessed on August 8, 2017.

Vakil, A. C., 1997, "Confronting the Classification Problem: Toward a Taxonomy of NGOs," *World Development*, 25(12): 257–270.

Windell, K., 2006, *Corporate Social Responsibility under Construction: Ideas, Translations, and Institutional Change*, Doctoral Dissertation No. 123 from the Department of Business Studies, Uppsala: Uppsala University.

Zadek, S., 2004, "The Path to Corporate Responsibility," *Harvard Business Review*, 82(12): 125–132.

6 Scrutinizers: Media

Helena Buhr, Stefan Arora-Jonsson and Josef Pallas

The authors are grateful to Maria Grafström and Pernilla Petrelius Karlberg for their input to the chapter.

Introduction

Chapters 3–5 have indicated, among other things, that media organizations play significant roles in the field of corporate governance. In the present chapter, we will focus on media organizations as scrutinizing and assessing corporations and their activities. Particularly important for our analysis is the rise of specialized business media that cover events, actors and processes in different sectors, industries and even entire economies. However, before doing so, a few words should be said about the relationships between media and organizations in more general terms and then how these relationships can be situated into a context of corporate governance.

Media—here broadly defined in terms newspapers, TV, radio and social media technologies created for the production, circulation and sharing of information, facts and opinions (Couldry 2012)—speak not only to those that are financially and materially interested in corporations, for example investors, customers, employees, labor unions, regulators and a variety of NGOs. Media coverage and scrutiny is relevant also for intermediaries such as those that we mentioned in previous chapters in this book: business analysts, advisors, lobbyist, consultancies and think tanks. Through their extensive reach and importance for the multiplicity of corporate stakeholders and those mediating between these stakeholders and corporations, media are highly involved in influencing and structuring the web of actors that constitute the landscape in which corporations of various types navigate and operate. But media are by no means fully independent and unaffected by the organizations they cover and scrutinize. Media live in a complicated symbiosis with those they cover, not only by being dependent on corporations for revenue reasons (e.g., advertising) and as a primary source of information on which media report (Olasky 2013). The extant public relations and strategic communication literature suggests that media can be approached also as a tool (i.e., channel) or as an arena that can be used to serve interests and agendas of the actors being covered by the media (see Frandsen and Johansen 2017 for an overview).

At a more general level, we can understand such a dual role of media (i.e., shaping the landscape in which organizations operate and being subject to attempts on the part of the very organizations that are covered) in terms of institutional embeddedness, thereby recognizing the relationship between media and organizations as situated in collectives, amidst a set of relations that influence how the two types of actors act vis-à-vis each other (Ihlen and Pallas 2014). This perspective allows us to situate the role(s) of media into an analytical space between individual actions and societal structures. Or, as Couldry and Hepp (2016) argue, social reality in most contemporary societies is to be seen as medially constructed not only with respect to how media coverage frames what people, in their various roles, talk about and how they understand it but also as a tool or platform for human interaction (for instance when using social media such as Twitter, Facebook, Snapchat, etc.)—that is, tools and structures with their own sets of rules and norms about what such an interaction should look like. In a context of corporate governance, two important aspects are essential in such a perspective, namely media's influence on the *structural* and *cognitive* characteristics of the institutional environment in which organizations operate. The structural aspect puts the emphasis on relationships and interconnectedness between media and other societal actors in terms of shared relational, technological and spatial dependencies between media and the subjects of their scrutiny. The cognitive aspect directs our attention toward common systems of beliefs, values and meaning as holding together what media and their audiences recognized as relevant, legitimate and proper behavior. The cognitive aspect also captures that these shared systems of value and meaning are not static but evolve over time, and as a consequence of the conflicting—or often even incompatible—expectations societies have both on the media and on organizations. Together these two aspects suggest that the degree to which media and organizations internalize and make sense of the competing expectations will be decisive for how the results of media coverage form not only the behavior of individual organizations but also the structures within which shared norms, rules, practices and prescriptions for adequate organizational behavior, and the way it should be understood, evaluated and acted upon, are developed, proliferated and legitimized (Schultz, Suddaby and Cornelissen 2014).

The ways in which media shape social realities—and thereby also governing structures in which organizations are embedded—are by no means disconnected from purposeful as well as unintended efforts by corporations and their representatives who deal with the media in activities ranging from daily work to long-term strategic planning. The relationship of corporations with the media differs, however, from the systems of governance that were analyzed in Chapters 3–5. First, as we argued earlier, through their scrutiny and subsequent public judgments, media bring new stakeholders and their values and preferences into interaction with corporations. The media's role in expanding the stakeholder groups is well-known from the political sphere (cf. Baum 2002; Esser and Strömbäck 2014) as well as from the corporate one (Jonsson and Buhr 2011; Bednar 2012). But similar developments can also be observed in areas such as science (Pallas and Wedlin 2013), the public sector (Schillemans 2012) or religion (Lövheim and Lynch 2011). The media and the mediatization of these spheres not only raise awareness of new types of audiences (i.e., stakeholders), the rationales of the media also indicate what adequate or possible responses to these audiences can be expected. Second, and relatedly, although most news-producing actors are incorporated as profit-seeking firms, the media sphere is penetrated by distinct journalistic values, preferences and work routines that emphasize scrutiny and independence from economic interests (Gamson et al. 1992; Altheide and Snow 1979). These ideals make interactions between the media and corporations highly contested (Pallas and Fredriksson 2013). As we hinted earlier, both parties live in an uneasy symbiosis with each other, not least due to the fact that corporations and the media also share common technological platforms that enable them to partake in each other's production and distribution of symbolical means (Raviola and Norbäck 2013).

While recent scholarship has uncovered particular aspects of the interactions between the media and corporations, few comprehensive reviews of the topic have been undertaken. Rather, the existing literature on relations between the media and business organizations is split into many theoretical camps, including strategic communication and public relations, organizational institutionalism, population ecology, strategic management and the reputation literature. Due to such theoretical partitioning, limited attention has been paid to the embeddedness of the media and corporations. In line with the general thesis of this book, we propose in this chapter that the various interfaces between corporations and the media—though they may appear as separate at first glance—inform one another in powerful ways. To fully understand the role of the media for the governance of corporations and the impact of those interactions on field-level processes, we need to take a broad perspective that transcends traditional analytical levels and a priori theoretical boundaries (Pallas, Jonsson and Strannegård 2014).

Our argument will proceed as follows. First, we will set the stage for our analysis by giving a historical overview of the growth of specialized business media as well as business coverage in the traditional media. Next, we will present an inventory of different roles by which media influence contemporary organizations and the values, norms and practices that guide the governance of modern corporations. Thereafter, we will discuss how corporations respond to and negotiate the mediatized environments in which these different roles play out. The chapter concludes with a discussion about the nature of governance that arises in the interactions between the media and corporations.

The Global Expansion of the Business Media

As already indicated, over the past few decades the business media have undergone a significant expansion throughout the Western world (see, e.g., Duval 2005; Kjaer and Slaatta 2007; Carroll 2010; Grafström and Windell 2012). Today the business media transcend geographical boundaries and are important carriers of information in the global economy. Specialized business outlets have gained a prominent position not only among journalists but also among corporations and in society at large (Gavin 1998; Slaatta 2003; Machin and Niblock 2010). Business newspapers, in particular in the English language, have evolved into global voices that reach broad audiences. The *Financial Times*, for instance, since 2015 owned by the Japanese Nikkei Co., is published in five editions—the United Kingdom, Continental Europe, the United States, Asia and Middle East—and is printed in 40 countries on six continents. Its distinct pink paper has evolved into a widely recognized symbol for business news. In addition, the US-based *Wall Street Journal* is found in offices, business schools as well as homes around the globe. Besides traditional printed outlets, the web media and television constitute other growing providers of business news.

Alongside global media organizations, national media outlets have developed into important bridges between global and local economies. Since the 1960s, for instance, national business press organizations in Europe have met in their shared professional association, the European Business Press (EBP), a federation with 43 members in 23 European countries. In addition to the *Wall Street Journal Europe*, prominent members are the German *Handelsblatt*, the French *Les Echos* and *EurActiv* (EBP 2017). Among the newly founded business media in Europe, we find business newspapers in transition economies such as Estonia, Latvia, Lithuania, Russia, Poland and Slovenia. During the 1990s, the Swedish media conglomerate, Bonnier Group, exported its concept of the business daily, *Dagens industri* (Industry Today), by founding sister newspapers in eight countries (Risberg and Ainamo 2007).

The expansion of business news has also made broader imprints in the structures of news production. Recent longitudinal studies on business news developments show an expansion of business news not only in specialized newspapers but also in the general media. One of the best-documented examples of how the general newspapers started to pay more attention to economic issues comes from a comparative longitudinal study of the Nordic countries of Denmark, Finland, Norway and Sweden. In these countries, the number of articles on economic issues in the main business and general dailies increased on average by 150% from 1960 to the 2000s (Kjaer, Erkama and Grafström 2007: 137). This development reached also other media outlets, and the large broadcast and cable networks have introduced separated business shows. Therefore, the recent expansion of business news would be even more impressive if broadcast, cable, and the web media were also included. The emergence of new business news platforms on the web is rapid, and the number of new outlets—such as the Internet version of the *Financial Times*, *The Economist*, *Les Échos*, *La Tribune*, *Handelsblatt*—has dramatically escalated (cf. Thurman and Myllylahti 2009). These and similar websites, blogs, forums and communities discussing business and financial news have grown rapidly during the last decade, often at the expense of traditional newspapers, thereby dramatically changing the landscape of the business news market (cf. Adams 2007; Thurman and Myllylahti 2009). Such developments also have far-reaching consequences for the way business news is produced, delivered and presented to the audience (Raviola 2010). Chaffee and Metzger (2001) thus suggest that the expansion of media channels—including among other things the Internet and other portable technologies—leads to demassifying and individualizing of communication (Chaffee and Metzger 2001: 369; Hodkinson 2007). Similarly Kline and Burstein (2005) argue that political, business and culture news reporting is—due to the emergence of technological means such as blogs or wikis—increasingly relying on user-produced content (Thorsten 2008; Grafström and Windell 2010). These new technologies not only direct a change in the form and content of business news but also challenge the established relations between business, the media and their audiences. (For further historical accounts of management media, see Engwall, Kipping and Üsdiken 2016.)

Four Roles of the Business Media

We started this chapter by arguing that there are different roles by which the media influence contemporary organizations and the values, norms and practices in which governance of corporations is embedded. Among these roles, that of scrutinizing is particularly significant of course. However, three other roles are equally important for the shaping of corporate behavior, namely *informing*, *agenda-setting* and *legitimizing*. In the following, we will examine these four roles in turn as they have been summarized and discussed by Fredriksson and Pallas (in press).

Scrutinizing

The role as scrutinizer extends the work of media with providing information to include critical accounts of events, issues and activities and to expose misconduct, injustices, power abuse and other moral, ethical, economic and social ills and wrongdoings to a wider public (Ettema and Glasser 1998). As argued earlier, the level and extent of what information the media provide to their readers and listeners, and the willingness and ability to scrutinize such information critically, is dependent on the media system within which media organizations operate. In media studies, scrutinizing journalists attempt search to uncover the "true nature" of reality where such reality is altered for purposes of power elites, for instance. Media scrutiny is about choosing topics from a stance of what is morally right and wrong but based on thorough and evidence-based research. However, the moral stance of media does not reflect universal values but rather interpretations of what such values mean in relation to the public interest (de Burgh 2000).

However, for corporations, the critical and investigative media scrutiny is decisive for a slightly different effect. Broadly speaking, media scrutiny of organizations finds expression at two levels: evaluation and judgment of individual organizations and an aggregated assessment of collectives of organizations, such as sectors or industries. This phenomenon is commonly used in branding, for instance, whereby the positive associations of a particular brand are strategically employed to brand another unrelated product (Wernerfelt 1988; Jonsson, Greve and Fujiwara-Greve 2009). But such an associative and aggregated effect also works in opposite direction—that is, a negative effect of media scrutiny is not restricted to the individual organizations being scrutinized. Because of their influence on public perceptions, the media can tarnish the reputation of entire classes of organizations. Attractive and commonly held images produced by the media can easily become available and transferable for assessing and judging other organizations (Kuran and Sunstein 1999). Literature on media rankings is another illustrative example of the dynamics through which the media influence organizations both individually and collectively (Fombrun 1998; Espeland and Sauder 2007). By way of constructing, proliferating and using variety of comparative tools for describing and assessing specific aspects of organizations (such as sales performance, workplace inequality, financial stability or capacity to innovate), the media translate individual performance into a metric evaluation than can be related to evaluations of other organizations. In other words, media scrutiny tends to judge organizations in terms of better or worse within a specific group of organizations. Again, a crucial argument here is also that the media as scrutinizers produce analytical tools that follow the working routines and preferences of the media. These tools reduce complexity by simplifying what is used as a basis for evaluation; they introduce elements that underpin general validity by way of standardizing measurements across different types or groups of organizations, and they create a sense of relevance to a variety of audiences by making their coverage and judgments readily accessible and dramaturgically popular (Pallas, Wedlin and Grünberg 2016; Pallas and Wedlin 2013).

Informing

Another fundamental role of media is to gather and provide information on various accounts. From a democratic perspective, societies and their citizens are dependent on media for information about relevant aspects of their lives (Kovach and Rosenstiel 2001). This includes coverage of events, issues and developments within areas that relate to peoples' political, economic, social, environmental and cultural realities. In such a role, the media not only serve as a source of information within these areas but also provide their audiences with important input into processes by which they form their opinions and values and upon which attitudes, general perceptions and behaviors are built (Dimbleby and Burton 1992). Transforming such a general and democratic role into a context of corporate governance, this process implies that organizations craft their structures, activities, relations and decisions based on the activities, events and issues that the media include in their coverage (Einwiller, Carroll and Korn 2010). Media reporting on regulatory frameworks within the pharmaceutical industry, disruptions on commodity markets, development of housing and labor prices or scientific progress in various disciplines are examples of areas where organizations are dependent on their provision of mediated information.

However, media scholars are generally reluctant to regard media reporting as free from the agendas, interests and preferences of media organizations—especially when these are commercial news-producing entities. For instance, in national contexts dominated by market mechanism (i.e., a liberal media system) with a low share of public service media, the information provided by media actors populating such a context is characterized by a greater focus on commercial qualities of the information provided. Aalberg, Van Aelst and Curran (2010) argue here that the soft news (e.g., news focusing on entertainment, disasters, accidents) has grown at the expense of fact-based news coverage of public affairs, and, obviously, this trend is not only significant in the market-liberal societies. Several studies show also that the development of the information-providing role of the media follows certain general patterns, such as media convergence and increased interdependencies between news-producing and news-consuming actors (Jenkins 2004). In a context of political and financial reporting, to mention just two examples, research shows that economic and political actors are increasingly central as a primary source of information that the media deliver to their audiences (Knowles, Phillips and Lidberg 2017).

Agenda-Setting

Media do not simply transfer information to and between various societal actors. They also select what information is newsworthy and relevant to pay attention to, thereby shaping cognition and making some issues more salient than others. Or, simply, people tend to focus more on areas and issues that have been introduced and proliferated through the work and coverage of the media. Communication and media studies commonly address such an impact of news media on people and other societal actors within the framework of "agenda-setting theory." In the original writings of McCombs and colleagues, agenda-setting is studied in a context of political reporting where, by selecting and focusing on specific political areas and issues, the media influenced and shaped the attention and attitudes of voters. Or, as it was put by McCombs and Shaw (1972: 176), "The pledges, promises and rhetoric encapsulated in news stories, columns, and editorials constitute much of the information upon which a voting decision is made."

Analogously, underlying the agenda-setting influence of the media on corporations is the argument that social reality of organizations and those interested in these organizations is to a large extent medially constructed by the information accessible via news reporting. Research on the emergence and spread of new managerial practices is one area of empirical work that has illustrated how the attention of organizations to new areas, issues or models can be associated with the proliferation of these issues and models in the media (Alvarez 1998). In this literature, a few examples of medially diffused managerial methods, including, among others things, quality management models (i.e., Six Sigma), corporate social responsibility practices (i.e., Global Compact Performance Model) or accounting and financial control tools (i.e., the Balanced Scorecard), have been extensively covered by the media, and organizations of various types have not been late to adopt these methods. By paying extensive and explicit attention to these and many other managerial models, the media indicate to their readers not only what practices, activities, values or priorities should or should not be paid attention to. These models also need to be presented in media-friendly format to increase the probability of being noticed by the audience (Sahlin-Andersson and Engwall 2002). In this process, agenda-setting is also a transformative process in that it reduces the complexity of the issues covered, focusing on aspects that are appealing and easy to pick up by a variety of actors populating the shared contexts in which corporations operate.

However, the agenda-setting role of the media is not limited to bringing up and making certain issues and topics more salient and accessible, which constitutes first level of agenda-setting. News media are also involved in second-level and third-level agenda-setting (Guo, Vu and McCombs 2012). Whereas the media exert an impact on the scrutiny and judgments of individual as well collective audiences by way of directing attention to a selection of relevant issues, the second level of agenda-setting is closer to the notion of framing and priming (Scheufele and Tewksbury 2007). Simply put, in the framing and priming processes media introduce and attach not only normative stands (e.g., positive or negative) regarding what is being subjected to media coverage and scrutiny. The media also offer the readers clues and suggestions how these stands are to be interpreted and acted upon. Thus the media directly influence how the public evaluates and judges selected issues, topics or activities. Moreover, there is also evidence of third-level agenda-setting. This is a process through which media interconnect scrutiny and social judgment of certain issues or behavior with other issues. In other words, media provide audiences with ideas and suggestions how individual issues and perceptions of these issues relate to each other, and how such a totality of judgment should be understood and acted upon.

Legitimizing

As argued earlier, news coverage concerns not only issues and topics with an eye to informing audiences about individual issues, topics, events or activities. Media also seek to approach the subject of their scrutiny from a position where it can be presented, understood, evaluated and judged in relation to what is perceived as appropriate within a relevant context and based on the subject's degree of conformity with the norms, values and rules permeating and governing such a context. Thus, media coverage legitimizes or delegitimizes the subject of scrutiny by connecting it to a generalizable phenomenon or category within different areas of social life, such as politics, culture, business, family, religion or science (Curran and Gurevitch 2005). For instance, film critics working for a newspaper not only review films on the films' own premises (as it would in a case of ranking). Films are described and evaluated also based on the film's qualities as belonging to predefined categories (genres) of movies. But the legitimizing process is not only about ascribing and explaining specific topics, issues and events as belonging to preset categories. Legitimizing also highlights how media coverage influences the very subject of their scrutiny by giving it recognizable and normative meaning and values. Taking the example of film criticism again, when a film is presented as belonging to a specific genre (e.g., political thriller), certain expectations are created that both the audience and filmmakers have to relate to in both their current and their future work. Thus, how a political thriller movie will perform depends to a certain degree on how it lives up to the audience's definition (here formed by the film critics) of a good political thriller.

In the management literature, the legitimizing role of media is about evaluating and judging the behavior of an organization in relation to taken-for-granted and widely accepted norms, rules, values and expectations that are common to the majority of actors populating a given industry, market or field (Pollock and Rindova 2003). Important mechanisms by which the media legitimize organizations and their behavior are simplification, stereotyping and categorization. Simplification refers to reducing the number and complexity of aspects and characteristics used for evaluation and judgment; by stereotyping, media are able to use criteria for scrutiny and judgment that are widely recognizable and accepted; and categorization serves to interpret the scrutiny within a context of preset categories such as industry classifications (Jonsson, Greve and Fujiwara-Greve 2009). These mechanisms facilitate sense-making and reduces the uncertainty that shareholders might experience when facing scrutiny of new stock exchange opportunities, for instance, as Pollock and Rindova (2003) nicely illustrated in their work. The core argument here is that organizations that fall neatly into predefined categories are often considered more legitimate, whereas those that do not suffer loss of legitimacy.

Recent work on the development of the Swedish mutual fund market in the period 1990–2005 is another example of how the media have contributed to the generation of aggregate market structures through the formation of micro-level actor behavior. Jonsson and Buhr (2011) found that the media influenced the very criteria that investors used when evaluating financial products. Investors that initially were not price-sensitive became so after the media taught them to pay attention to price. As a result, high-price firms lost market shares in the aggregate market.

Three Roles of Corporations in Relation to the Media

So far, we have discussed how the media change meaning systems in line with their four roles (scrutinizing, informing, agenda-setting, legitimizing). However, these roles of the media are not autonomous and independent from the efforts and influences exercised by the subject of media attention (e.g., corporations). The question arises then—how do modern corporations contribute to shaping the field-level governance structures in the course of their interaction with the media? In answering such a question, we need to move beyond professionalization of corporate media activities within a context of specialized communication and media units and to regard corporate understanding of responses to media as a part of ongoing field practice. These efforts are prevalent in recent and ongoing studies of business corporations (Pallas and Fredriksson 2013), political parties (Esser and Matthes 2013), health sector organizations (Blomgren, Hedmo and Waks 2016), universities (Engwall 2008; Lövgren 2017) and public bureaucracies and governmental agencies (Schillemans 2012; Fredriksson and Pallas 2016). In empirical terms these studies suggest three main roles through which organizations within different societal sectors partake in shaping their individual as well as field-level media practices and interactions—namely, (1) production and circulation of media material: *the news providing role*, (2) organizing of interaction settings: *the media interaction role* and (3) introduction of professional routines and practices: *the media practice building role.*

The News Providing Role

Existing research suggests that the materials that corporations—and organizations in general—circulate to the media have a significant impact on content as it finally appears in the media (e.g., Cantelmo 2001; Grünberg and Pallas 2013; Craig and Deephouse 2014; Laursen and Valentini 2015). However, when designing such material, corporations are affected by a spectrum of external pressures, including expectations on what content that should appear in various outlets. The material that corporations circulate covers different aspects of their financial performance, but also non-financial topics such as social and environmental engagement or changes in management. Further, analyses of corporate texts find that corporations often adjust to the requirements of specific audiences (cf. Callison 2003; Fredriksson 2014; Rehnberg 2014). Corporate texts, presentations and stories play an important role in building relations with strategic audiences such as shareholders, customers, competitors and the media. Yet other studies support such a view by seeing the texts, signs and other symbolic artifacts produced by organizations as a way of expressing compliance with ideas that attract the interest of not only the various stakeholder groups but also (and even primarily) the media (Schillemans 2012; Esser and Matthes 2013; Strömbäck and Van Aelst 2013). In this context, Kjaer (2007) and Ihlen and Pallas (2014) argue that corporations respond (e.g., by way of media training, recruitment of professionals such public relations consultants or former journalists, development of internal communication guidelines, etc.) to the pressures and interest of the media. Such a response finds expression mainly through an increased orientation toward news material that is relevant for public scrutiny in terms of evaluation and assessment.

For instance, Pallas (2007) argues that corporate news material, while seemingly heterogeneous, follows an underlying logic and exhibits significant similarities. Despite the fact that news frames used by corporations are selected on the basis of the intended audience and with specific outcomes in mind, the corporate media texts arise in relation to a field-level practice, values and preferences regarding how news material should be produced (both in terms of content and format) and distributed (see also Pallas and Fredriksson 2011). This finding is corroborated by other empirical studies (cf. Curtin and Rhodenbaugh 2001; Kjaer and Langer 2003; Schultz, Castelló and Morsing 2013) that suggest a blending of the expectations of external stakeholders and journalistic standards of assessments of newsworthiness—that is, media logic in the production of corporate media material. One important consequence of this close collaboration and co-production of corporate news is the provision to the media of material that can be directly used in the media production processes, which fits in with an ever-increasing marketization of news production (cf. Grafström et al. 2006; Czarniawska 2011; Grünberg and Pallas 2013).

In sum, by way of the production and distribution of press releases, quarterly and annual reports, press kits, stories, pictures and written comments the business organizations actively take part in the activities that shape the form and content of information that is available to different stakeholder groups. The characteristics of corporate media material suggest that, even if corporations are also highly involved in providing and supporting their own views and preferences, the dominant discourse in the corporate messages is relatively consistent with the prevailing values, preferences and working routines of the media.

The Media Interaction Role

Corporations are also involved in shaping the organizational settings for their interactions with the media. In their studies of business news development

Grafström et al. (2006) and Grünberg and Pallas (2013) show that interactions between various news-producing actors such as news agencies and financial analysts are highly organized and coordinated (see also Czarniawska 2011). Most important are the organizing activities that take place at the borders between organizations and their environments. These occur in what we, inspired by Thompson (1967), refer to as boundary-spanning units (cf. also Grünberg and Pallas 2009 and further in Chapter 7) that are rapidly introduced as a response to increasing media activities and the need to retain good corporate brand, political support or financial resources (for empirical examples, see Pallas 2007; Engwall 2008; Grandien and Johansson 2016).

Such corporate units that are established to deal with the media are naturally influenced and shaped by legal requirements, from existing professional norms, and by imitations of other successful examples found in the field (Engwall 2008: 33). Furthermore, there are strong dependency relations that are reflected in the setup of corporate—media interactions. A study of corporate websites conducted by Kent, Taylor and White (2003) shows that organizations that are dependent on a specific audience for their survival tailor their communicative and media-oriented components closely to what this audience may need. Similarly, Callison (2003) points out that highly ranked and more medially exposed companies are more likely than lower-ranked and less medially exposed companies to provide press rooms including media texts and other material supporting their interactions with the media representatives. The medially exposed companies are also more likely to adapt to requests from the media as regards the standardization of the material provided from the press rooms as well as the structure, labeling, and accessibility of their Internet sites (*ibid.*: 30, 36–38; see also Schillemans 2012 and Lövgren 2017 for examples from the public sector).

According to Ericson, Baranek and Chan (1989), the organizational arrangements, conditions and strategies are necessary components of company—media interactions and negotiations (see also Gammal 1997; Pallas 2007; and Grandien and Johansson 2016 for similar reasoning). These authors introduce different types and levels of regions or stages and closures available to organizations in their negotiations with the media. These illustrate the different ways in which corporations and the media interact with one another depending on the way information or knowledge is defined in specific situations. "Front regions" are open to public scrutiny, and the organizations make information about activities conducted within these regions accessible to the media either with full publicity or partially, with some degree of censorship. Information defined as secret or confidential belongs to the "back regions," where private business is conducted and media journalists have limited or no access (Pallas 2007: 184).

A number of empirical studies also suggest that the way corporations manage their interactions with the media should be examined with regard to different organizational levels. Here it is argued that we should pay attention to interactions between organizations and the media as greatly affected by the separation of various communication units or functions (e.g., media communications, public affairs communications, financial communications and CSR communications) within the organizations (cf. Christensen and Langer 2009). Such separation affects the internal coordination of the media activities and has direct consequences for the way the interactions with the media are organized. These consequences include, among other things, the quality and the amount of information being handled and exchanged between the organization and the media as well as the character and type of personal relations between the company spokespersons and specific journalists (cf. Nierenberg 2004; Dozier, Grunig and Grunig 2013). Through direct relations and personal ties to journalists, corporations take an active part in influencing the way in which the interactions with media are structured and carried out. This is the case not only in specific contexts but also if we regard more long-lasting arrangements. Employment of former journalists and other media professionals with extensive personal ties to leading media outlets is here again a widely recognized corporate strategy that has been documented in a number of studies (cf. de Lange 2000; Neijens and Smit 2006, Westphal and Deephouse 2011).

Thus, corporations are to be seen as active organizers of media interactions. Through the aforementioned activities and structural arrangements, the organizations provide physical, relational and situational settings in which the media are treated and responded to not only with specific news in mind but also in accordance with routinized and formalized practices and processes that journalists and their organizations recognize as professional and based in their own production conditions. In that sense, the interactions between corporations and the media are both well structured and organized while also enabling spontaneous encounters and engagements.

The Media Practice Building Role

Corporate activities aimed at successful interactions with the media concern not only involvement in the production of content and creation of influential organizational contexts. It also includes formation of professional values and norms guiding both the specific interactions and their long-term preconditions. The professionalization of relationships between corporations and the media have been analyzed by Tuchman (1978) and Cook (1998), who have argued that we should regard news production—including the relations and activities between the media and their sources—as a part of an institutional practice in which the news media and their sources interact with one another. Such institutional practice refers not only to specific organizational and relational conditions but also to professional rules and norms (Pallas and Fredriksson 2011). Grafström (2006), in her study of the development of business news, gives support to the notion of business—media relations as an institutional practice, as she suggests that the professional logics of general journalists and the educational background of business professionals who enter the field of journalism—together with various organizational platforms and boundaries—have provided guidelines for the performing and organizing of the new institutional practice of business journalism (Grafström 2006: 186–187). Research on mediatization supports such a notion by arguing that different media outlets (including the specialized business press) develop their own working practices, values and routines while also partaking in a more general media logic (Landerer 2013; Klinger and Svensson 2015).

Engwall (2008) points out that professional associations, sectors or clearly defined industries exercise powerful normative pressures on organizations to consider and handle the creation or introduction of media practices that are perceived as effective and matching the expectations of other relevant affiliated parties, as seems to be the case of the higher-education field. He argues that the introduction of professional media and other communication-related activities in the Swedish universities is largely the result of the mimetic and coercive pressures followed by the incorporation of interest on the part of other actors such as the local community, the general public, special-interest groups, decision makers, employees, students and alumni (Engwall 2008: 42). Also, Petrelius Karlberg (2007) illustrates how such a proliferation of professional norms is involved in presenting and explaining organizations to the media. In a survey on the interaction between media and a highly exposed CEO, she found that the ideals of media logic were strong within the studied company, at the levels of communication staff, executive teams and the CEO herself. The media were expecting the spokespersons of the organization to be "trained in media interaction" and the lack of such performance is regarded as a failure to follow professional norms and expectations.

However, corporations are by no means to be perceived as passive in adapting and adopting to these field practices. As has been shown in a study of 13 major Swedish corporations, corporate communication departments and their media professionals are actively involved in influencing entire field practices of business—media interactions. Here it is evident that corporations partake in the content and form of business news through long-term collaboration with and adaptation to the media, rather than through struggles over specific news items. The corporations were also found to be actively involved in influencing established norms and ideas governing news production—that is, norms that transcend the context of individual news items or relations of the organizations with specific media outlets (Pallas 2007: 194–195). For example, through their membership in various professional associations and organizations or their participation in providing seminars and training programs, companies contributed to the promotion of their own solutions within the framework of the field practice. They also participated on a regular basis in external seminars, industry meetings, public debates and research projects, in all of which they described their own experience of—and their reflections upon—the conduct of the activities between their organizations and the media. The corporate communication managers and their media relations officers were active in this context particularly often. These people helped present and introduce their company media practices to a wide range of actors—including the media themselves.

These corporate engagements in the formation of field practice illustrate that we cannot regard the media and their business news production solely as an independent institution in its own right (cf. Hjarvard 2008), but rather as closely tied to the activities of other societal actors (Couldry and Hepp 2016). The empirical evidence suggests that corporations (as well as any types of organizations) have a significant part not only in adjusting to the external requirements on the way their media activities should be organized and performed; the organizations also play an important role as constituents and co-creators of such requirements (Pallas and Fredriksson 2013).

Interactions Between the Media and Corporations in the Field of Governance

Pulling together the threads of the different strands of literature, it is clear that the relationship between media organizations and corporations extends far beyond that of the scrutinizer and the scrutinized. Management literature usually explains corporate behavior by examining the multitude of actors surrounding a focal corporation (Freeman 1984; Donaldson and Preston 1995). This positioning of the individual firm at the center of the analysis provides an understanding of the media as invading the corporate territory. Traditional media research, on the other hand, starts from the opposite direction by emphasizing the influences and pressures on media organizations and their work. While this literature conceptualizes the interaction between the media and organizations in terms of political processes, power games and struggles over the control of resources and information, its chief concern is with changes in "the what" and "the how" of media reporting. Hence, such a perspective represents the flipside of the management literature by center staging the media.

As argued throughout this book, our aim is to foreground a perspective with blurred boundaries between organizations and their environment, and in the case of this chapter, between organizations and the media. Instead of one party controlling and managing the other party's behavior and actions, our empirical research reveals that the media and corporations continuously negotiate what is to be regarded as leadership, business and what pieces of information will be turned into news. Media organizations are not omnipotent actors in the agenda-setting process—as is sometimes projected in organization literature. Organizations work consciously to be at the top of the minds of the media in their agenda-setting activities of media (Deephouse 2000). At the same time, business leaders consume media images of themselves and other business leaders and learn the aesthetics, ideals and norms of mediated leadership presentations. In these interaction processes, corporations to a great extent incorporate the logic of media production.

An illustrative example of this reciprocal process is the co-production of the most "routine" and mundane of business reporting: quarterly results. A close look at how this is actually done reveals a stunning degree of reciprocal interactions between corporations and the media. Ethnographically inspired trackings of the actual chain of events from release of quarterly results of 141 corporations Grafström et al. (2006) and Grünberg and Pallas (2013) show how different actors struggled for attention and how the media and corporations meaningfully orient activities toward each other. The production of this piece of business news is a complex process that includes several different actors with both competing and common interests. The interactions were guided by well-established routines. The different actors specifically were addressing the genre of the quarterly report, meaning that they knew not only what to do but also when, where and with whom to do it. In its bare essence, a quarterly result report is a set of numbers. The way these were translated into business news is guided by a set of routines.

One central routine was that the coverage of corporate quarterly reports was organized around common principles of news value and time. What constituted news value differed across the media organizations, depending on their specialization and their target audiences; likewise, they differed in their views on time. For news agencies, time of distribution was absolutely critical, and the publication process was optimized to literally gain seconds. For analysts in business magazines, on the other hand, the exact same numbers were turned into business news over a time horizon of a week or so. All actors involved knew whom they were interacting with and the needs of those partners, generating a complex system of interlocking needs and services (see also Czarniawska 2011).

Our studies show that media interact with corporations in a far broader sense than setting time lines and negotiating the content and precision of quarterly reporting. As discussed, the media provide information to a variety of corporate stakeholders; they set the agenda and direct attention to specific questions and issues; they scrutinize individual corporations as well as whole industries, and they legitimize new firms and organizational forms. Corporations, at the same time, are involved in reciprocal media-related activities. They contribute input for media material through subunits specializing in communication and public relations. There is also evidence that other actors—such as business and financial analysts, non-governmental organizations (NGOs), customer groups, and associations—are highly involved in affecting the way the media and business organizations interact with each other. These actors provide the media with opinions, interpretations and evaluations of the corporation and its leaders. Thereby these actors constitute an important facilitator or destructive force influencing the corporate image, reputation and legitimacy.

Our institutional approach, considering a field of governance with media as an important actor, sheds light on these complex interactions. Institutional literature pays attention to activities and interests of actors beyond the immediate outcome of their interactions with each other, placing the influences of business-media interactions on broader social orders such as organizational fields or institutional practices (cf. DiMaggio 1983; Lawrence and Phillips 2004). Hence, interactions between the media and corporations are characterized by embedded agency (cf. Seo and Creed 2002; Thornton and Ocasio 2008). Journalists and business people alike are located in a context of norms, structures and meaning that enable their actions. Such actions, at the same time, are the building blocks of field dynamics.

Through our studies, we see corporate-media interactions as reproducing field structures and sometimes, when it is malleable, also altering the field. We see three dimensions as particularly important in this. *First*, the duality between field structures and practices appears to be particularly salient in times of change. Historical shifts in the field have important implications for business and media interactions; in periods of turmoil, routines for media interactions are no longer taken for granted (Pallas and Fredriksson 2011, 2013). Similar findings are reported in earlier institutional literature. For instance, Glynn and Lounsbury (2005) found that changes in media reviews of the Atlantic Symphony Orchestra corresponded to a broader shift from an aesthetic to a market logic following a strike among musicians in 1996. *Second*, we find that other actors in the field of governance—such as clients, suppliers and shareholders—are directly or indirectly influenced by the interactions between corporations and the media. Under other circumstances, such actors have the power to influence the interaction. For example, media content on corporations often contains quotes from security analysts, consultants, customers, state officials and NGOs. Our effort to position the interactions between corporations and the media in the field of governance stresses the importance of multiple types of actors. Future research needs to flesh out how different actors in the field can influence the interaction between corporations and the media.

Third, our findings point to the importance of power and status games, as these are unifying, though still under-examined, themes in the literature on fields, corporations and the media. While political approaches to the media as well as the traditional literature in media and communication studies have started to address these questions, we nevertheless need more research on this topic. Recent research on fields has also started to address the role of politics and contestations in situations where competing interests, logics and rule systems are available (e.g., Thornton, Ocasio and Lounsbury 2012; Cloutier and Langley 2013).

Conclusions

In this chapter, our concern has been to inventory extant research in the intersection of media and organization studies to provide a more coherent theory for how corporations and the media relate to one another. Specifically, we have discussed the emergent governance structures that arise from the interactions between the media and corporations. Over the past decades, organizational researchers have made important progress in understanding the relations between business and the media. However, prior research has focused on individual aspects of this relation and failed to see how interactions between different roles and relationships constitute a broader context of governance.

Our view is that the relation between the media and business is multiplex and subject to ongoing field negotiations. We have presented the media as (1) critical scrutinizers offering their audiences tools and knowledge to critically examine and assess organizations and their activities, (2) providing their audiences with expected and relevant issues and accounts, (3) agenda-setters that influence attention structures and interpretations and (4) legitimizers of new markets, organizational forms, and practices. Through these mechanisms, the media shape how corporations act, how they are managed and the way they are structured. From the perspective of corporations, communication departments are a central tool for actively structuring the media landscape. We have shown that corporations, through these departments, are acting as (1) news providers, (2) media interaction organizers and (3) media practice builders. In this way, corporations are involved not only in the form and content of business news but also in the creation of the institutional practices that guide the long-term media—business interactions. We find that the different roles and activities of the media and corporations are not isolated from one another, but rather are complementary and interwoven.

These conclusions point to the importance of taking a field approach when analyzing interactions between the media and corporations. Instead of focusing on attributes and activities of individual organizations, we are concerned with the ongoing construction of field-wide norms, regulations and meanings systems. Drawing on recent research in organizational institutionalism, we have outlined the dual relationship between business—media interactions and field structures. Interactions between corporations and the media are situated in the field of governance, yet they also shape the structures and culture of that field.

References

Aalberg, T., Van Aelst, P. and Curran, J. P., 2010, "Media Systems and the Political Information Environment: A Cross-national Comparison," *The International Journal of Press/Politics*, 15(3): 255–271.

Adams, J. W., 2007, "U.S. Weekly Newspapers Embrace Web Sites," *Newspaper Research Journal*, 28(4): 36–50.

Altheide, D. L. and Snow, R. P., 1979, *Media Logic*, Beverly Hills, CA: Sage.

Alvarez, J. L. (ed.), 1998, *The Diffusion and Consumption of Business Knowledge*, Basingstoke: Macmillan.

Baum, J. A. C., 2002, *The Blackwell Companion to Organizations*, Oxford: Blackwell.

Bednar, M. K., 2012, "Watchdog or Lapdog?: A Behavioral View of the Media as a Corporate Governance Mechanism," *Academy of Management Journal*, 55(1): 131–150.

Blomgren, M., Hedmo, T. and Waks, C., 2016, "Being Special in an Ordinary Way: Swedish Hospitals' Strategic Web Communication," *International Journal of Strategic Communication*, 10(3): 177–194.

Callison, C., 2003, "Media Relations and the Internet: How Fortune 500 Company Web Sites Assist Journalists in News Gathering," *Public Relations Review*, 29(1): 29–41.

Cantelmo, D. P., 2001, "How PR People Distribute—And the Media Prefer to Receive—News Releases and Other Public Relations Information: The Myth Versus Reality," *Public Relations Quarterly*, 56(3): 15–17.

Carroll, C. E., 2010, *Corporate Reputation and the News Media: Agenda-setting Within Business News Coverage in Developed, Emerging, and Frontier Markets*, London: Routledge.

Chaffee, S. R. and Metzger, M. J., 2001, "The End of Mass Communication?" *Mass Communication and Society*, 4(4): 365–379.

Christensen, L. T. and Langer, R., 2009, "PR and the Strategic Use of Transparency: Consistency, Hypocrisy and Corporate Change," in: Toth, E. L., Heath, R. L. and Waymer, D. (eds.), *Rhetorical & Critical Approaches to Public Relations*, London: Taylor & Francis, pp. 129–153.

Cloutier, C. and Langley, A., 2013, "The Logic of Institutional Logics: Insights From French Pragmatist Sociology," *Journal of Management Inquiry*, 22(4): 360–380.

Cook, T., 1998, *Governing With the News: The News Media as a Political Institution*, Chicago: University of Chicago Press.

Couldry, N., 2012, *Media, Society, World: Social Theory and Digital Media Practice*, Cambridge: Polity Press.

Couldry, N. and Hepp, A., 2016, *The Mediated Construction of Reality*, Cambridge: Polity Press.

Craig, C. E. and Deephouse, D. L., 2014, "The Foundations of a Theory Explaining Organizational News: The VT4 Framework of Organizational News Content and Five Levels of Influence on Its Production," in: Pallas, J., Strannegård, L. and Jonsson, S. (eds.), *Organizations and the Media: Organizing in a Mediatized World*, London: Routledge, pp. 81–95.

Curran, J. P. and Gurevitch, M., 2005, *Mass Media and Society*, 4th ed., London: Hodder Arnold.

Curtin, P. A. and Rhodenbaugh, E., 2001, "Building the News Media Agenda on the Environment: A Comparison of Public Relations and Journalistic Sources," *Public Relations Review*, 27(2): 179–195.

Czarniawska, B., 2011, *Cyberfactories: How News Agencies Produce News*, Cheltenham: Edward Elgar.

de Burgh, H., 2000, "The Emergence of Investigative Journalism," in: de Burgh, H. (eds.), *Investigative Journalism: Context and Practice*, London: Routledge, pp. 32–53.

de Lange, R., 2000, "Public Affairs Practitioners in the Netherlands: A Profile Study," *Public Relations Review*, 26(1): 15–29.

Deephouse, D. L., 2000, "Media Reputation as a Strategic Resource: An Integration of Mass Communication and Resource-Based Theories," *Journal of Management*, 26(6): 1091–1112.

DiMaggio, P. J., 1983, "State Expansion and Organizational Fields," in: Hall, R. H. and Quinn, R. E. (eds.), *Organizational Theory and Public Policy*, Beverly Hills, CA: Sage, pp. 147–161.

Dimbleby, R. and Burton, G., 1992, *More than Words: An Introduction to Communication*, London: Taylor & Francis.

Donaldson, T. and Preston, L. E., 1995, "The Stakeholder Theory of the Corporation: Concepts, Evidence, and Implications," *Academy of Management Review*, 20(1): 65–91.

Dozier, D. M., Grunig, L. A. and Grunig, J. E., 2013, *Manager's Guide to Excellence in Public Relations and Communication Management*, London: Routledge.

Duval, J., 2005, "Economic Journalism in France," in: Benson, R. and Neveu, E. (eds.), *Bourdieu and the Journalistic Field*, Cambridge: Polity Press, pp. 135–155.

EBP, 2017, "The European Business Press Federation (EBP)" <www.business-press.org> accessed on April 28, 2017.

Einwiller, S. A., Carroll, C. E. and Korn, K., 2010, "Under What Conditions Do the News Media Influence Corporate Reputation?: The Roles of Media Dependency and Need for Orientation," *Corporate Reputation Review*, 12(4): 299–315.

Engwall, L., 2008, "Minerva and the Media: Universities Protecting and Promoting Themselves," in: Mazza, C., Quattrone, P. and Riccaboni, A. (eds.), *European Universities in Transition: Issues, Models, and Cases*, Cheltenham: Edgar Elgar, pp. 31–48.

Engwall, L., Kipping, M. and Üsdiken, B., 2016, *Defining Management: Business Schools, Consultants and Media*, New York: Routledge.

Ericson, R. V., Baranek, P. M. and Chan, J. B. L., 1989, *Negotiating Control: A Study of News Sources*, Milton Keynes: Open University Press.

Espeland, W. E. and Sauder, M., 2007, "Rankings and Reactivity: How Public Measures Recreate Social Worlds," *American Journal of Sociology*, 113(1): 1–40.

Esser, F. and Matthes, J., 2013, "Mediatization Effects on Political News, Political Actors, Political Decisions, and Political Audiences," in: Kriesi, H., Bochsler, D., Matthes, J., Lavenex, S., Bühlmann, M. and Esser, F. (eds.), *Democracy in the Age of Globalization and Mediatization*, Hampshire: Palgrave Macmillan, pp. 177–201.

Esser, F. and Strömbäck, J., 2014, *Mediatization of Politics: Understanding the Transformation of Western Democracies*, New York: Palgrave Macmillan.

Ettema, J. S. and Glasser, T. L., 1998, *Custodians of Conscience: Investigative Journalism and Public Virtue*, New York: Columbia University Press.

Fombrun, C. J., 1998, "Indices of Corporate Reputation: An Analysis of Media Rankings and Social Monitors' Ratings," *Corporate Reputation Review*, 1(4): 327–340.

Frandsen, F. and Johansen, W. (eds.), 2017, *The International Encyclopedia of Strategic Communication*, New York: Wiley.

Fredriksson, M., 2014, "Crisis Communication as Institutional Maintenance," *Public Relations Inquiry*, 3(3): 319–340.

Fredriksson, M. and Pallas, J., 2016, "Diverging Principles for Strategic Communication in Government Agencies," *International Journal of Strategic Communication*, 10(3): 153–164.

Fredriksson, M. and Pallas, J., in press, "Media," in: Frandsen, F. and Johansen, W. (eds.), *The International Encyclopedia of Strategic Communication*, New York: Wiley.

Freeman, R. E., 1984, *Strategic Management: A Stakeholder Approach*, Boston: Pitman.

Gammal, D. L., 1997, *Relations Between British Government and the Media in Wartime: An Analysis of the Falklands War, 1982 and the Gulf War, 1991*, Doctoral Dissertation from the Faculty of Social and Political Sciences, University of Cambridge.

Gamson, W. A., Croteau, D., Hoynes, W. and Sasson, T., 1992, "Media Images and the Social Construction of Reality," *Annual Review of Sociology*, 18(1): 373–392.

Gavin, N. T., 1998, *The Economy, Media and Public Knowledge: Studies in Communication and Society*, London: Leicester University Press.

Glynn, M. A. and Lounsbury, M., 2005, "From the Critics' Corner: Logic Blending, Discursive Change and Authenticity in a Cultural Production System," *Journal of Management Studies*, 42(5): 1031–1055.

Grafström, M., 2006, *The Development of Swedish Business Journalism: Historical Roots of an Organisational Field*, Doctoral Dissertation No. 121 from the Department of Business Studies, Uppsala: Uppsala University.

Grafström, M., Grünberg, J., Pallas, J. and Windell, K., 2006, *Ekonominyhetens väg: Från kvartalsrapporter till ekonominyheter* (The Route of the Business News: From Quarterly Reports to Business News), Stockholm: SNS Förlag.

Grafström, M. and Windell, K., 2010, "Nyhetsproduktion i det sociala landskapet" (News Production in the Social Landscape), in: Pallas, J. and Strannegård, L. (eds.), *Medialisering av näringslivet* (The Medialization of Business), Malmö: Liber, pp. 58–76.

Grafström, M. and Windell, K., 2012, "Newcomers Conserving the Old: Transformation Processes in the Field of News Journalism," *Scandinavian Journal of Management*, 28(1): 65–76.

Grandien, C. and Johansson, C., 2016, "Organizing and Disorganizing Strategic Communication: Discursive Institutional Change Dynamics in Two Communication Departments," *International Journal of Strategic Communication*, 10(4): 332–351.

Grünberg, J. and Pallas, J., 2009, "Barbarians at the Gates? Organizations Protection and Promoting their (Non)Technical Cores Through Institutional Boundary Spanning," in: Wedlin, L., Sahlin, K. and Grafström, M. (eds.), *Exploring the Worlds of Mercury and Minerva: Essays for Lars Engwall*, Acta Universitatis Upsaliensis. Studia Oeconomiae Negotiorum 51, Uppsala: Uppsala University, pp. 243–256.

Grünberg, J. and Pallas, J., 2013, "Beyond the News Desk: The Embeddedness of Business News," *Media, Culture & Society*, 35(2): 216–233.

Guo, L., Vu, H. T. and McCombs, M., 2012, "An Expanded Perspective on Agenda-Setting Effects: Exploring the Third Level of Agenda Setting," *Revista de Comunicación*, 11: 51–68.

Hjarvard, S., 2008, "The Mediatization of Society: A Theory of the Media as Agents of Social and Cultural Change," *Nordicom Review*, 29(2): 105–134.

Hodkinson, P., 2007, "Interactive Online Journals and Individualization," *New Media Society*, 9(4): 625–650.

Ihlen, O. and Pallas, J., 2014, "Mediatization of Corporations," in: Lundby, K. (ed.), *Mediatization of Communication*, Berlin: De Gruyter Mouton, pp. 423–441.

Jenkins, H., 2004, "The Cultural Logic of Media Convergence," *International Journal of Cultural Studies*, 7(1): 33–43.

Jonsson, S. and Buhr, H., 2011, "The Limits of Media Effects: Field Positions and Cultural Change in a Mutual Fund Market," *Organization Science*, 22(2): 464–481.

Jonsson, S., Greve, H. R. and Fujiwara-Greve, T., 2009, "Lost Without Deserving: The Spread of Legitimacy Loss in Response to Reported Corporate Deviance," *Administrative Science Quarterly*, 54(2): 195–228.

Kent, M. L., Taylor, M. and White, W. J., 2003, "The Relationship Between Web Site Design and Organizational Responsiveness to Stakeholder," *Public Relations Review*, 29(1): 63–77.

Kjaer, P., 2007, "Changing Constructions of Business and Society in the News," in: Kjaer, P. and Slatta, T. (eds.), *Mediating Business: The Expansion of Business Journalism*, Copenhagen: Copenhagen Business School Press, pp. 159–186.

Kjaer, P., Erkama, N. and Grafström, M., 2007, "The Expansion and Transformation of Business News Content," in: Kjaer, P. and Slaatta, T. (eds.), *Mediating Business: The Expansion of Business Journalism*, Copenhagen: Copenhagen Business School Press, pp. 131–158.

Kjaer, P. and Langer, R., 2003, *The Negotiation of Business News: A Study of Journalist-Source Interaction*, Paper presented at the 19th EGOS Conference in Copenhagen.

Kjaer, P. and Slaatta, T. (eds.), 2007, *Mediating Business: The Expansion of Business Journalism*, Copenhagen: Copenhagen Business School Press.

Kline, D. and Burstein, B., 2005, *Blog!: How the Newest Media Revolution Is Changing Politics, Business, and Culture*, New York: CDS Books.

Klinger, U. and Svensson, J., 2015, "The Emergence of Network Media Logic in Political Communication: A Theoretical Approach," *New Media & Society*, 17(8): 1241–1257.

Knowles, S., Phillips, G. and Lidberg, J., 2017, "Reporting the Global Financial Crisis: A Longitudinal Tri-nation Study of Mainstream Financial Journalism," *Journalism Studies*, 18(3): 322–340.

Kovach, B. and Rosenstiel, T., 2001, *The Elements of Journalism: What News People Should Know and the Public Should Expect*, New York: Crown Publishers.

Kuran, T. and Sunstein, C. R., 1999, "Availability Cascades and Risk Regulation," *Stanford Law Review*, 51(4): 683–768.

Landerer, N., 2013, "Rethinking the Logics: A Conceptual Framework for the Mediatization of Politics," *Communication Theory*, 23(3): 239–258.

Laursen, B. and Valentini, C., 2015, "Mediatization and Government Communication: Press Work in the European Parliament," *The International Journal of Press/Politics*, 20(1): 26–44.

Lawrence, T. B. and Phillips, N., 2004, "From Moby Dick to Free Willy: Macro-Cultural Discourse and Institutional Entrepreneurship in Emerging Institutional Fields," *Organization*, 11(5): 689–711.

Lövgren, D., 2017, *Dancing Together Alone: Inconsistencies and Contradictions of Strategic Communication in Swedish Universities*, Uppsala: Uppsala University (dissertation).

Lövheim, M. and Lynch, G., 2011, "The Mediatisation of Religion Debate: An Introduction," *Culture and Religion*, 12(2): 111–117.

Machin, D. and Niblock, S., 2010, "The New Breed of Business Journalism for Niche Global News: The Case of Bloomberg News," *Journalism Studies*, 11(6): 783–798.

McCombs, M. E. and Shaw, D. L., 1972, "The Agenda-Setting Function of Mass Media," *Public Opinion Quarterly*, 36(2): 176–187.

Neijens, P. and Smit, E., 2006, "Dutch Public Relations Practitioners and Journalists: Antagonists No More," *Public Relations Review*, 32(3): 232–240.

Nierenberg, A., 2004, "Positive Networking Techniques for Media Relations," *Public Relations Tactics*, 11(5): 11–15.
Olasky, M. N., 2013, *Corporate Public Relations: A New Historical Perspective*, New York: Routledge.
Pallas, J., 2007, *Talking Organizations: Corporate Media Work and Negotiations of Local Practice*, Doctoral Dissertation, 133 from the Department of Business Studies, Uppsala: Uppsala University.
Pallas, J. and Fredriksson, M., 2011, "Providing, Promoting and Co-opting: Corporate Media Work in a Mediatized Society," *Journal of Communication Management*, 15(2): 165–178.
Pallas, J. and Fredriksson, M., 2013, "Corporate Media Work and Micro-dynamics of Mediatization," *European Journal of Communication*, 28(4): 420–435.
Pallas, J., Jonsson, S. and Strannegård, L. (eds.), 2014, *Organizations and the Media: Organizing in a Mediatized World*, London: Routledge.
Pallas, J. and Wedlin, L., 2013, "Governance of Science in Mediatized Society: Media Rankings and the Translation of Global Governance Models for Universities," in: Drori, G. S., Höllerer, M. A. and Walgenbach, P. (eds.), *Global Themes and Local Variations in Organization and Management: Perspectives on Glocalization*, New York: Routledge, pp. 295–308.
Pallas, J., Wedlin, L. and Grünberg, J., 2016, "Organizations, Prizes and Media," *Journal of Organizational Change Management*, 29(7): 1066–1082.
Petrelius Karlberg, P., 2007, *Den medialiserade direktören* (The Medialized Manager), Doctoral Dissertation from the Stockholm School of Economics, Stockholm: EFI.
Pollock, T. G. and Rindova, V. P., 2003, "Media Legitimation Effects in the Market for Initial Public Offerings," *Academy of Management Journal*, 46(5): 631–642.
Raviola, E., 2010, *Paper Meets Web: How the Institution of News Production Works on Paper and Online*, JIBS Dissertation Series 65, Jönköping: Jönköping International Business School.
Raviola, E. and Norbäck, M., 2013, "Bringing Technology and Meaning Into Institutional Work: Making News at an Italian Business Newspaper," *Organization Studies*, 34(8): 1171–1194.
Rehnberg, H. S., 2014, *Organisationer berättar: Narrativitet som resurs i strategisk kommunikation* (When Organizations Tell Stories: Narrativity as a Resource in Strategic Communication), Doctoral Dissertation 90 from the Department of Scandinavian Languages, Uppsala: Uppsala University.
Risberg, A. and Ainamo, A., 2007, "Expansion of the Nordic Business Press," in: Kjaer, P. and Slaatta, T. (eds.), *Mediating Business: The Expansion of Business Journalism*, Copenhagen: Copenhagen Business School Press, pp. 101–130.
Sahlin-Andersson, K. and Engwall, L., 2002, "Carriers, Flows, and Sources of Management Knowledge," in: Sahlin-Andersson, K. and Engwall, L. (eds.), *The Expansion of Management Knowledge: Carriers, Flows, and Sources*, Stanford, CA: Stanford University Press, pp. 3–32.
Scheufele, D. A. and Tewksbury, D., 2007, "Framing, Agenda Setting, and Priming: The Evolution of Three Media Effects Models," *Journal of Communication*, 57(1): 9–20.
Schillemans, T., 2012, *Mediatization of Public Services: How Organizations Adapt to News Media*, Frankfurt: Peter Lang.

Schultz, F., Castelló, I. and Morsing, M., 2013, "The Construction of Corporate Social Responsibility in Network Societies: A Communication View," *Journal of Business Ethics*, 115(4): 681–692.

Schultz, F., Suddaby, R. and Cornelissen, J., 2014, "The Role of Business Media in Constructing Rational Myths of Organizations," in: Pallas, J., Strannegård, L. and Jonsson, S. (eds.), *Organizations and the Media: Organizing in a Mediatized World*, London: Routledge, pp. 13–32.

Seo, M.-G. and Creed, W. E. D., 2002, "Institutional Contradictions, Praxis, and Institutional Change: A Dialectical Perspective," *Academy of Management Review*, 27(2): 222–247.

Slaatta, T., 2003, *Den norske medieorden: Posisjoner og privilegier* (The Nordic Media Order: Positions and Privileges), Oslo: Gyldendal.

Strömbäck, J. and Van Aelst, P., 2013, "Why Political Parties Adapt to the Media: Exploring the Fourth Dimension of Mediatization," *International Communication Gazette*, 75(4): 341–358.

Thompson, J. D., 1967, *Organizations in Action*, New York: McGraw-Hill.

Thornton, P. H. and Ocasio, W., 2008, "Institutional Logics," in: Greenwood, R., Oliver, C., Sahlin, K. and Suddaby, R. (eds.), *The SAGE Handbook of Organizational Institutionalism*, London: Sage, pp. 99–129.

Thornton, P. H., Ocasio, W. and Lounsbury, M., 2012, *The Institutional Logics Perspective: A New Approach to Culture, Structure and Process*, Oxford: Oxford University Press.

Thorsten, E., 2008, "Journalistic Objectivity Redefined?: Wikinews and the Neutral Point of View," *New Media and Society*, 10(6): 935–954.

Thurman, N. and Myllylahti, M., 2009, "Taking the Paper Out of News," *Journalism Studies*, 10(5): 1–18.

Tuchman, G., 1978, *Making News: A Study in the Construction of Reality*, New York: Free Press.

Wernerfelt, B., 1988, "Umbrella Branding as a Signal of New Product Quality: An Example of Signalling by Posting a Bond," *RAND Journal of Economics*, 19(3): 458–466.

Westphal, J. D. and Deephouse, D. L., 2011, "Avoiding Bad Press: Interpersonal Influence in Relations Between CEOs and Journalists and the Consequences for Press Reporting About Firms and their Leadership," *Organization Science*, 22(4): 1061–1086.

7 Governance Relations

Lars Engwall, Jaan Grünberg, Josef Pallas, Kerstin Sahlin, Linda Wedlin, Stefan Arora-Jonsson, Helena Buhr, Katarina Buhr, Magnus Frostenson, Ingemund Hägg, Laurence Romani, Lars Strannegård and Karolina Windell

Introduction

The preceding four empirical chapters have extensively illustrated how corporations and other organizations in the governance field come to forge relations. The examples further underscored the extensive range of forms the relations could take and the dynamic character of these relations and their forms. In the present chapter, these findings will be more extensively related to the framework presented in Chapter 2. This chapter will particularly focus on how the different kinds of relations, and their dynamics, can be identified in the preceding four chapters. We then move on to a discussion of the intermediaries in the field of governance—that is, various kinds of organizations, commercial and non-commercial—that take part in the field of governance. Subsequently, we turn to the corporate actions in relation to the three types of governors, and identify corporate strategies and discuss the phenomenon of the editing corporation.

Throughout the chapter, we will deal with the broad question of what brings order to the corporate governance field. Our observation of the corporate governance field as complex and dense with actors and heterogeneous, paraphrasing the classic book title of Robert Dahl (1961), prompts the question: Who governs the corporation?

Governance Relations

Modes of Relations

The evidence provided in Chapters 3–6 allows us to specify two basic types of direct governor relations (cf. Table 7.1): (1) unilateral relations and (2) bilateral relations. The first of these (second column of Table 7.1) is manifested through the power of regulators, market actors and scrutinizers to impose governance measures on corporations. Manifestations of this are formal rules provided by regulators through legislation and allocation decisions by market actors. As far as scrutinizers are concerned, the major expression of unilateral relations of non-governmental

Table 7.1 Types of Relations in the Field of Governance

Relations *Governors*	*Unilateral*	*Bilateral*
Regulators	Legislation	Consultation
Market Actors (Investors)	Allocation Decisions	Negotiations
Scrutinizers (NGOs)	Critique	Dialogue
Scrutinizers (Media)	Scrutinizing	Legitimizing

organnizations (NGOs) is their critique of businesses and other formal organizations, even states, and for the media their scrutinizing. These manifestations primarily depend on formal mechanisms of applying power, and for all these interactions there are well-specified arenas and processes. In our framework, these relations are salient in the governance field, and, when taken together, which entails handling legislation, allocation decisions, critiques and the scrutinizing of the media, they present multiple challenges for the business corporation.

In contrast to unilateral relations, bilateral relations involve interpersonal exchanges between corporations and governance actors (third column in Table 7.1). Our studies clearly show that these relations are an integral part of the governance field. In Chapters 3–6, we saw examples that showed that an essential part of governance was the creation of arenas for interaction, that is, where actors met and discussed governance matters. In terms of regulators we have seen consultations and, for market actors, negotiations with corporations. Scrutinizers, in turn, have exhibited the bilateral relations of dialogue (NGOs) and of legitimizing (media), respectively. The setting of these relations, in rather open arenas, also means that more than one group of governors is often present in one arena.

Our studies have also pointed to the indirect influence on corporations from regulators through the diffusion of norms and ideas from other fields as well as the branding of corporations by market actors. Similarly, scrutinizers are part of a more general norm setting (NGOs) and image making (media). We will return to these indirect relations next in a discussion of intermediaries.

Relational and Governor Dynamics

The large range of governance relations portrayed in the previous chapters also illustrated that the business corporation handles a multitude of relations simultaneously. This in itself entails considerable complexity. Earlier, we recognized that various forces create incentives for actions of the governors. This in turn may lead to dynamics of two significant types in their relations. First, there are *relational dynamics* through which the governance relations may move between the unilateral and the bilateral modes. This was most clearly brought out in Chapter 5, which discussed the role of NGOs, but similar dynamics were present in the other relations between governors and business corporations. For example, we can consider how the unilateral relations between investors and a corporation changed into bilateral relations when the actions of the corporation were assessed as less than proper in relation to established or newly introduced norms (which may involve performance and standards of conduct).

Second, there is the possibility of *governor dynamics* where the corporate governance matters move between the different types of governors. The corporate governance codes discussed in Chapter 4 are examples of situations where corporate scandals that have erupted in the media are debated by scrutinizers in the form of NGOs, leading to a tension of whether there should be self-regulation by market actors or formal law issued by regulators. As a matter of fact, regulators may have reasons to be very favorably inclined toward scrutinizers criticizing certain phenomena for at least two reasons. *First*, attention through scrutinizers will work much faster than the legislative process. *Second*, the criticism of scrutinizers may pave the way for future legislation, or make such legislation unnecessary. In the same way, market actors and scrutinizers may use each other to promote their interests.

Although we have not been able to investigate the aforementioned dynamics in-depth in Chapters 3–6, we can see that in the field of governance, bilateral relations represent opportunities for governors to exert influence beyond what is prescribed in their formal roles (described by the unilateral relations in Table 7.1). Governor dynamics are thus dependent on relational dynamics. By using bilateral relations, concrete issues of governance can be pursued even when the formal channels for influence are closed. A case in point is the importance of having media coverage.

The dynamics of the field of governance is not only an effect of what are called relational dynamics and governance dynamics, however. Another contributing element is the vast number of intermediaries that are active in the field of governance. We will therefore in the following section turn to a discussion of these organizations.

Intermediaries

Introduction

The term intermediaries is traditionally associated with the financial sector and the opportunities for such organizations to address both transaction costs and asymmetric information (Allen and Santomero 2001). When introducing an organizational rather than financial perspective on intermediaries, there are a number of consequences. First, the character of the relation between parties become social, which is underscored by Zucker's observation that intermediaries play a role in establishing trust among organizations (Zucker 1987: 454):

> Since intermediaries "manufacture" trust as a commodity and market it, the actual transaction cost increases, since it often substitutes for "free" trust generated by kin ties or ethnic group membership.

Second, the intermediaries play a role in structuring the social relations in a given field (Suchman 2000). Third, the intermediaries can develop and shape concepts, categories and discourses that are central to structuring a field or a market (Khaire and Wadhwani 2010). However, it is clear that the intermediaries that we identify in the field of governance have a much wider variety of functions in channeling relations, demands and representations. They serve as links between corporations and other actors, but they also mediate among the latter and among themselves. Just as is true for the corporations, these intermediaries are institutionally embedded. Thus the formation of these organizations can be understood as an outcome of institutional processes (cf. Meyer 2009: 46–47). Moreover, these organizations in turn develop their interests, modes of acting, and relations. This means that when they translate stakes, expectations and responses among governing counterparts, they do so against the backdrop of the institutional forces that both frame and constitute their interests and identities. In this way, the intermediaries are active in organizing as well as in the managing of meaning in the field of governance.

To further our understanding of the intermediaries' role in corporate governance, next we will develop an argument concerning first the types of intermediaries and then their function. In so doing, we can make a first distinction between (1) commercial and (2) non-commercial intermediaries. Among the former, we find consultants, and among the latter various kinds of organizations representing corporate members, such as corporate interest organizations.

Commercial Intermediaries

A number of commercial intermediaries have been mentioned in Chapters 3–6. These are formed as business corporations, striving for profit and include financial analysts, news agencies, screening institutes and rating institutes. Many of them have a long record and are thus not new players. The first public relations bureau in the world "the Publicity Bureau," for instance, was founded in 1900 and has since the 1920s, together with other bureaus, constituted an integrated feature of the media and corporate landscape (Ewen 1996).

Many of the commercial intermediaries are consultancies. The previous four chapters pointed to consultants who specialized in investor relations (IR), corporate social responsibility (CSR), media and public relations and consultants specializing in the translation of and response to standards and to scrutinizing activities. We also saw lobbyists who assisted corporations or groups of corporations in their efforts to seek to influence regulatory schemes and political decisions. After World War II, we thus witnessed the development of communication consultants that operate both in the public and private sectors (L'Etang 1999; Johansen 2001). In addition to these more or less specialized commercial intermediaries, modern corporations are surrounded by and work closely together with many management consultancy firms (see further, e.g., Kipping and Engwall 2002; Kipping and Clark 2012; Engwall, Kipping and Üsdiken 2016).

As Meyer and Rowan (1977: 35) noted, "Highly professionalized consultants who bring external blessings on organizations are often difficult to justify in terms of improved productivity, yet may be very important in maintaining internal and external legitimacy." Such an insight suggests that consultant services go beyond that of "extra-worker" or specialized productivity improver. As some extant research suggests, consultants tend to be important carriers of symbolic values (Czarniawska-Joerges 1990). They infuse new meanings to practices within organizations. Such an idea partly contrasts with a traditional view of the consultant as someone who diagnoses a problem and proposes a solution. Rather, consultants tend to engage in "the manipulation of symbolic values" (Fincham 2006: 17). This means that consultants are active in constructing the services that they offer. The intangibility of the services that they provide also implies the construction of the success criteria for their own services. To convince clients of their superiority, a central feature of consulting activities is dramatization of the services that they provide (Clark and Salaman 1998; Berglund and Werr 2000). In our studies, the organizing of meetings and arenas can be interpreted as the production of rituals that confirm and celebrate the efficacy of governance.

These results show, as do the examples from Chapters 3–6, that consultancies—and commercial intermediaries more generally—play important roles in mediating corporate governance. They are active in (1) shaping the activities and responses performed by corporations, (2) representing and presenting stakes placed on corporations and (3) legitimizing corporations and the choice of organizational structure that these corporations form. The presence of commercial intermediaries shows that they are able to turn mediation into commerce. The commercial intermediaries are able to relay and transform information, relations and images that add value and legitimacy to both corporations and governance parties.

Non-commercial Intermediaries

Among non-commercial intermediaries, a significant group is constituted by *corporate interest organizations*—that is, organizations that corporations belong to in order to represent their interests. These are federations of industries, federations of employers, industry associations, etc. However, corporations are also increasingly becoming members of intermediary organizations that have been formed by groups of stakeholders—that is, stakeholder-interest organizations. Examples of the latter that perform a critical function were provided in Chapter 5. Many of these organizations are active in the transnational arena (cf. Djelic and Sahlin-Andersson 2006: 387).

However, Chapters 3–6 also clearly demonstrated that many organizations transcend the distinction mentioned earlier. The Global Compact initiative, analyzed in Chapter 3, is a good example of an organization that was formed in and by an intergovernmental organization. Nevertheless, business corporations, (NGOs) and governmental organizations together formed a network that organizes work on and demands for CSR. This network in turn diffused a normative framework within which corporate operations are assessed and formed.

Many of the NGOs referred to in Chapter 3 have corporations as members, thereby providing the opportunities for dialogue. Consisting of more than 150 national standards institutes, the ISO (International Organization for Standardization) considers itself a network non-profit organization that constitutes a link between the public and private sectors (cf. Chapter 5). Another example of an intermediary that clearly transcends the public-private distinction is the GRI (the Global Reporting Initiative), also examined in Chapter 5. It works closely together with an active multi-stakeholder network to ensure the continuous relevancy and applicability of its guidelines. The formal governance bodies of the GRI include representatives of hundreds of different stakeholders from business, civil society, labor and professional institutions. From 2003 onwards, stakeholder involvement grew as the organizational stakeholder membership program of the GRI was launched, while a stakeholder council, a "Parliament" for the organizational stakeholders, was founded.

As an additional example of the same type of organization, we can mention the European Corporate Governance Institute (ECGI) discussed in Chapter 4, which organizes academics and corporate governance practitioners. In so doing, this institute arranges conferences and projects where ideas about governance develop and are disseminated, for example through their report series.

Even though the organizations mentioned earlier have different constituencies, members, interests and relations with stakeholder groups, corporations and governments, they do share some features. They are largely what Ahrne and Brunsson (2006, 2008) have termed meta-organizations. Their members are other organizations—such as corporations, various stakeholder groups or the like—and their "identity and status are contingent upon the identity and status of the identity and status of [these] members" (Ahrne and Brunsson 2006: 90). Hence, reciprocal relations and interdependences among the many organizations in the field evolve partly because organizations in the field can be at the same time independent of each other as well as organizations and members of intermediary organizations that are important in the governing of these same organizations. The European Public Relations Education and Research Association, the International Public Relations Association (IPRA), and the Public Relations Society of America (PRSA) are examples of such intermediary meta-organizations that are active in media governance relations.

Roles of Intermediaries

On the basis of our empirical work, we have identified three roles of intermediaries (Table 7.2): (1) corporate agents, (2) governor agents and (3) brokers. In

Table 7.2 Roles of Intermediaries

Type of Intermediary	*Corporate Agents*	*Governor Agents*	*Brokers*
Commercial	Lobbyists and Consultancies	Proxy Advisory Services	Financial Analysts
Non-Commercial	Corporate Interest Organizations	Interest Organizations	Think Tanks

terms of corporate agents, we have found among commercial intermediaries, lobbyists and consultancies and among non-commercial intermediaries, corporate interest organizations (second column in Table 7.2). As for governor agents—that is, agents for regulators, market actors or scrutinizers—we have seen proxy advisory services as an example of commercial intermediaries and governor interest organizations among non-commercial intermediaries (third column in Table 7.2). Brokers, our third category, can be exemplified for the two types of intermediaries by financial analysts and think tanks, respectively (fourth column in Table 7.2).

However, the agency of intermediaries is not as straightforward as this typology may suggest. Intermediaries belong to a group of organizations that Meyer (1996) labels as "Others," which "discuss, interpret, advise, suggest, codify, and sometimes pronounce and legislate [and] develop, promulgate, and certify" (Meyer 1996: 244). In later writings, Meyer has described them as "scriptwriters, telling actors how to posture and behave in the good of the whole collective, rather than [functioning as] the interested actors of realist theory" (Meyer 2009: 44). This reasoning points to the importance of those intermediaries in the construction of meaning in the field of governance and in ordering processes in the field.

Irrespective of their commercial orientation and regardless of the three basic roles, intermediaries may act more or less visibly. In the terms of Ervin Goffman (1959) they may operate either backstage or frontstage. In the first instance, they act as scriptwriters and editors and in the second instance as interest-driven actors.

Backstage: Scriptwriters and Editors

Working backstage, intermediaries mediate stakes, demands and expectations on corporations, and mediate responses and demands from the corporations on their various stakeholders. In doing so, we have pointed out that they represent and present various interests, activities and responses. Another way of characterizing their role in governance is to consider these intermediaries as carriers (Sahlin-Andersson and Engwall 2002). They carry the governing efforts and responses between those who seek to govern and those who are governed. When carrying these messages, the carriers also influence and reshape what they mediate. This is important to note, since even when those carriers—or intermediaries—may present themselves as neutral mediators, they engage in activities that are crucial for the circulation and translation of ideas. Such intermediaries not only mediate ideas; they also influence and shape the activities that take place under their auspices. Therefore, in order to analyze how carriers translate and mediate ideas, Sahlin-Andersson (1996) conceptualized them as editors (see also Sahlin and Wedlin 2008). These editors not only report on and transmit ideas and experiences but also formulate and reformulate and thus frame and reshape them in the process. Moreover, they teach (Finnemore 1996)—more or less directly—other organizations how to act in order to be acknowledged as legitimate. Studies of accreditation and ranking bodies (Hedmo 2004; Hedmo, Sahlin-Andersson and Wedlin 2005; Wedlin 2006) and of international organizations such as the OECD (Sahlin-Andersson 2000) have revealed how such editors form prototypes that drive imitation processes and templates that form the basis for assessments of what is good, bad, proper and desirable (Wedlin 2006). Chapter 3 gave two examples (the UN Global Compact and the European Union Emissions Trading Scheme, EU ETS) of regulatory processes where such teaching and learning played a part.

In their role as scriptwriters and editors, in the terms of Goffman (1959), the intermediaries thus act backstage. They are often not situated in the center of corporate presentations or of analysis of corporate developments. They often stay in the background rather, but the mere organizing as such, as well as the editing of messages carried, orders and rationalizes the field. When acting upon the taken-for-granted and institutionalized forces that permeate the field, intermediaries also take part in the self-reproducing processes that characterize institutionalized settings. Intermediaries channel specific interests as well as broad institutions. Meyer noted that scriptwriters "are not really actors, in the standard senses, but rather agents of wider principles—they tell actors how to be and what to do" (Meyer 2009: 44).

However, our studies also suggest that corporations demonstrate the use of intermediaries to legitimize the corporation as well as the actions taken. This has to do with another role that intermediaries are ascribed and promote. They are largely seen as experts on the specific kind of governing relations where they act. Hence, media consultants are experts on the media, financial analysts are experts on IR, CSR consultants are experts on corporate social responsibility and other consultants uphold identities as experts on regulations of various kinds. Therefore, for corporations it sometimes appears important to demonstrate the use of and relation to these experts, so that their activities appear well grounded (cf. Jacobsson 2000; Jacobsson and Sahlin-Andersson 2006).

In their analysis of global orders, Ahrne and Brunsson (2006) point to two additional interlinked modes of ordering in addition to organizing: shared understandings and standardizing. Applying these to our object of study here, we find that the corporate field of governance is ordered by shared understandings—institutional forces—regarding the basis for governance and by shared understandings of the nature or identity of the corporation. In the earlier analysis, we pointed to the intermediaries as scriptwriters and editors. Through such processes, carried messages are represented and reformulated based on these shared understandings. The organizing processes also create order, and, as is shown in Chapter 3 on regulators, these organizations do issue and carry a number of standards and more generally soft regulations.

Frontstage: Interest-Driven Actors

Intermediaries also work frontstage, then being more active and interest-driven. From our analysis, it follows that even those intermediaries who present themselves as interest-less or as "Others" rather than as actors, also develop interests and identities. Previous studies have also shown that intermediaries are not often so actor-less after all. One primary interest that has been shown to guide the developments and activities of such organizations is the interest in organizational survival (Hedmo 2004). When such organizations are being evaluated, they too tend to be assessed in light of the widely spread scripts of what proper organizations should look like, as discussed by Drori, Meyer and Hwang (2009). Hence, even intermediaries at times tend to develop into being bounded and rationalized actors. In addition, intermediaries may develop policy-related interests of their own. One example provided in Chapter 4 on market actors were the proxy advisory services that prescribe what suitable corporate governance practices might be, but at the same time, they are exposed to challenges from regulators. They thus do not always remain the interest-less mediator, but sometimes develop into actors seeking to drive operations in the field more actively in certain directions.

Even if intermediaries often act covertly on behalf of their members or clients, over time they may develop interests and desires of their own, and can develop close relations with various other organizations active in the field. Their activities appear both to be part of ordering processes but also to give rise to quests for ordering. Consultants and industrial associations are no longer necessarily covert actors. Rather, it can be claimed that within several fields, intermediaries are high-profile organizations (e.g., rating agencies), whose brands are used to enhance the credibility of business corporations and their stakeholders.

Intermediaries, Agency and Institutions

Earlier, we showed how the many intermediaries serve to channel demands, expectations and stakes among corporations and their environment. When channeling these demands, expectations and stakes, they thus act as script-writers or editors, and they reflect and reinforce the institutional forces and serve to order and hold together the field of governance. We have characterized those intermediaries at the same time as reflecting and reinforcing institutional forces backstage and being active and interest-driven frontstage. Such a characterization speaks directly to the discussion in organizational institutionalism on the relation of agency and institutions—sometimes understood as a paradox (see Lawrence, Suddaby and Leca 2009).

Indeed, intermediaries are institutionally embedded, and they reflect their environments. These intermediaries, as well as corporations, seek legitimacy as a means of surviving, and such survival depends on whether they are seen legitimate, thus not breaking the taken-for-granted features of the institutional environment (cf. Meyer and Rowan 1977). Therefore, it is central to our analysis to emphasize that the many organizations studied are both institutionally embedded and active. They are interest driven, but the interests are institutionally molded. These findings point to the importance of further research designed to follow the activities and interrelations of the myriad intermediaries in the field of governance, and to analyze how the interests and stakes of these organizations develop with their activities and relations. The organizations in the field at the same time reflect and reinforce dominant institutions, and they seek to shape and drive the field in certain directions; thus while they are institutionally embedded, they perform institutional work (cf. Lawrence and Suddaby 2006; Lawrence, Suddaby and Leca 2009).

Our view of the duality of agency and institutional embeddedness resembles and is illuminated and inspired by the clarification of this relation as formulated by Lawrence, Suddaby and Leca (2009) as well as Battilana and D'Aunno (2009). In line with these authors, we find that in order to explore and elucidate the dynamics of this combined activity, interest-driven behavior, we should develop a multi-contextual analysis, acknowledging the importance of field-level, organizational and individual activities and embeddedness. However, based on our empirical studies we conclude that the very processes of organizing and editing should be brought into the very center of the analysis of corporate governance. It is through the processes of organizing that some stakes are emphasized and some relations are put forward at the expense of others. Frameworks for the carrying and editing of certain demands, presentations and identities are shaped through the processes of organizing, where actors and their institutional embeddedness are formed. Our analysis of governance relations has pointed to both bilateral direct relations and indirect relations that represent sectors of the governance field that are not as heavily institutionalized as unilateral relations, thereby providing settings for institutional development and change through organizing and editing.

Corporate Actions

Our approach thus implies that we emphasize the interaction, that is, what we call governance exchanges, between corporations and the three types of governors in the field of governance. As already pointed out earlier, this does not mean that corporations are passive recipients of governing signals from regulators, market actors or scrutinizers. Instead, in line with work on organizational fields and organizational responses (Kodeih and Greenwood 2013), our research suggests that corporations are both reactive and proactive in these relations. In this context, as should be obvious from the earlier section, intermediaries play a significant role. The commercial intermediaries (i.e., consultancies) add to their competence and capacity by dealing with issues that a specific company wants to address. Similarly, the non-commercial intermediaries (primarily corporate interest organizations) act in the governance field in the interest of their members. Corporations thus use different kinds of intermediaries to handle their external relations. They do this in order to avoid surprising events not only from politics and markets but also from various scrutinizers. In this way, corporations may get information about challenges that may arise and also be able to communicate their views to regulators, market actors and scrutinizers. They may not be able to avoid measures they dislike, but, through their interaction, they may first postpone them and, with the passage of time, negotiate changes in their interest.

However, even if both commercial intermediaries and non-commercial intermediaries may provide very valuable services to corporations, they alone are not sufficient when it comes to corporate responses in the field of governance. In addition, as our research has demonstrated, corporations form elaborated formal organizational structures as reflections of the institutional embeddedness and as ways of responding to and seeking to influence the governing processes and governing relations. Special organizational units have thus been observed in corporations for handling relations to regulators, market actors and scrutinizers.

The creation of these organizational units is in line with the observations that constituted the very start of the theoretical development of organizational institutionalism as formulated by Meyer and Rowan (1977) (cf. also Greenwood et al. 2008). Elaborated formal organizational structures are thus an often-observed outcome of institutionalization (cf. Drori and Krücken 2009; Meyer 2009). Those dynamics of organization are also associated with the organizational dynamics that Power (2007) has pointed to in his studies of how organizations organize uncertainty.

Boundary-Spanning Units

The organizational units that corporations set up to handle uncertainty have many of the features in common with the buffering efforts discussed by Thompson (1967: 20): "Under norms of rationality, organizations seek to buffer environmental influences by surrounding the technical cores with input and output components." Obviously, this statement refers to production processes, and the technical cores relate to production facilities, which can be protected from environmental disturbances by stocks of input goods as well as stocks of finished products. However, it is equally appropriate, we argue, to consider that the strategic apex of organizations, that is, its top management, has to be protected as a technical core. Our research thus shows that top managers use buffering for the "adjustment to constraints and contingencies not controlled by the organization—to what the economist calls exogenous variables" (Thompson 1967: 67). This means that we extend the use of the term from units directly involved in the production. As far as services are concerned, Thompson (1967: 96) himself mentioned sales units in business firms, interviewers in employment agencies, tellers in banks, classroom instructors in schools or universities, caseworkers in welfare agencies, or purchasing agents. Likewise, our research, as illustrated in Chapters 3–6, suggests that the modern corporation is making more and more arrangements to protect the work of top managers. One way for this is the creation of boundary-spanning units, that is, organizational units that are not involved in "coordination (of variables under control) but *adjustment* to constraints and contingencies not controlled by the organization" (Thompson 1967: 67). Many large corporations thus have created such boundary-spanning units to handle governing relations and governing bodies. There are units handling government relations, IR, public relations and media relations, respectively. These in turn require expertise in the areas of law and politics, finance, ethics and journalism (cf. also Scott 1987: 250).

The aforementioned points back to Meyer and Rowan (1977) and their findings that elaborated formal organizational structures were built as reflections of the institutional environment of organizations, and these formal structures tended to be decoupled from the core activities of the organizations. Similarly, we have seen how these special units were created as reflections of the institutional environment and how they were used as ways of taking care of certain stakeholders and certain institutional forces of the environment, thus protecting the management and production units from such forces and often contradictory external demands.

However, the role and dynamics of the boundary-spanning units that we have identified are more complex. We have found that they not only protect the core of the organization but just as much channel and edit those expectations and demands from the environment to the top management of the corporations. For instance, our studies on market actors in Chapter 4 have demonstrated how units for handling IR not only looked after these relations but also organized and staged the relations between top management, the board and investors. Similar examples could be provided for the other governance relations.

Corporate actions thus often meant that the corporate executives had to be activated in representing the corporations, by appearing at meetings or in expressing the corporate view. Likewise, the special corporate information units responded and related to the media but also staged and organized media relations between top management and the media. Moreover, they had very close relations with media organizations. And they shared many of the same ideas and ideals with those working in the intermediary organizations. This becomes especially clear as corporations often recruit their experts for such boundary-spanning units from regulators, market actors and scrutinizers, as well as intermediaries in the field (cf. Engwall 2006:

172 for evidence). There is thus increasing incidence of a phenomenon that is quite parallel to what the French call "pantouflage" (from *pantoufles* = slippers) and what the Americans label "revolving doors" (Etzion and Davis 2008). While the original use of the French term referred to the move between public service or government positions to corporations, we see today many forms of *pantouflage*. People formerly employed within governments (even high-level politicians), NGOs, investment companies and media companies tend to be hired by corporations in order to deal with their former colleagues. For instance, media and public relations units have been built and populated by former journalists and public relations consultants (Pallas 2007; Cornelissen 2008; Tyllström 2010, 2013). As a result, networks of relationships are created between actors in boundary-spanning units and actors in the field of governance. Such relationships are to the advantage of corporations for two reasons. First, the former employees of other organizations bring with them the expertise of their former field of employment and therefore know how their former colleagues reason and work. Second, they are well connected to significant actors in their part of the field of governance. This makes it easier to bridge gaps and to generate initiatives on both sides.

Corporate Strategies

Boundary-spanning units thus clearly function as both buffering and bridging units between the corporations and their governors. They thereby handle and organize the corporate actions to the governing relations and the many demands and expectations of the governors. However, they are also actively seeking to influence and shape the expectations, interests and identities that develop in the field.

Referring to the model we presented in Chapter 2, on the basis of our research we can now identify three strategies that corporations use in combination in their relations to regulators, market actors and scrutinizers (Figure 7.1; see further Engwall 2014). Considering the unilateral relations that we identified, our research has discerned three types of corporate strategies: persuasion, promotion and protection.

The first strategy, *persuasion* is used to influence regulators. As pointed out, these govern through rules and may punish those who do not follow the rules. It is therefore in the interest of corporations to change rules to their advantage, to avoid restrictions on their operations and to avoid punishment. As a result, by means of boundary-spanning units as well as intermediaries, corporations make efforts to persuade regulators to adopt rules that are as advantageous as possible for them. This strategy is often referred to in everyday language as lobbying (cf., e.g., Bouwen 2002).

The second strategy, *promotion*, consists of efforts to communicate to market actors the reputation of the corporation. This strategy includes signaling a positive corporate image, both to customers and providers. In terms of the

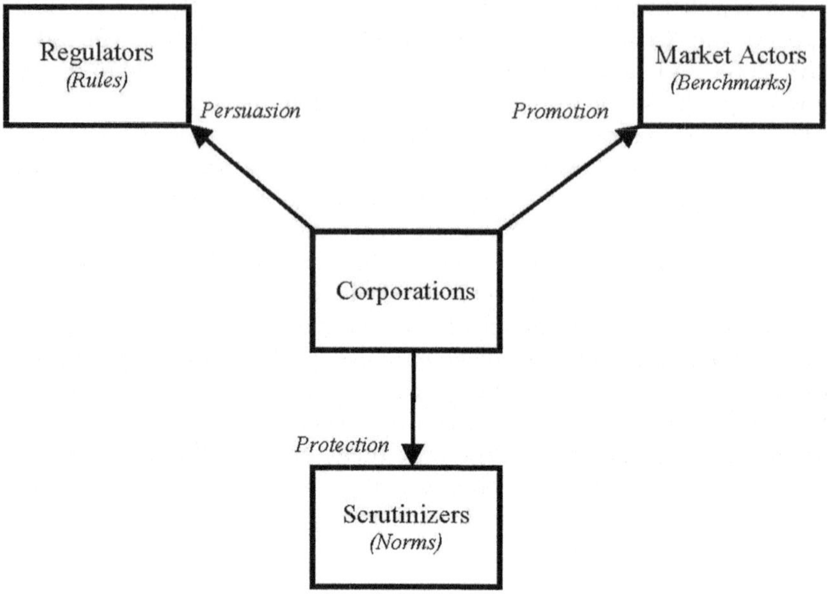

Figure 7.1 Corporate Actions in Relation to Governors

first group, it is a question of influencing the preferences of customers so they choose the particular goods and services of the corporation. And, with respect to providers, it is important to communicate trust to financial markets in order to facilitate their investments. Similarly, signals to the labor market are important for the recruitment of personnel and to suppliers so that deals will be kept.

The third strategy, *protection*, refers to handling criticism from scrutinizers in order to avoid naming and shaming. This strategy often has strong proactive elements. These include the training of top management and other significant corporate actors to deal with scrutinizers as well as the creation of special units to help prepare for scrutiny. In this context, we can expect corporations to respond to the upgrading of certain scrutinizing bodies by adding organizational expertise of their own.

The identification of bilateral and indirect relations complicates the clarity of the three strategies. We have recognized that the relations, and consequently corporate responses as well, are embedded in the field of governance, and the complexity of the relations thus indicates that multiple strategies are likely to be employed. Consider for example how Chapter 6 showed that corporations responded to the media by providing news (promotion), establishing settings for media interaction (persuasion) and influencing media practice through values and norms (protection).

In conclusion, our analysis has thus shown that in addition to intermediaries, boundary-spanning units constitute buffers for the corporate leadership. In the same way as we found that there are bilateral relationships between corporations, regulators, market actors and scrutinizers, in the previous and this section we have identified a similar reciprocity with respect to intermediaries and boundary-spanning units. The intermediaries and boundary-spanning units also activate executives to perform frontstage, using their scripts. In this way, they are instrumental for a significant role in the modern corporation: managing meaning. Needless to say, our discussion of boundary-spanning is equally relevant for other types of organizations than the business corporation, which has been the focus of our discussion.

The use of boundary-spanning units and intermediaries are related. *First*, of course, the task of the boundary-spanning units is to handle relations with other actors in the field of governance. *Second*, it should be noted that individuals in various parts of the field of governance, be they regulators, market actors, or scrutinizers, often know each other to a large extent through their education and earlier employment.

The Editing Corporation

The earlier arguments, and the evidence we provided in Chapters 3–6, point to the critical role of communication for the processes that play out in the field of governance. The intermediaries and boundary-spanning units are all concerned with, and driven by, the importance attached to the way corporations are presented and represented. Representation is thus at the heart of corporate management, and it transcends the role an individual leader plays in managing a corporation. The reciprocal relations and governance processes are concerned with translating activities and operations into texts, speeches, and events, but these activities also lead to communication, organizing and power relations.

As a result, it can be concluded that the critical role of such activities can be seen as constitutive of the contemporary business corporation, which as a result could be characterized as *the editing corporation* (Engwall and Sahlin 2007). This underlines that activities of the units in question are geared to the editing of texts picked up by the corporation from the environment—management ideas, market information, news of competitors and so on—or texts about the company intended for its stakeholders or for other uses. Further, the term *editing* suggests the presence of reciprocal processes in which several individuals and units inside and outside the corporation interact with one another. Moreover, we want to emphasize the fact that such models, ideas, beliefs and texts are often shaped—in fact, edited—according to more or less clearly established procedures and day-to-day routines or, to put it another way, according to certain sets of editing rules.

Looking at the editing work of the corporation as a question of buffering and bridging, we are assuming the existence of a core that requires protection from the pressures to which it is exposed by various governing bodies. Boundary-spanning units partly buffer the corporation from the many governing stakes, but they also channel those demands and expectations to corporate managers. Likewise, intermediaries edit presentations of corporations, and they edit expectations and demands posed on the corporation in the field of governance. In addition, these intermediaries, like the boundary-spanning units, provide both buffering and bridging. In their editing, they may emphasize, for example, some demands or presentations and may play down others; they combine some demands and presentations and disregard others. In this way, as argued earlier, they are important bodies in the governing of corporations, and they largely influence this governing through editing work.

The editing corporation, then, is an organization clearly embedded in the field of governance; it is a corporation in which a great many activities are devoted to managing and organizing for this embeddedness, and to editing work. To take one example from Chapter 6 on the media: the supply of information and routinely planned forms of reporting of quarterly reports (Grafström et al. 2006). Largely these corporations exploit the expected timing and rhythm of the media's news reporting as a means of controlling their own planned media—corporate events. We expect the editing corporation to become increasingly common in a mediatized society.

The edited presentation of a corporation and its activities is not directed at an external audience only. The governors and intermediaries function as mirrors, where the editing corporation appears in an auto-communicative process in which corporate activities are presented, which in turn informs people in the corporation about their own situation and operations. The editing corporation is thus a corporation in which the very core of the corporate business is the representations of it: its brand and its reputation. This has the result that any presentation and report in the media may potentially have a direct and profound impact on the corporate business.

The conception of the editing corporation implies that corporations are found to have wider capabilities to produce and interpret meaning than were considered in earlier research (see, e.g., Fligstein and McAdam 2012: 218). The studies we have presented show that the governance field is structured and organized by multiple organizations that are involved in such meaning production. However, to be successful, corporations need to communicate to their advantage through these structures, thereby participating in a continuous negotiation process among actors in an extended field of governance constituted by regulators, market actors and scrutinizers. These negotiations are often not formal in nature, but rather characterized by efforts to communicate preferred images of the organizations and points of view on specific issues through various channels. They take place in arenas that have evolved considerably in the past decades through the development of media technology and the increased demands for transparency and accountability. In these arenas, persuasion, presentation and protection constitute basic strategies. Like scientists, although with fewer requirements regarding rigor, organizations provide their own arguments as well as counterarguments to arguments they eschew. In this way collaborations between different actors may emerge, develop and fade away.

The concept of the editing corporation thus has implications for more profound discussions of governance. In terms of the critical capabilities of a business corporation, it suggests that two such capabilities are important: (1) capabilities in editing—that is, resources to deal with stories, brands and narratives of the corporation—and (2) capabilities in diffusion, that is, the ability to build relations and channels for dissemination. These capabilities can then build up assets in a pool of reputation, brands and narratives, which in turn can reinforce these capabilities.

Conclusions

Throughout this volume, we have argued that the notion of a governance field is central to the understanding of modern corporate governance. Although the conception of field can be used analytically to analyze a number of settings for collective action (Fligstein and McAdam 2012), we have employed the term governance field in a more specific way. The structures of relations and the structures of organizations that we have identified in our analysis point to patterns that are similar across the governance relations that we have analyzed—that is, regulators, market actors, and scrutinizers.

We also claim that intermediaries play a significant role in the field of governance. For corporations they, like boundary-spanning units, offer modern corporations buffering against signals from governors. As a result, modern top managers have working conditions that differ from those of their predecessors. It may even be an explanation for the findings by Tengblad (2002) that top managers are disturbed by unplanned activities to a much lesser extent than they were according to earlier studies by Carlson (1951), Stewart (1967), Mintzberg (1973) and Kotter (1982). On the other hand, as also shown by Tengblad (2002), they are out of their office more, which should be interpreted a sign of the increasing demand for their appearance in the field of governance to interact with the three types of governors.

Our research also illuminates the classic discussion of how policy and practice can become decoupled in corporate governance. This is in line with findings regarding the creation of boundary-spanning units for the contacts with investors (Adrem 1999; Rao and Sivakumar 1999), which has facilitated what Westphal and Zajac (1998) have labeled the symbolic management of shareholders. Their study demonstrates how long-term incentive plans may be adopted and announced by companies and, although not implemented, still have positive effects on share performance and in fending off other kinds of governance reforms. Similar dynamics apply when it comes to stock repurchase, where CEO power is one of the strong predictors of decoupling (Westphal and Zajac 2001). While our research identifies several mechanisms that may drive decoupling (e.g., buffering), it also shows that the complex web of relations in the field of governance involves a multitude of dynamic relations where it is likely that one measure of decoupling provides the opportunity for governors to exert influence.

Our research also suggests that corporations seek to influence the activities in the field—for example, by contracting consultants or by making use of corporate interest organizations. This will be further evident in the next and final chapter, as we return to the three basic features of our analysis: the field of governance, embeddedness and reciprocity. In addition, we will discuss implications for management theory and practice.

References

Adrem, A. H., 1999, *Essays on Disclosure Practices in Sweden: Causes and Effects*, Lund Studies in Economics and Management, 51, Lund: The Institute of Economic Research, Lund University.

Ahrne, G. and Brunsson, N., 2006, "Organizing the World," in: Djelic, M.-L. and Sahlin-Andersson, K. (eds.), *Transnational Governance: Institutional Dynamics of Regulation*, Cambridge: Cambridge University Press, pp. 74–94.

Ahrne, G. and Brunsson, N., 2008, *Meta-organizations*, Cheltenham: Edward Elgar.

Allen, F. and Santomero, A. M., 2001, "What Do Financial Intermediaries Do?" *Journal of Banking & Finance*, 25(2): 271–294.

Battilana, J. and D'Aunno, T., 2009, "Institutional Work and the Paradox of Embedded Agency," in: Lawrence, T. B., Suddaby, R. and Leca, B. (eds.), *Institutional Work: Actors and Agency in Institutional Studies of Organizations*, Cambridge: Cambridge University Press, pp. 31–58.

Berglund, J. and Werr, A., 2000, "The Invincible Character of Management Consulting Rhetoric: How One Blends Incommensurates While Keeping Them Apart," *Organization*, 7(4): 633–655.

Bouwen, P., 2002, "Corporate Lobbying in the European Union: The Logic of Access," *Journal of European Public Policy*, 9(3): 365–390.

Carlson, S., 1951, *Executive Behaviour*, Stockholm: Strömbergs.

Clark, T. and Salaman, G., 1998, "Telling Tales: Management Gurus' Narratives and the Construction of Managerial Identity," *Journal of Management Studies*, 35(2): 137–161.

Cornelissen, J., 2008, *Corporate Communication: A Guide to Theory and Practice*, London: Sage.

Czarniawska-Joerges, B., 1990, "Merchants of Meaning," in: Turner, B. A. (ed.), *Organizational Symbolism*, Berlin: W. de Gruyter, pp. 139–150.

Dahl, R. A., 1961, *Who Governs?: Democracy and Power in an American City*, New Haven, CT: Yale University Press.

Djelic, M.-L. and Sahlin-Andersson, K., 2006, "Institutional Dynamics in a Re-ordering World," in: Djelic, M.-L. and Sahlin-Andersson, K. (eds.), *Transnational Governance: Institutional Dynamics of Regulation*, Cambridge: Cambridge University Press, pp. 375–397.

Drori, G. S. and Krücken, G., 2009, "World Society: A Theory and a Research Program in Context," in: Krücken, G. and Drori, G. S. (eds.), *World Society: The Writings of John W. Meyer*, Oxford: Oxford University Press, pp. 3–35.

Drori, G. S., Meyer, J. W. and Hwang, H., 2009, "Global Organization: Rationalization and Actorhood as Dominant Scripts," in: Meyer, R. E., Sahlin, K., Ventresca, M. J. and Walgenbach, P. (eds.), *Institutions and Ideology: Research in the Sociology of Organizations*, 27, Bingley: Emerald, pp. 17–43.

Engwall, L., 2006, "Global Enterprises in Fields of Governance," in: Djelic, M.-L. and Sahlin-Andersson, K. (eds.), *Transnational Governance: Institutional Dynamics of Regulation*, Cambridge: Cambridge University Press, pp. 161–179.

Engwall, L., 2014, "Corporate Governance and Communication," in: Pallas, J., Strannegård, L. and Jonsson, S. (eds.), *Organizations and the Media: Organizing in a Mediatized World*, London: Routledge, pp. 220–233.

Engwall, L., Kipping, M. and Üsdiken, B., 2016, *Defining Management: Business Schools, Consultants and Media*, New York: Routledge.

Engwall, L. and Sahlin, K., 2007, "Corporate Governance and the Media: From Agency Theory to Edited Corporations," in: Kjaer, P. and Slaatta, T. (eds.), *Mediating Business: The Expansion of Business Journalism*, Copenhagen: Copenhagen Business School Press, pp. 265–284.

Etzion, D. and Davis, G. F., 2008, "Revolving Doors?: A Network Analysis of Corporate Officers and US Government Officials," *Journal of Management Inquiry*, 17(3): 157–161.

Ewen, S., 1996, *PR! A Social History of Spin*, New York: Basic Books.

Fincham, R., 2006, "Knowledge Work as Occupational Strategy: Comparing IT and Management Consulting, New Technology," *Work and Employment*, 21(1): 16–28.

Finnemore, M., 1996, *National Interests in International Society*, Ithaca, NY: Cornell University Press.

Fligstein, N. and McAdam, D., 2012, *A Theory of Fields*, Oxford: Oxford University Press.

Goffman, E., 1959, *The Presentation of Self in Everyday Life*, New York: Doubleday.

Grafström, M., Grünberg, J., Pallas, J. and Windell, K., 2006, *Ekonominyhetens väg: Från kvartalsrapporter till ekonominyheter* (The Route of the Business News: From Quarterly Reports to Business News), Stockholm: SNS Förlag.

Greenwood, R., Oliver, C., Sahlin, K. and Suddaby, R. (eds.), 2008, *The Sage Handbook of Organizational Institutionalism*, London: Sage.

Hedmo, T., 2004, *Rule-making in Transnational Space*, Doctoral Thesis No. 109 from the Department of Business Studies, Uppsala University.

Hedmo, T., Sahlin-Andersson, K. and Wedlin, L., 2005, "Fields of Imitation: The Global Expansion of Management Education," in: Czarniawska, B. and Sevón, G. (eds.), *Global Ideas: How Ideas, Objects and Practices Travel in the Global Economy*, Malmö: Liber and Copenhagen Business School Press, pp. 190–212.

Jacobsson, B., 2000, "Standardization and Expert Knowledge," in: Brunsson, N., Jacobsson, B. and Associates (eds.), *A World of Standards*, Oxford: Oxford University Press, pp. 40–49.

Jacobsson, B. and Sahlin-Andersson, K., 2006, "Dynamics of Soft Regulations," in: Djelic, M.-L. and Sahlin-Andersson, K. (eds.), *Transnational Governance: Institutional Dynamics of Regulation*, Cambridge: Cambridge University Press, pp. 247–265.

Johansen, P., 2001, "Professionalisation, Building Respectability, and the Births of Canadian Public Relations Society," *Journalism Studies*, 2(1): 55–71.

Khaire, M. and Wadhwani, R. D., 2010, "Changing Landscapes: The Construction of Meaning and Value in a New Market Category—Modern Indian Art," *Academy of Management Journal*, 53(6): 1281–1304.

Kipping, M. and Clark, T. (eds.), 2012, *The Oxford Handbook of Management Consulting*, Oxford: Oxford University Press.

Kipping, M. and Engwall, L. (eds.), 2002, *Management Consulting: The Emergence and Dynamics of A Knowledge Industry*, Oxford: Oxford University Press.

Kodeih, F. and Greenwood, R., 2013, "Responding to Institutional Complexity: The Role of Identity," *Organization Studies*, 35(1): 7–39.

Kotter, J. D., 1982, *The General Managers*, New York: Free Press.
Lawrence, T. B. and Suddaby, R., 2006, "Institutions and Institutional Work," in: Clegg, S., Hardy, C., Lawrence, T. and Nord, W. (eds.), *The Sage Handbook of Organization Studies*, London: Sage, pp. 215–254.
Lawrence, T. B., Suddaby, R. and Leca, B., 2009, *Institutional Work: Actors and Agency in Institutional Studies of Organizations*, Cambridge: Cambridge University Press.
L'Etang, J., 1999, "Public Relations Education in Britain: An Historical Review in the Context of Professionalisation," *Public Relations Review*, 25(3): 261–289.
Meyer, J. W., 1996, "Otherhood: The Promulgation and Transmission of Ideas in the Modern Organizational Environment," in: Czarniawska, B. and Sevón, G. (eds.), *Translating Organizational Change*, Berlin: Walter de Gruyter, pp. 241–252.
Meyer, J. W., 2009, "Reflections: Institutional Theory and World Society," in: Krücken, G. and Drori, G. S. (eds.), *World Society: The Writings of John W. Meyer*, Oxford: Oxford University Press, pp. 36–63.
Meyer, J. W. and Rowan, B., 1977, "Institutionalized Organizations: Formal Structure as Myth and Ceremony," *American Journal of Sociology*, 83(2): 340–363.
Mintzberg, H., 1973, *The Nature of Managerial Work*, New York: Harper & Row.
Pallas, J., 2007, *Talking Organizations: Corporate Media Work and Negotiations of Local Practice*, Doctoral Dissertation No. 133 from the Department of Business Studies, Uppsala: Uppsala University.
Power, M., 2007, *Organized Uncertainty: Designing a World of Risk Management*, Oxford: Oxford University Press.
Rao, H. and Sivakumar, K., 1999, "Institutional Sources of Boundary-Spanning Structures: The Establishment of Investor Relations Departments in the Fortune 500 Industrials," *Organization Science*, 10(1): 27–42.
Sahlin-Andersson, K., 1996, "Imitating by Editing Success: The Construction of Organizational Fields," in: Czarniawska, B. and Sevón, G. (eds.), *Translating Organizational Change*, Berlin: Walter de Gruyter, pp. 69–92.
Sahlin-Andersson, K., 2000, "Arenas as Standardizers," in: Brunsson, N., Jacobsson, B. and Associates (eds.), *A World of Standards*, Oxford: Oxford University Press, pp. 100–113.
Sahlin-Andersson, K. and Engwall, L. (eds.), 2002, *The Expansion of Management Knowledge: Carriers, Flows and Sources*, Stanford, CA: Stanford University Press.
Sahlin-Andersson, K. and Wedlin, L., 2008, "Circulating Ideas: Imitation, Translation and Editing," in: Greenwood, R., Oliver, C., Sahlin, K. and Suddaby, R. (eds.), *The Sage Handbook of Organizational Institutionalism*, London: Sage, pp. 218–242.
Scott, W. R., 1987, *Organizations: Rational, Natural, and Open Systems*, Englewood Cliffs, NJ: Prentice-Hall (Second edition).
Stewart, R., 1967, *Managers and their Jobs*, Maidenhead: McGraw-Hill.
Suchman, L., 2000, "Organising Alignment: A Case of Bridge-building," *Organization*, 7(2): 311–327.
Tengblad, S., 2002, "Time and Space in Managerial Work," *Scandinavian Journal of Management*, 18(4): 543–565.
Thompson, J. D., 1967, *Organizations in Action*, New York: McGraw-Hill.
Tyllström, A., 2010, "PR-konsultbranschens framväxt i Sverige" (The Rise of the PR Consulting Industry in Sweden), in: Pallas, J. and Strannegård, L. (eds.), *Företag och medier* (Corporations and the Media), Malmö: Liber, pp. 169–191.
Tyllström, A., 2013, *Legitimacy for Sale: Constructing a Market for PR Consultancy*, Doctoral Thesis No. 162 from the Department of Business Studies, Uppsala: Uppsala University.

Wedlin, L., 2006, *Ranking Business Schools: Forming Fields, Identities and Boundaries in International Management Education*, Cheltenham: Edgar Elgar.

Westphal, J. D. and Zajac, E. J., 1998, "Symbolic Management of Stockholders: Corporate Governance Reforms and Shareholder Reactions," *Administrative Science Quarterly*, 43(1): 127–153.

Westphal, J. D. and Zajac, E. J., 2001, "Explaining Institutional Decoupling: The Case of Stock Repurchase Programs," *Administrative Science Quarterly*, 46(2): 202–228.

Zucker, L. G., 1987, "Institutional Theories of Organization," *Annual Review of Sociology*, 13: 443–464.

8 Conclusions

Lars Engwall, Jaan Grünberg, Josef Pallas, Kerstin Sahlin, Linda Wedlin, Stefan Arora-Jonsson, Helena Buhr, Katarina Buhr, Magnus Frostenson, Ingemund Hägg, Laurence Romani, Lars Strannegård and Karolina Windell

Introduction

Our aim with this volume is to provide a deeper understanding of the governance of modern corporations and the role of modern corporations in governance. To this end, we formulated the research question as follows:

> *What are the significant characteristics of modern corporate governance?*

To answer this question, we argued from the outset in Chapter 1 that there is a need to develop and complement existing models of corporate governance by focusing on three groups of actors: regulators, market actors and scrutinizers. In Chapter 2, we presented our approach further by pointing to three significant features of the analysis. First, we argued for the appropriateness of focusing on a field of governance consisting of corporations and the three types of governors. Second, we pointed out that this field of governance is characterized by the embeddedness of these organizations. Third, the relations between these organizations are to a considerable extent reciprocal—that is, signals are not only unilateral but often bilateral and even multilateral.

Against this background, in this final chapter, we will now go back to the mentioned three features of the analysis in order to provide our answer to the research question. Finally, we will discuss the implications of our analysis for organizations other than corporations, but also for organization theory, for management education, and for management. In some concluding remarks, we will also elaborate on possible further studies.

An Embedded Field of Governance With Reciprocal Relations

The Field of Governance

Our approach means that we have been able to present a number of significant findings regarding corporate governance on the basis of extant literature and our empirical studies. A basic point of departure for these has been the idea that modern corporate governance encompasses much more than the hierarchical relationship between the principal and the agent. Instead, corporations are parts of a field of governance with a multitude of actors with different interests that interact in more or less symbiotic ways. In this field of governance we have been able to show that, while market actors are important for corporate governance, significant roles are also played by two other types of governors—namely, regulators and scrutinizers (such as non-governmental organizations (NGOs) and the media).

We have also demonstrated that the field of governance is populated by a number of intermediaries that are not part of either the corporations or the governors but nevertheless have important functions in corporate governance. Among these intermediaries, a first category that we have identified is commercial organizations—that is, consultancies directed toward investor relations (IR), corporate social responsibility (CSR), and media and public relations, as well as general management consultants. A second category of intermediaries identified in our research is non-commercial organizations. These are corporate interest organizations and stakeholder-interest organizations. We have also been able to conclude that irrespective of their commercial orientation intermediaries play three basic roles, as corporate agents, governor agents and brokers.

Embeddedness

Chapters 3–6 have portrayed the multitude of actors, activities and governing relations that make up the field of corporate governance in contemporary society. They have demonstrated the institutional embeddedness of corporations and governors. This means that the evidence presented in the previous chapters provides a view of corporate governance that has established how corporations take part in endlessly complex organizing processes. Chapters 3–6 have also established the mobilization of a number of intermediaries and their embeddedness in the field of governance. At the same time, and partly in response to the organizing in the field, the chapters also report on the formation of corporate organizational units and of elaborated formal organizational structures. They present evidence of a more and more densely organized field and more complex formal organizing of corporations. Organizing in the field of governance therefore appears to be a prominent feature of corporate governance. In this way, corporations and governors are becoming increasingly embedded in the field of governance.

We have thus seen in Chapters 3–6 that corporations take part in active processes of organizing and that the governing relations of modern corporations are highly organized. It has also become evident that those many actors are mutually seeking to influence each other and to respond to actions taken by others. In all these cases, stabilized relations evolve between corporations and the multitude of organizations in their environment that represent various stakes. Moreover, corporations as well as those many organizations activate themselves in developing common frameworks, standards, and scrutinizing activities that together form the embedded corporate field of governance. With these processes of organizing, interactions stabilize and strengthen. At the same time new interests, relations and meanings develop with these processes of organizing. Organizing, therefore, appears to be a basic way for actors to respond to various problems—namely, to demonstrate a willingness to act on certain demands and to mobilize actions or resistance. These processes of organizing provide frameworks for actors and activities in the field, thereby creating order in a field characterized by increasing embeddedness.

Our findings of proliferating organizing efforts are also consistent with other research. For example, elaborations of social movement theories have clearly pointed to the importance of organizing for mobilizing and influencing action (Davis et al. 2005). Organizing should therefore be considered a form of mobilizing action, of asserting influence and of ordering contemporary societies. Hence, we argue that it is of fundamental importance for social scholars and social knowledge to portray and explain organizing, its dynamics and its consequences.

Many scholars have also noted the dramatic expansion of organizations in all parts of our society (see, e.g., Drori, Meyer and Hwang 2006, 2009). New organizations, alliances and networks are emerging everywhere. This development once prompted Perrow (1991) to characterize the modern world as a society of organizations. In a later book, where he portrays and analyzes the dramatic expansion of organizations in America, he even declared, "The most important feature of our social landscape is the large organization, public or private" (Perrow 2002: 1). Particularly salient during the post-World War II era is the almost exponential growth of international organizations (e.g., Boli and Thomas 1999), which, according to Drori, Meyer and Hwang (2006), are a dominant feature of globalization. In relation to this development Djelic and Sahlin-Andersson (2006a, 2006b), note the especially active processes of organizing in transnational contexts and demonstrate that an important task for many of these organizations is to issue rules, although they may also be involved in elaborating and activating processes to monitor the adoption and implementation of those rules. Our studies indicate that the presence of these intermediary organizations is a salient aspect of contemporary governance, constituting a relatively novel aspect of organizational society. These intermediaries are not necessarily either large organizations or rule-producing membership organizations. They may very well have small staffs, but they nevertheless wield significant capabilities in carrying messages and scripts between contexts and relations.

In conclusion, we have thus found organizing to be a fundamental institutional force in corporate governance. This occurs in response to problems, new situations and developments. As a result, corporations and governors become increasingly embedded in the field of governance. In this way, organizing shapes organizational actors, their interests, and their stakes.

Reciprocity

Chapters 3–6 have also shown that the three types of governors (regulators, markets actors and scrutinizers) not only influence corporations but also reciprocally impact each other through regulation, benchmarks, and norm setting, as well as influencing and being influenced by corporations through their efforts to promote, persuade, and protect.

Our studies have thus demonstrated the importance of paying particular attention to the reciprocity that characterizes governance relations. This reciprocity means that self-reproducing and self-reinforcing spirals develop so that, for example, as shown in Chapter 6, media attention leads to the formation of media units in the corporations and of corporate strategies for managing media. This, in turn, triggers attention, organizing and strategies from media actors. Along similar logics, corporations have been shown to react to new regulations with special organizing efforts, management and strategies for handling such regulations and with lobbying for or against new regulations among the multiple actors involved (cf. Chapter 3). As demonstrated in Chapter 4, investor relations similarly develop self-reinforcing activity spirals. Strategies are devised for dealing with various groups of investors, and certain activities, such as road shows, are formed as part of corporate relations with investors, both directly and indirectly through media and financial analysts. Lastly, activities involving CSR have clearly escalated with the interplay of corporations and the many organizations and actors in the environment (cf. Chapter 5). Thus when certain issues, such as CSR, arose as a focus of attention among corporations and other organizations alike, this gave rise to extended organizing efforts. Furthermore, as non-governmental and governmental organizations initiated scrutinizing as well as collaborative activities with corporations, this also gave rise to a market for consultancies. New consultancies were created and already-established ones were mobilized within these fields. In this way, various kinds of commercial and non-commercial intermediaries and corporate organizing activities formed and developed in relation to each other. These organizing responses to organizing efforts created the complex—but also ordered—organizational landscape that constitutes the fields of governance.

The reciprocal processes identified result in a large number of organizations and relations, which may give the impression of considerable complexity. Nevertheless, we have not found the field of governance to be anarchical. Rather, our studies show that the organizations in the field use various mechanisms to create order and to appear highly skilled in handling the complexity. Moreover, our institutional analysis has pointed to the fact that the field is "filled with shared understandings of nature, humans, and society" (Meyer 2009: 37). One important shared understanding—with global outreach—is actually, as shown by Drori (2006), the very notion of governance itself. She demonstrated that many organizing and re-organizing efforts are motivated by the need for more and better governance. Likewise, we see the reciprocity of governing and organizing. Organizing forms governance relations and governance relations are framed and shaped by organizing.

Our analysis has focused on the active process of organizing that shapes fundamental aspects of the corporate response to governing efforts as well as important aspects of the processes of governance. Active organizing efforts were found in the field and in the corporations studied. Moreover, these processes of organizing developed in response to each other. Thus, as mentioned earlier, when an organization was created or mobilized in the field, these efforts gave rise to further organizing activities in the field and among the companies in the field. Our research also suggests that there are forces active in pulling governors together. It thus seems to suggest a field-level isomorphism—that is, governance fields have come to evince similar forms of organizing, similar kinds of actors, and the same kinds of interactional patterns. Significant observations of this included the presence of exchange relations across all variants of corporate relations with governors.

Field conceptions of organizing often emphasize the blurring of boundaries and roles. Our studies instead pinpoint a number of organizing processes that produce distinct orders in the governance field. The ordering processes that we have identified may be seen in relation to a number of dominant views of comparative corporate governance studies (e.g., varieties of capitalism or the law and finance perspective). In these, a fundamental assumption has been that national contexts provide a strong institutional grounding that has a lasting influence on governance practices. Our field perspective points to mechanisms that may be driving institutional change. The force of these mechanisms is that they are active in multiple institutional sectors, both nationally and transnationally. In this way, intermediaries are agents in creating mobility for governance ideas, practices and regulation. Thus, we propose that intermediaries and boundary-spanning practices are gradually changing the institutional setup for corporate governance (and other kinds of governance in society).

Our Findings in a Nutshell

To make a long story short, the aforementioned, and the book as a whole, can now be summarized in four points:

First, our analysis has clearly demonstrated that modern corporate governance is much more than the hierarchical relationship between the principal and the agent. Instead, corporations are embedded in a field of governance with a multitude of actors with different interests that interact reciprocally in more or less symbiotic ways.

Second, while regulators and market actors are important for corporate governance, we have identified a third, increasingly important, type of governors—namely, scrutinizers such NGOs and the media.

Third, the three types of governors (regulators, markets actors and scrutinizers), not only influence corporations but also in a symbiotic way influence each other through regulation, benchmarks and norm setting, as well as influencing and being influenced by corporations in various ways.

Fourth, we have shown that corporations act in the field of governance in order to balance uncertainty and freedom of action by employing intermediaries in the field as well as through the creation of boundary-spanning units internally. These arrangements protect top managements through buffering but also activate them in the managing of meaning.

Implications of Our Results

Beyond the Corporation

In this volume, the business corporation has been the central focus. At this point, it is appropriate to reflect on the implications of our results for other systems of governance. Take the regulatory system as an example. Our analysis has indicated a substantial role for backstage work for intermediaries in creating regulation and arenas in order to select groups in bringing regulation about. We have thus confirmed that organizations are appearing and forming everywhere; a number of organizations and organizing efforts are constantly taking shape and shaping governing relations. In line with those previous studies referred to earlier, we also note that organizing appears to be a more or less taken for granted and self-producing response to challenges, problems, incidents and organizing itself. Moreover, the way in which organizations are formed also appears to follow taken-for-granted and widely spread norms or scripts (Brunsson and Sahlin-Andersson 2000; Drori, Meyer and Hwang 2009). Lastly, operations are often monitored and assessed based on how they are organized and on their organizational form. For example, in his studies of the audit society, Power (1997: 82–87) showed that many times the organizing of operations is audited as a proxy for assessing and scrutinizing the operations themselves. Such procedures are partly based on economic reasoning, as it may appear too difficult and too costly to audit operations as such (Power 1997: 88). Furthermore, and of special interest for our reasoning here, there is a widespread fundamental view in society that certain ways of organizing are needed and are supportive of good practices. This fundamental—and widely taken-for-granted view—on the virtues of organizing has been even more clearly demonstrated in Power's studies of risk management and of organizing for uncertainty in society (Power 2007). During the past decade, the setting up of risk committees—the organizing for risk management—has become a widely diffused practice and a given model against which corporations are being assessed and monitored (Power 2007: 153–154). We thus see how the elements of audit are present in the governance field and employed in governance. But we also identify how relational processes are present.

Not only has organizing been shown to be an institution (Zucker 1983), that is, a widespread and more or less taken-for-granted practice in contemporary society. Based on studies of reforms in the public sector, Brunsson and Sahlin-Andersson (2000) directed our attention to the widely spread ideas of what a "real organization" was expected to look like. These widely spread notions of how well-functioning organizations should be formed are not limited to the public sector—but there are more widely diffused notions of "real" or "proper" organizations in society (Meyer and Jepperson 2000; Ahrne and Brunsson 2006). As noted by Drori, Meyer and Hwang (2009: 18) "modern organizations are expected to be bounded, purposive, and rationalized sovereign actors, with great capabilities for effective action towards goals."

All this suggests that organizing is not only a widespread activity with profound consequences but also that organizing is an institutionalized as well as an institutionalizing activity. In characterizing organizing as an institutional force, we also acknowledge that organizing evolves in self-reproducing processes. Significant for these are the many organizations and intermediaries that are formed and mobilized in the field as part of, or in reaction to, specific governing attempts. They mediate between the many actors, activities and relations that make up the field of governance. At the same time, they are subject to forces similar to those we have identified for corporations.

Organization Theory

Our observation of the fundamental importance of organizing was actually one of the important foundations for organizational institutionalism. However, somewhat paradoxically, it may seem, this aspect of institutionalization appears to have been taken for granted also by institutional and organizational scholars, so it has not attracted as much interest as other aspect of organizations. The results presented in this volume not only exemplify that organizations are formed as reflections of institutional environments and of rationalized myths in these environments, we have also seen much of the dynamics through which those elaborated organizational structures are built and self-sustained. It is therefore appropriate to elaborate somewhat on how our results could serve as a basis for the development of theories and insights of organizational institutionalism.

Our field perspective highlights the distributed character of governance. It is through routines, practices, rituals, meetings and dialogues that governance processes play out. The critical capacity of institutional analysis should therefore not fall into the trap of viewing field power as lodged in concentrated units such as command posts and internal governance units (Zald and Lounsbury 2010) or the classical concept of elites (Pettigrew 1992). In keeping organizing and organizations in focus the critical capacity of theory is not displaced. Organizations are staffed, have policies and resources, and have accountable officials and managers, which is essential since accountability is the very point of critique. The centrality of the intermediaries in the field of governance is one topic that deserves such critical analysis.

In order to emphasize the fundamental importance of organizing, Greenwood et al. (2008a) used the term "organizational institutionalism" to characterize the institutional theory that has developed from Meyer and Rowan's seminal article in 1977. These authors remind us of the fact that this line of research started with questions primarily posed around observations of rationalization, diffusion of formal bureaucracies, and the development of elaborated formal organizational structures. Hence, theories of institutionalism presuppose organizing processes, and at the heart of this theory lie research questions concerning how and why organizing evolves. Meyer and Rowan (1977) claimed that elaborated formal organizational structures could not be explained with "prevailing theories [that] assume that the coordination and control of activity are the critical dimensions on which formal organizations have succeeded in the modern world" (Meyer and Rowan 1977: 342). Instead, they showed that such elaborated bureaucratized "formal organizational structures arise as reflection of rationalized institutional rules." The answer furthermore pointed to legitimacy as the fundamental driver for these organizations; thus, "the development of formal rationalized structures is driven not by the pursuit for efficiency, but rather by the pursuit for legitimacy from the environment in which organizations are embedded" (Drori and Krücken 2009: 8). This clearly implies that in order to understand and explain the development of organizational formal structures we need to focus on the interface of such structures and the rules, norms and ideologies of the wider society (Meyer and Rowan 1977). This is particularly important, since, as organizations are created, they develop and elaborate interests, activities and relations, which in turn create new reactions, etc.

While the main body of research that followed Meyer and Rowan (1977) dealt with developments in the "institutional environment" (cf. Greenwood et al. 2008a; Drori and Krücken 2009), not much attention has been paid to analyzing the specific dynamics of organizing in the modern world. This is especially clear when we look at studies of the corporate world. Indeed, studies in the 1980s and early 1990s dealt primarily with individual organizations, their striving for legitimacy, their elaborated formal organizational structures and the decoupling of such structures from their daily activities. Those studies mainly focused on public or non-profit organizations, as these organizations were presumed to be especially sensitive to institutional influences (Greenwood et al. 2008b: 9). Later on, studies in the field of organizational institutionalism expanded to include the corporate sector as well, and the interplay of various kinds of organizations, how ideas and "rationalized myths" travel and diffuse across sectors and around the world. With this development, however, research turned to focus more on the overall patterns of developments in and across fields rather than on the organizing processes of individual organizations. Organizations are often taken for granted also in research. And this may not be so surprising, because, as Brunsson and Sahlin-Andersson (2000) note, social science tends to take its objects of study—individuals, organizations, states and the like—as given (see also Strang and Meyer 1993). A crucial task for future research is therefore to analyze how and why people construct organizations rather than other social forms.

In the research reported in this volume, we combined studies of individual organizations with field-wide studies. We have been able to show how and why individual corporations develop elaborated organizational structures in response to mediated external demands and in response to taken-for-granted notions in the field. Moreover, we have claimed, and illustrated, that organizing itself is just such a taken-for-granted notion that shapes expectations, ideals, interests and activities among corporations as well as other actors in the field. This means, *first*, that to organize—to build organizations or to build certain units within established organizations—is a taken-for-granted and repetitive response to experienced problems or demands for action. *Second*, specific ideas—or rationalized myths—permeate the organizations, the field and the governing processes regarding what proper organizations look like. This rational myth of organizations gives rise to recurrent organizational reforms or, in short, organizing.

Management Education

Academic management education is an innovation in the academic system that started to develop in the late nineteenth century and the beginning of the twentieth century (Engwall 2009: Chapter 1; Engwall, Kipping and Üsdiken 2016: Chapter 4). Since then such education has proliferated and constitutes today a significant part of academic institutions all over the world. This development has not occurred without resistance and criticism, however. Particularly in the early years, representatives of established disciplines expressed deep concern that universities were including business in their curriculum (Engwall and Gunnarsson 1994: Chapter 1; Engwall, Kipping and Üsdiken 2010). Later on, programs of management education were criticized for not meeting academic standards, something that was made particularly public through the reports from the Carnegie Corporation and the Ford Foundation in 1959 (Gordon and Howell 1959; Pierson 1959). This in turn led to the recruitment of behavioral scientists as well as mathematically trained scholars to US business schools (Augier and March 2011). As a result, these became multidisciplinary institutions with increasingly strong publishing ambitions. This development prompted views that business schools had become too academic (Porter and McKibbin 1988), starting a discussion about the tension between rigor and relevance in business schools that has continued ever since. Locke (1996) thus argued that "the American management mystique" had collapsed, while Mintzberg (2004) and Pfeffer and Fong (2002, 2004) questioned what business schools offered. At the centenary of Harvard Business School, Khurana (2007) concluded that the orientation of business education has fundamentally gone in the wrong direction through too strong a focus on market logic. More recently, Locke and Spender (2011) have even claimed that the business schools have thrown our lives out of balance.

The present volume fits nicely into the earlier debate. Our analysis and our findings point to a need to reconsider the curricula of business schools. Although there is always a need for business graduates to be able to gather and interpret accounting figures as well as to perform different kinds of analyses of significant corporate features, a significant implication of this volume is that there are also considerable needs for other types of knowledge and skills in modern corporations.

First, it is clear that the tendency in modern society for presentations of various kinds calls for a stronger need for *critical training*—that is, classical academic training to sort out what is true and what is not true. This, in turn, relates to a basic feature of journalist training, namely to always crosscheck and to have at least two independent sources before believing a story. Such a working rule is of course particularly significant in times when journalistically trained people have "changed sides" and work to disseminate certain images rather than questioning them.

Second, it should be evident from our research that future business education would benefit from a stronger focus on *social and political aspects* of business. It is crucial in the systems we have been analyzing that managers have a basic understanding of the dynamics of the formation of rules, benchmarks and norms. This is particularly important for managers working in transnational corporations facing different cultures around the globe. However, such understanding is also truly essential in domestic markets. This is especially the case for ethical issues, as Khurana (2007) stressed, and in the years after the publication of his book, this has become even more obvious through various corporate scandals.

Third, it seems obvious that *communication skills* need to be stressed even more than before. In the media society of today and tomorrow, it is crucial that managers be able to communicate convincingly in speech and in writing. Rhetoric and language training therefore stand out as important ingredients in future management education.

Management

In the same way as we argue that our findings have implications for management education, they appear to have implications for the recruitment of and demands on executives. The tendencies we have observed may thus imply a new step in the recruitment patterns observed by Fligstein (1990) in his study of corporate control in large US corporations. Our research indicates that a new breed of CEOs may succeed the earlier masters of corporations: first engineers and then marketing specialists, followed by financial managers. This would be a reflection of a change in the corporate environment to a situation, where a number of key functions—production, marketing, and finance—have been handled by routines in specialized units, at the same time as the presenting and defending of the corporate image is becoming more and more urgent. As a result, we would expect increased demands for CEOs to constantly be on stage, and to perform well. This development could lead to the recruitment and promotion of persons with a background in media, communication consulting or even entertainment. At least it will pave the way for the increased involvement of communication consultants preparing and supporting top executives in their work. Media training and communication advice appear to have permanently invaded the field of governance.

Concluding Remarks

In terms of our theoretical foundations, it must be evident by now that we consider the field approach to be highly fruitful for the study of corporate governance. This also means that we suggest that future research in the organization and management field would benefit from extensive use of this approach. Our studies particularly point to the importance of studying processes over time, and we believe that this should be taken further through historical perspectives on the organizing processes in the governance field. In this way, it would be possible, among other things, to shed more light on processes that led to the current situation, thereby also giving some hints regarding future developments.

This means that we are pleading for more in-depth studies into various processes through which rules for corporate behavior are determined. Such studies require extensive research efforts and will require sophisticated social-scientific methods to deal with various kinds of data. Using cross-disciplinary competence, they would contribute to a further development of the framework we have suggested in the present volume. In this way, it would in due course be possible to formulate propositions regarding expected relationships in the field of governance—that is, to point out under what circumstances different kinds of actions are likely to happen. For instance, the interaction of bridges and decoupling mechanisms deserves further study. Such studies may contribute to the debate on the convergence of governance structures. A hypothesis might be that there is partial convergence in areas where there are dense populations of intermediaries.

To be more specific, it appears that more research in the intersection between organizations and governors can explain how tensions between them emerge and how these tensions can be resolved. By attending to these topics, we would for instance learn more about the increasingly significant interaction between corporations and the media. However, the focus on the interaction between business and media can also further our understanding of how corporations are structured and how they act. In particular, future research needs to address questions of how and when media activities reproduce field structures, and when the field is malleable and subject to change.

Those questions are critical for understanding how the media make the modern corporation possible.

Further studies to develop extant approaches to corporate governance are particularly important since the corporate world is continuously changing. Approaches that were once appropriate have therefore become less so over time. This is important to keep in mind also in relation to our own arguments. What we have presented should therefore be considered as a beginning of a new approach, which we—and hopefully others inspired by this volume—will develop and revise as time goes by. For we consider it important always to keep in mind the words attributed to the 1947 Nobel Laureate in Literature André Gide: "Believe those who are seeking the truth. Doubt those who find it."

References

Ahrne, G. and Brunsson, N., 2006, "Organizing the World," in: Djelic, M.-L. and Sahlin-Andersson, K. (eds.), *Transnational Governance: Institutional Dynamics of Regulation*, Cambridge: Cambridge University Press, pp. 74–94.

Augier, M. and March, J. G., 2011, *Roots, Rituals, and Rhetorics of Change: North American Business Schools After the Second World War*, Stanford, CA: Stanford University Press.

Boli, J. and Thomas, G., 1999, *Constructing World Culture*, Stanford, CA: Stanford University Press.

Brunsson, N. and Sahlin-Andersson, K., 2000, "Constructing Organizations: The Example of Public Sector Reform," *Organization Studies*, 21(4): 721–746.

Davis, G. F., McAdam, D., Scott, W. R. and Zald, M. N. (eds.), 2005, *Social Movements and Organization Theory*, Cambridge: Cambridge University Press.

Djelic, M.-L. and Sahlin-Andersson, K., 2006a, "Introduction: A World of Governance: The Rise of Transnational Regulation," in: Djelic, M.-L. and Sahlin-Andersson, K. (eds.), *Transnational Governance: Institutional Dynamics of Regulation*, Cambridge: Cambridge University Press, pp. 1–28.

Djelic, M.-L. and Sahlin-Andersson, K., 2006b, "Institutional Dynamics in a Re-ordering World," in: Djelic, M.-L. and Sahlin-Andersson, K. (eds.), *Transnational Governance: Institutional Dynamics of Regulation*, Cambridge: Cambridge University Press, pp. 375–397.

Drori, G. S., 2006, "Governed by Governance: The Institutionalization of Governance as a Prism for Organizational Change," in: Drori, G. S., Meyer, J. W. and Hwang, H. (eds.), *Globalization and Organization: World Society and Organizational Change*, Oxford: Oxford University Press, pp. 91–118.

Drori, G. S. and Krücken, G., 2009, "World Society: A Theory and a Research Program in Context," in: Krücken, G. and Drori, G. S. (eds.), *World Society: The Writings of John W. Meyer*, Oxford: Oxford University Press, pp. 3–35.

Drori, G. S., Meyer, J. W. and Hwang, H., 2006, *Globalization and Organization: World Society and Organizational Change*, Oxford: Oxford University Press.

Drori, G. S., Meyer, J. W. and Hwang, H., 2009, "Global Organization: Rationalization and Actorhood as Dominant Scripts," in: Meyer, R. E., Sahlin, K., Ventresca, M. J. and Walgenbach, P. (eds.), *Institutions and Ideology: Research in the Sociology of Organizations*, 27, Bingley: Emerald, pp. 17–43.

Engwall, L., 2009, *Mercury Meets Minerva*, Stockholm: EFI; Extended second edition of *Mercury Meets Minerva*, 1992, Oxford: Pergamon.

Engwall, L. and Gunnarsson, E. (eds.), 1994, *Management Studies in an Academic Context*, Acta Universitatis Upsaliensis. Studia Oeconomiae Negotiorum 35, Uppsala: Almqvist & Wiksell.

Engwall, L., Kipping, M. and Üsdiken, B., 2010, "Public Science Systems, Higher Education, and the Trajectory of Academic Disciplines: Business Studies in the United States and Europe," in: Whitley, R., Gläser, J. and Engwall, L. (eds.), *Reconfiguring Knowledge Production: Changing Authority Relationships in the Sciences and their Consequences for Intellectual Innovation*, Oxford: Oxford University Press, Chapter 11, pp. 325–353.

Engwall, L., Kipping, M. and Üsdiken, B., 2016, *Defining Management: Business Schools, Consultants, Media*, New York: Routledge.

Fligstein, N., 1990, *The Transformation of Corporate Control*, Cambridge, MA: Harvard University Press.

Gordon, R. A. and Howell, J. E., 1959, *Higher Education for Business*, New York: Columbia University Press.

Greenwood, R., Oliver, C., Sahlin, K. and Suddaby, R. (eds.), 2008a, *The Sage Handbook of Organizational Institutionalism*, London: Sage.

Greenwood, R., Oliver, C., Sahlin, K. and Suddaby, R., 2008b, "Introduction," in: Greenwood, R., Oliver, C., Sahlin, K. and Suddaby, R. (eds.), *The Sage Handbook of Organizational Institutionalism*, London: Sage, pp. 1–46.

Khurana, R., 2007, *From Higher Aims to Hired Hands: The Social Transformation of American Business Schools and the Unfulfilled Promise of Management as a Profession*, Princeton, NJ: Princeton University Press.

Locke, R. R., 1996, *The Collapse of the American Management Mystique*, Oxford: Oxford University Press.

Locke, R. R. and Spender, J. C., 2011, *Confronting Managerialism: How the Business Elite and their Schools Threw Our Lives Out of Balance*, London: Zed.

Meyer, J. W., 2009, "Reflections: Institutional Theory and World Society," in: Krücken, G. and Drori, G. S. (eds.), *World Society: The Writings of John W. Meyer*, Oxford: Oxford University Press, pp. 36–63.

Meyer, J. W. and Jepperson, R. L., 2000, "The Actors of Modern Society: The Cultural Construction of Social Agency," *Sociological Theory*, 18(1): 100–120.

Meyer, J. W. and Rowan, B., 1977, "Institutionalized Organizations: Formal Structure as Myth and Ceremony," *American Journal of Sociology*, 83(2): 340–363.

Mintzberg, H., 2004, *Managers Not MBAs: A Hard Look at the Soft Practice of Managing and Management Development*, San Francisco: Berrett-Koehler.

Perrow, C., 1991, "A Society of Organizations," *Journal Theory and Society*, 20(6): 725–762.

Perrow, C., 2002, *Organizing America*, Princeton, NJ: Princeton University Press.

Pettigrew, A. M., 1992, "On Studying Managerial Elites," *Strategic Management Journal*, 13(S2): 163–182.

Pfeffer, J. and Fong, C. T., 2002, "The End of Business Schools: Less Success than Meets the Eye," *Academy of Management Learning and Education*, 1(1): 78–95.

Pfeffer, J. and Fong, C. T., 2004, "The Business School 'Business': Some Lessons From the US Experience," *Journal of Management Studies*, 41(8): 1501–1520.

Pierson, F. C. (ed.), 1959, *The Education of American Businessmen*, New York: McGraw-Hill.

Porter, L. W. and McKibbin, L. E., 1988, *Management Education and Development: Drift of Thrust Into the 21st Century?* New York: McGraw-Hill.

Power, M., 1997, *The Audit Society: Rituals of Verification*, Oxford: Oxford University Press.

Power, M., 2007, *Organized Uncertainty: Designing a World of Risk Management*, Oxford: Oxford University Press.

Strang, D. and Meyer, J. W., 1993, "Institutional Conditions for Diffusion," *Theory and Society*, 22(4): 487–511.

Zald, M. N. and Lounsbury, M., 2010, "The Wizards of Oz: Towards an Institutional Approach to Elites, Expertise and Command Posts," *Organization Studies*, 31(7): 963–996.

Zucker, L. G., 1983, "Organizations as Institutions," in: Bacharach, S. B. (ed.), *Research in the Sociology of Organizations*, vol. 2, Greenwich, CT: JAI Press, pp. 1–42.

Index

For Product Safety Concerns and Information please contact our EU representative GPSR@taylorandfrancis.com Taylor & Francis Verlag GmbH, Kaufingerstraße 24, 80331 München, Germany

Printed and bound by CPI Group (UK) Ltd, Croydon, CR0 4YY
14/09/2026
02216224-0004